Watching

Contemporary Psychoanalytic Studies
4

Editor
Jon Mills

Associate Editors
Roger Frie
Gerald J. Gargiulo

Editorial Advisory Board

Neil Altman
Howard Bacal
Alan Bass
John Beebe
Martin Bergmann
Christopher Bollas
Mark Bracher
Marcia Cavell
Nancy J. Chodorow
Walter A. Davis
Peter Dews
Muriel Dimen
Michael Eigen
Irene Fast
Bruce Fink
Peter Fonagy
Peter L. Giovacchini
Leo Goldberger
James Grotstein

Otto F. Kernberg
Robert Langs
Joseph Lichtenberg
Nancy McWilliams
Jean Baker Miller
Thomas Ogden
Owen Renik
Joseph Reppen
William J. Richardson
Peter L. Rudnytsky
Martin A. Schulman
David Livingstone Smith
Donnel Stern
Frank Summers
M. Guy Thompson
Wilfried Ver Eecke
Robert S. Wallerstein
Otto Weininger
Brent Willock
Robert Maxwell Young

Watching and Praying

Personality Transformation in
Eighteenth Century British Methodism

Keith Haartman

Rodopi

Amsterdam - New York, NY 2004

Cover illustration:
John Wesley Preaching on His Father's Grave. (Library of Congress Prints and Photographs Division)

Cover Design: Studio Pollmann

The paper on which this book is printed meets the requirements of "ISO 9706:1994, Information and documentation - Paper for documents - Requirements for permanence".

ISBN: 90-420-1853-4
©Editions Rodopi B.V., Amsterdam - New York, NY 2004
Printed in the Netherlands

For my dear friend Dan Merkur,
whose unique grasp of religious experience has guided this book

Contents

Introduction, *by Gerald J. Gargiulo, Ph.D.*		vii
Preface		ix
1	Early British Methodism and Personality Change	1
2	Trauma and Conflict in Eighteenth Century British Childrearing	11
3	Wesley's Stages of Spiritual Development	33
4	Repentance	49
5	Justification and the New Birth	89
6	Inflation and Depression	133
7	The Practice of the Presence	155
8	Watching and Praying: The Paired Meditations of Sanctification	171
9	Concluding Reflections	211
Bibliography		221
Index		235

Introduction

Gerald J. Gargiulo, Ph.D.

For anyone interested in hearing the dialogue between psychoanalysis and religion in a new key, the present text will be deeply rewarding. There are many bridges being built today between these two formerly antagonistic disciplines, an antagonism that was much to each other's loss. Psychoanalysis hovers near a functionalistic, mechanistic approach to human experience, while religion frequently fosters a denial of human ambiguity and conflict. Dr. Keith Haartman's bridge, so to speak, is solidly built and brings the reader to an informed appreciation not only of John Wesley's Methodism but also of the essential role psychoanalysis plays in understanding the intrapsychic issues at stake in his religious method. Using Maslow's concepts of self-actualization, Haartman studies the vicissitudes of superego/ego-ideal and ego reaction to understand Wesley's contributions to his religious followers. Haartman details the effect not only of the expectable life issues that Wesley's followers experienced, but particularly the pervasive childhood bereavement traumas they were subject to in eighteenth century England and its effect as evidenced in their religious experiences.

Wesley taught that God's grace and kingdom were to be experienced in the here and now rather than exclusively in the hereafter, that "salvation" was a graduated process with many turns in the road and that continued self-awareness were to be its constant companion. Psychoanalysis, for its part, teaches that the fruits of one's labors for insight have to eventuate in an integrated life in the here and now, marked by an experience of personal meaning and creative interaction with one's world. And, of course, that the formal ending of any personal analysis is only the beginning of a life long task. Without compromising the fact that Christian religious beliefs and psychoanalysis are radically different in content, Haartman shows, with remarkable clarity, how psychoanalysis supplies the tools for understanding the *process* of such religious beliefs. Along the way the author's mastery of psychoanalytic concepts, particularly the work of Melanie Klein, is evident. Dr. Haartman achieves his study of Methodism without the all too common reductionistic approach that still mars psychoanalytic scholarship.

Dr. Haartman is no apologist for any religious belief, his interest is in showing how personal internal harmony, expressed in Wesley's practices, achieved an integration that is similar to the secular, non-religious experience which psychoanalysis offers. The human quest for integration is at work in both these human experiences; such a quest, of course, is as old as humanity itself. Dr. Haartman in this careful, respectful and penetrating analysis offers the reader a model of applying psychoanalytic concepts that deepens their understanding. Both psychoanalysts, as well as those interested in studying western religious traditions, will be grateful to Dr. Haartman for what this text offers.

Preface

John Wesley, the eighteenth century founder of British Methodism, created a unique theology that synthesized ideas from a variety of Christian traditions. He also devised a comprehensive, systematic *method* of personality change that reflected an implicit yet highly astute understanding of depth psychology. Wesley, the evangelical reformer, clearly worked with the idea of a dynamic unconscious. Employing theological language, he formulated the equivalent of concepts such as repression, defense, sublimation, and working through.

This book examines closely the developmental stages and contemplative techniques that comprised Wesley's model of spiritual transformation. I use a psychoanalytic perspective to explain the pastoral effectiveness of the method. Wesley's view of spiritual growth was both therapeutic and transformative as measured by the standards of contemporary psychoanalysis.

In each successive stage of religious development, Wesley's scriptural metaphors deftly portrayed psychodynamic processes. Drawing on studies of parent-child relationships in eighteenth century Britain, I show how "repentance," the first phase in Wesley's model, figuratively expressed conflicts that trace back to childhood and infancy. Here, as in clinical psychoanalysis, Wesley's method relied heavily on the "transference." His gospel message evoked an existential crisis, a potentially healing "transference neurosis" whose emotional roots lay in the past, in the early traumas of family life, and whose current manifestation took shape within the powerfully evocative, symbolic idioms of theology. Arlow has pointed out that the God imago may serve as a transferential figure (Grossman, 1993, p. 760). In Methodism, the transference neurosis, as well as the therapeutic alliance, focused primarily on culturally mediated notions of divinity. During repentance, as individuals awakened to their sinfulness and their longing for forgiveness, previously unconscious conflicts—those centering on issues of parental punishment, unresolved grief and separation anxiety—emerged into consciousness, where they now found opportunities for resolution.

The second stage, deemed "justification," involved a "perceptible inspiration"—what Taves (1993, p. 206) refers to as a "displacement of ordinary consciousness." Ideally, the crisis of repentance led to a unitive ecstasy, a confirmation of divine acceptance and love. Here the ecstatic sense of God's omnipresence throughout the created world brought previously unconscious moral insights—ego-ideals—into view. In turn, the moral insights of conscience bolstered self-esteem and initiative, and provided a highly therapeutic sense of purpose and meaning.

In the final phases of the model, the meditative techniques of "watching" and "praying," consisting, respectively, of introspection and the practice of the presence, aided in the gradual, long-term integration of conscience and led to the spiritual achievement of sanctification. These combined meditations compare to the two chief paradigms in current psychoanalytic technique: the insight-uncovery approach and the supportive-empathic approach.

This study presupposes a multifaceted and sophisticated understanding of religious experience that does not intrinsically pathologize the data (for example, Fauteux, 1994; Merkur, 1998a). The role of ideals and idealization play a particularly important role in this regard. According to Bacal and Newman (1990, p. 260), psychoanalytic views on idealization prior to Kohut's work on narcissism underscored conflict and resistance—the need to defend against contempt and hostility. For example, Klein emphasizes the relation between idealization and splitting (Hinshelwood, 1991, p. 319). Idealization wards off aggression prompted by the pressures of the death drive. Reich (1953; 1954; 1960) and Chasseguet-Smirgel (1985), who both see the ego-ideal as a regressive precursor of the superego, hold that idealization destroys the reality principle, perpetuates omnipotence, and cripples the ego's ability to recognize and accept its limitations. Kohut, by contrast, argues that idealization represents a basic and fundamental need in psychological development. Idealized self objects provide an "enfeebled self" with growth promoting "nutrients" (Bacal & Newman, 1990, p. 260). In a similar vein, Eigen (1993, p. 91) writes: "In instances of serious personality impoverishment, contact with ideal images can genuinely nourish the ego, build supplies, and restore hope, as well as stimulate and support the need for meaningful work." When Freud (1914) first introduced the concept of the ego-ideal, he claimed that it facilitated sublimation. Moreover, despite Klein's primary view of idealization as a defense, she too understood that "a stable psychic development also requires the preservation and enhancement of the imago of the idealized good parent or parents" (Sagan, 1988, p. 189).

Religious ecstasies and unitive experiences act as crucial ingredients in Methodist spirituality. Because unitive ecstasies represent states of ideality, psychoanalytic writers have pathologized them along lines that resemble negative views of idealization. Unitive states are regarded as forms of manic denial involving a regressive fusion with the idealized maternal breast (Lewin, 1951; Hartocollis, 1974, 1976); as elaborate reaction formations against aggression (Hartocollis, 1974, 1976); and as Oedipal triumphs and pathological destructions of the reality principal (Chasseguet-Smirgel, 1985). In line, however, with Waelder's (1930) principle of multiple function, I suggest that the uses and functions of idealization are variable, complex and overdetermined. Judgments whether idealizing transferences or unitive raptures are *inherently* adaptive or pathological lose sight of the subtle and multidetermined array of human motivations. Either-or perspectives are myopic at best. Kakar (1991, p. 28) makes the same point when he states that mysticism and ideal experiences "can be deployed defensively as has been spelled out in the Freudian literature, but [they are] not coterminus with defense."

No doubt, idealization may function as a resistance. Just as importantly, however, these terms may be reversed. Individuals may just as easily resist healthy forms of ideal experience (Hartmann & Loewenstein, 1962, pp. 62-63; Eigen, 1993, p. 68; Siegel, 1996, p. 77). The same applies to unitive ecstasies in that they may be both the outcome and object of defense (for example, Fauteux, 1994, pp. 52-82; Merkur, 1998, p. 95; 1999a, pp. 114-123). Because states of ideality are central to the Methodist pursuit of "perfection," we see the same dynamics at work. Although Methodist ecstasies present the ego with ideals that sponsor greater degrees of psychic integration, repression may hinder their emergence. Or, when the ideals manifest, they may not only enhance certain facets of psychological functioning, but also simultaneously reinforce dissociative trends. In some instances, unresolved unconscious conflicts directly attach themselves to otherwise healthy and non-conflicted ideals and convert them into non-integrative neurotic compromise formations (Haartman, 2001).

As in the dream work, the diversity of conscious and unconscious meanings, motivations and processes involved in the determination of unitive experiences requires a subtle and differentiated analysis. Therefore my approach matches Fauteux's (1994) "dialectic perspective" in which religious experiences hover between poles of pathology and adaptation, conflict and resolution, regression and progression. Although unitive experiences may help to achieve greater wholeness, they may also cater to "hidden fears" and "childish needs" (pp. 1-2).

Throughout the study, I employ phrases such as "the approval of the superego" or the "ego-ideal's acceptance of the ego." Although these phrases imply an anthropomorphism, a reification of Freud's structural model, I use them as a *convenient shorthand* for a process of self-observation that transpires in the ego. The superego's "approval" and the ego-ideal's "acceptance" refer to the pleasurable emotions that naturally arise when the ego observes that it has actively conformed and lived up to the loved and admired ideals of the superego.

The primary sources of historical data for the present study are twofold. I derive the phenomenological delineation of stages, dynamics and techniques in Wesley's model of spiritual development *primarily* from four volumes of sermons assembled in *The Bicentennial Edition of the Works of John Wesley*. I supplement this source with other data from related treatises, correspondences and memoirs.

One must bear in mind that Wesley's model and pastoral insights were, in large measure, shaped by direct observation of the experiences of his followers (Gunter, 1989, pp. 40, 209-211; Rack, 1989, pp. 157, 548-550). By the late 1750's, partly as a result of a second Methodist revival that climaxed in the following decade, Wesley's delineation of sanctification came to be almost entirely informed by others' accounts of their personal experiences. Therefore, along with Wesley's writings, I pay particular attention to Methodist autobiographical narratives that highlight spiritual development. A further rationale for the supplementation of this data is the inevitable distinction between the "ministry's teaching and laity's response" (Cohen, 1986, p. 21). For the most part, I avoid citing material from third person accounts in order to maximize the personal accuracy of written descriptions. Following Albin's (1985) lead, the primary source of first-hand accounts is Wesley's *Arminian Magazine*, first published in 1778 and continued as the *Methodist Magazine* after 1798. Autobiographical narratives appeared regularly in each issue. Citations from autobiographical texts published independently of the magazine—memoirs and diaries—are also included. Finally, I occasionally compare Methodist materials with those from related Christian traditions to clarify and amplify the phenomenology and psychology of early Methodist spirituality.

For their support and advice, as well as their generous editorial contributions, I am gratefully indebted to professors Morris Eagle, Phyllis Airhardt, James DiCenso and Don Carveth. I am particularly grateful to Dan Merkur who, for over a decade, has been an invaluable colleague and close friend. This book extends Merkur's work on the relation between religious experience, the superego and personality change.

Thanks to Ruth Mas for her constant encouragement, inspiration and laughter.

Thanks to all my friends and academic colleagues for their enthusiasm and support: Peter Jaeger, Guy Allen, Stephanie Bot, Jim Stieban and Janice Weston, Sam and Susan Boutzouvis, Stephen and Caroly Traub, Vivienne and Terry Pasieka, Thomas Neuspiel and Andrea Koziol, Tony Coleman and Margaret Meagher, Andy McNeill and Trudy Artman, Neil and Jill Campbell, Warren Spagn and Catherine Shepherd, Jon and Nadine Mills, Gerry and Julia Gargiulo, Christopher Nichols, Marc Lewis and Isabela Granic, Richard and Milena DeMarco, Lara Huntsman, John and Betty Keller, Stephen Liebow, and Jimmy Page.

One

Early British Methodism and Personality Change

John Wesley (1703-1791) was the founder of British Methodism, an evangelical movement within the Church of England that separated to become an independent church body only after Wesley's death. Wesley was born and raised in his father's parish at Epworth in the county of Lincolnshire. Wesley's ancestors had been Puritan non-conformists, but both of his parents converted to Anglicanism long before he was born. Wesley belonged to the Church of England until his death, and he regarded Methodism as both a legitimate expression and a necessary outgrowth of Anglican piety.

Following in his father's footsteps, Wesley was educated at Oxford where he received his orders as an Anglican priest. In the mid 1730's, after refusing to take up his father's post in Epworth, Wesley served as a clergyman in the colony of Georgia. Disillusioned by failed expectations and haunted by the belief that he did not possess an authentic faith, he returned to Britain in 1738. Under the influence of the Moravian Brothers Peter Bohler and Philip Molther, Wesley became convinced of the Moravian conception of faith as an instantaneous and immediate sense or witness of God's pardon. On May 24, 1738, Wesley himself received the witness of assurance during a sermon that he attended at a religious society in Aldersgate Street in London. Many view this event as the decisive turning point in his religious life and in his celebrated career as a preacher. Following a short-lived collaboration with the Moravians at Fetter Lane, Wesley, who could not accept their Calvinist precepts, formed his own society at Kingswood. Here he began field preaching to the Kingswood colliers in 1739.

Although Wesley was not the first to take his ministry into the field, he holds a place in history as perhaps the most important and successful early popularizer of open air revivalism. As the first Methodist revival took shape in the late 1730s and onward into the next decade, Wesley's travels as a preacher gradually spanned the whole of the British Isles. He tirelessly established a network of "Methodist" societies and preaching houses throughout England. He recruited both ordained and lay circuit preachers to assist him in his cause. With few exceptions, Wesley relegated all executive power to himself. He provided an extensive code of conduct for both preachers and society members, and he assiduously monitored the dissemination of what he regarded as the correct form of doctrine. For example, he took great liberties editing and revising Christian texts to align them with his own theological position. He was also the founder and sole editor of a Methodist journal, *The Arminian Magazine*.

Wesley's theology emphasizes the universal benevolence of God, and affirms the freedom of human will, as both prompted and guided by grace. His understanding of spirituality and salvation rested on the idea of development or growth in personal holiness. When believers were born anew, God not only forgave or "justified" them. He also rehabilitated their sensibilities with an infusion of grace and divine righteousness. By continually exercising this righteousness in daily affairs, believers gradually perfected their holiness until the values of Christian altruism, the law of love, exclusively informed their desires, intentions and actions. The perfection of holiness was Wesley's conception of sanctification, a soteriological doctrine that he viewed as central to scripture and one that he popularized through the revival. He held that the eradication of sin, a momentous transformation of the spirit, was possible in this life. Like the forgiveness of sins, sanctification was freely available to all who genuinely sought it.

Wesley's popularity may be attributed to several key factors: his charisma, his experiential rendering of the gospel, and his original method of prayer. Also, Wesley preached to a receptive audience. Large numbers, especially in the north country and in burgeoning industrial areas, had been seriously neglected by the Anglican Church. The spiritually disenfranchised eagerly received his message of hope. However, the Anglican Church, with its hierarchical strata of religious authority, condemned Wesley's ministry. They accused him of enthusiasm, of breaking church rule by encouraging the unordained to preach, and of violating jurisdictions already overseen by official clergy.

WESLEY AS PSYCHOLOGIST

Theological or doctrinal studies comprise most of the literature on Wesley and his teachings (Dimond, 1926; Cell, 1935; Knox, 1950; Bowmer, 1951; Hildebrant, 1951; Towlson, 1957; Green, 1961; Davies,1963; Outler, 1964; Monk 1966; Thompson, 1966; Semmel 1973; Whaling, 1981; Heitzenrater, 1989; Rack, 1989; Maddox, 1994). Dryer (1983) steps beyond these approaches, however, and gives a unique perspective. He argues that empiricism, informed largely by John Locke's epistemology, was a fulcrum, a central organizer in Wesley's synthesis of tradition. "Nothing is known," Dryer writes, "that cannot be felt" (p. 28). This principle, with its many psychological implications, characterized Wesley's theological stance as revealed in both his sermons, treatises and letters, as well as his most notable doctrinal disputes. For example, in opposition to Anglicans, Wesley held that personal discernment of justifying faith was not an intellectual exercise dependent solely on rational self-evaluation. Faith is experiential and immediately apparent to the senses. Epistemological and psychological concerns also highlighted his debate with the Moravians. Wesley refused to accept Molther's static view of faith. Molther held that the renewal of the whole person was instantaneous, entire, permanent and unchanging (Heitzenrater, 1989, pp. 123-24). Wesley instead formulated a *dynamic* model of spiritual growth that took note of degrees of faith and holiness and periods of regression and progression. It also allowed for differences in individual experience. Wesley's theology eventually accounted also for backsliding, variations in the content and intensity of assurance, and episodes of depression and doubt. Wesley's early break with the Moravians, and his abiding rejection of the central tenets of Calvinist doctrine stemmed from his willingness to prioritize psychological considerations. Dryer (1983, p. 14) writes: "The great controversies of his life all turned on points of psychology."

Wesley's empirical bent, combined with his belief in rigorous self-examination, promoted an acute psychological awareness that tempered all facets of his views. His sermons and letters reveal a remarkable pastoral sensitivity replete with insights consistent with basic psychoanalytic understandings of human motivation. For example, in explaining why an individual might remain oblivious to another's state of spiritual perfection, Wesley appeals to various psychological factors that impede perception: one's own lack of spiritual vitality; guilt over "unrepented sin"; the "overvaluation" or idealization of the other or conversely, the overestimation of one's self (Wesley & Wesley, 1981, p. 334).

With respect to guilt, Wesley understood the idea of the denial of conscience (compare: Rangell, 1974). In his sermon on *The Wilderness State*, he claims that unacknowledged sin may instill anxiety and depression, and compromise the pursuit of holiness. Once one identifies sin through introspection, one may anticipate the return of joy in the Holy Spirit (Wesley, 1984-87, II: pp. 208-221). Moreover, Wesley rejected the idea of "natural conscience," arguing instead that the Holy Spirit mediated moral "convictions." All individuals, even the morally bankrupt, possess some measure of "preventing grace" (Lindstrom, 1946, p. 48). Wesley claims, however, that the "generality of men stifle [their convictions] as soon as possible, and after a while forget, or at least deny, that they ever had them at all" (Wesley, 1984-87, II: p. 157). Commenting on the idea of prevenient grace, Outler (1984c) claims Wesley "pursues the self-excusing 'natural man' into the depths of his unconscious motives as if there were a conscience at their core" (p. 248).

Along with the denial of guilt, Wesley articulated other psychologically astute observations on the topic of sin. For example, immoral behavior and the denial of guilt require a self-deceptive rationalization in the form of collusion. A sinner needs to persuade others to behave similarly in order to further reinforce the rationalization (Wesley, 1984-87, II: pp. 556-557). Or, in connection with backsliding, Wesley realized that despair cripples one's sense of mastery. Appearances easily deceive. Those who persist in a course of sin may not necessarily do so out of presumption, but out of hopelessness (I: pp. 211-212).

Wesley was equally perceptive on the theme of love. The experiential sense of God's pardon and acceptance instills a reciprocal love for God and all his creatures. In psychological language, a good conscience creates a shift in the projective currents that distort interpersonal relations. Wesley writes,

> Love prevents a thousand provocations which would otherwise arise, because it thinketh no evil...One no longer infers evil where it does not appear, nor reasons about things which are not seen. [Love] tears up, root and branch, all *imagining* which we have not known. It casts out all jealousies, all evil surmisings, all readiness to believe evil. It is frank, open, unsuspicious; and as it cannot design, so neither does it fear evil (I: pp. 503-504).

Wesley's language resonates with Kleinian thought. Love eradicates suspicion. The consolidation of a good internal object mitigates both aggression and negative projections. Love conferred upon the ego by its identification with a good object prevents paranoid thinking and cultivates trust and gratitude (Klein, 1988, p. 353).

Consider Wesley's exegesis on forgiveness as it appears in the Lord's Prayer. He writes:

> All our trespasses and sins are forgiven us *if* we forgive, and *as* we forgive, others...So that if any malice or bitterness, if any taint of unkindness or anger remains, if we do not clearly, fully, and from the heart, forgive all men their trespasses, we far cut short the forgiveness of our own. God cannot clearly and fully forgive us. He may show us some degree of mercy. But we will not suffer him to blot out all our sins, and forgive all our iniquities (Wesley, 1984-87, I: p. 587).

Here again Wesley's thinking anticipates psychoanalytic theory. The superego refuses to pardon the ego, if the ego persistently harbors resentment and hostility. One cannot gain narcissistically what one is unprepared to give. Therefore, guilt remains.

Wesley's psychological mindedness is apparent not only in his pastoral insights, but also in his gradated model of spiritual development. The model presupposes what in modern parlance we call "personality change."

THE CENTRALITY OF PERSONALITY CHANGE

Personality change understood as growth in piety and holiness is pivotal in Methodism. Lindstrom (1942, p.102) holds that sanctification as an "ethical transformation of the heart and life of man" is the most important conception in Wesleyan theology. Sanctification encompasses both "inward" and "outward" holiness—a transformation of both subjectivity and behavior. Salvation involves a gradual process of growth that commences in the present:

> What is *Salvation?* The salvation which is here spoken of is not what is frequently understood by that word, the going to heaven, eternal happiness. It is not the soul's going to paradise...It is not a blessing which lies on the other side of death, or (as we usually speak) in the other world...It is not something at a distance: it is a present thing, a blessing which, through the free mercy of God, ye are now in possession of...the salvation which is here spoken of might be extended to the entire work of God, from the first dawning of grace in the soul till it is consummated in glory (Wesley, 1984-87, II: p. 156).

Similarly, in his long elucidation of the *Sermon on the Mount*, Wesley distinguishes between the present and final eschatological aspects of Christ's kingdom (I: pp. 581-582). The kingdom is "begun below, set up in the believer's heart" when he "repents and believes the gospel." Believers foster an ongoing regeneration of the soul by acting voluntarily on redemptive grace.

> He taketh unto himself his mighty power; that he may subdue all things unto himself. He goeth on in the soul conquering and to conquer, till he hath put all things under his feet, till 'every thought' is 'brought into captivity to the obedience of Christ'.

Wesley regards the full eschatological "kingdom of glory in heaven" as "the continuation and perfection of the kingdom of grace on earth."

Wesley called the kingdom the "immediate fruit of God's reigning in the soul" (I: p. 224). Clapper (1989) and Steele (1994) demonstrate that for Wesley the "fruits of the spirit" referred to a specific set of emotions that vitalize perception, promote happiness, and motivate believers to live in accordance with Christian values. The kingdom "within" is characterized by "righteousness, and peace and joy in the Holy Ghost," the love of God and all of mankind, and a calm serenity of soul (Wesley, 1984-87, I: p. 481).

Wesley continually insisted that the character traits associated with regeneration were clearly observable. The change is so thoroughly apparent that those born of the spirit cannot help but be exemplary. Their bearing and actions naturally have an evangelizing influence on others. Always careful to align his views with scripture, Wesley held that genuine Christians are the "salt of the earth," and the "light of the world."

> So long as true religion abides in our hearts it is impossible to conceal it...'Ye' Christians 'are the light of the world', with regard both to your tempers and actions. Your holiness makes you as conspicuous as the sun in the midst of heaven. As you cannot go out of the world, so neither can ye stay in it without appearing to all mankind...it is impossible to hide your lowliness and meekness and those other dispositions whereby ye aspire to be perfect...Love cannot be hid anymore than light; and least of all when it shines forth in action, when ye exercise yourselves in the labor of love, in beneficence of every kind (I: p. 539).

Wesley also pointed to the indisputable signs of dramatic characterological change in his followers. In his letters, he writes:

> The habitual drunkard that was is now temperate in all things; the whoremonger now flees fornication; he that stole, steals no more, but works with his hands; he that cursed and swore, perhaps at every sentence, has now learned to serve the Lord with fear and rejoice with him in reverence; those formerly slaved to various habits of sin are now brought to uniform habits of holiness...My Lord, can you deny these facts? (quoted in Lee, 1936, pp. 141-142).

The communal structure of Methodism reflected the centrality of personality change. The hierarchical cast of the Methodist societies embodied Wesley's conviction that holiness entailed personal growth and change. Wesley's stages of holiness, his *ordu salutis*, determined the pastoral design of group meetings (Rack, 1989, pp. 238-239). Those yet to receive the experiential witness of God's pardon (that is, justification) were placed in "classes" of 12, overseen by a spiritually advanced leader. Those justified and actively pursuing the gift of perfection assembled in "bands." A select number of the spiritually elite who had received the additional witness of entire sanctification met in "select societies" or "select bands." In addition to this three-tiered division, another band existed that ministered specifically to "penitentials" or backsliders "who were grown slack" (Heitzenrater, 1995, pp. 123-124). Rack (1989, p. 240) states that societal membership itself became a means for defining stages in spiritual development.

Various authors assess the effect of Wesley's regenerative vision on the lives of his disciples and followers. Church (1948, p. 2) stresses self-enhancement through the acquisition of a new standard of moral values.

Moral conviction brought confidence, purpose and peace to otherwise hopeless lives. Rammage (1967, p. 143) holds that conversion led to a "marked and permanent reformation of character and a general increase in personal contentment and efficiency." Rack (1989, p. 436), although wary of facile generalizations of the achievements of Methodism, claims it is reasonable to suppose that "an elite achieved a high degree of devotion and sacrificial service, and that a larger number achieved a more orderly, moral, civilized and indeed happier life than they would have without their faith."

SANCTIFICATION, SELF-ACTUALIZATION, AND PSYCHIC INTEGRATION

My translation from Wesley's religious language into the humanistic idioms of contemporary psychoanalysis involves important debts, however, to writers of other psychological orientations. At the turn of the twentieth century, Starbuck (1911) and James (1982), the founders of the psychology of religion, took up the problem of spiritual growth. Starbuck (1911), whose informants were predominantly American Methodists, viewed sanctification as a complete adaptation to religious ideals that manifest during conversion.

> At conversion, the person has accepted a new ideal as his own. It is vivid and real enough, but it exists largely as a possibility for future development...Sanctification is the step, usually after much striving and discontent, by which the personality is finally identified with the spiritual life which at conversion existed as a hazy possibility (pp. 383-384).

Sanctification is a state in which one is "cleansed" of former temptations and evil habits. According to Starbuck, because the sanctified have extensively resolved their conflicts, they abide consistently by their altruistic values. They feel that their lives are encompassed within a greater whole, often expressed as a deeper consciousness of God's presence.

James expanded Starbuck's observations by identifying a variety of crises that typically preceded conversion. On this basis, James (1982, pp. 127-258) created a generic typology. The sick soul aspires to achieve religious or existential ideals but feels woefully inadequate. The discrepancy between the state of the self and the imagined ideal leads to a depression characterized by ailments such as identity loss, malaise, guilt and anxiety. James set a historical precedent by formulating a depth-psychological understanding of conversion as an instance of conflict resolution. "Subliminal" influences in the "subconscious" incubate towards a solution that resolves the conscious problem. The gradual or instantaneous emergence of subconscious ideas constitutes the revelatory character of conversion, and the sick-soul enters the ranks of the "twice-born." If the rejuvenating effects of conversion remain permanent, the individual may go on to achieve "saintliness" (that is, asceticism, purity and charity), which may, in turn, be followed by mysticism.

Merkur (1996a) states that we can view Starbuck's and James's descriptions of spiritual progress in psychoanalytic terms as the integration of religious ideals within the sense of self. Although religious ideals may emerge passively during conversion, their actual integration within the personality occurs after a period of conscious consideration: "the manifestation of the ego-ideal—better, positive superego—materials and their integration within the ego is analogous to the psychoanalytic processes of acquiring insight and working it through" (pp. 2-3).

Following the pioneering work of Starbuck and James, academic research focused mainly on the problem of conversion. Interest in longitudinal post-conversion personality development resumed only with Maslow's (1970; 1971) work on "self-actualization," the fulfillment of the inborn potentials of the personality. For example, clinical researchers from both humanistic and transpersonal schools of psychology studied the relationship between "peak experiences" and personality transformations that coincided with the criteria of self-actualization (Pahnke et al, 1969; Kurland et al, 1973).

Maslow's work impacted on Wesleyan studies. Oakland (1981) and Carter (1981) pointed to a thematic convergence between Wesleyan sanctification and Maslowian self-actualization. Oakland (1981, p. 162) identifies several areas of general overlap. Faith implies freedom from internal tension, or Carl Rogers' notion of "trusting one's own organism." Oakland sees "union with Christ" or the "indwelling of the Spirit" as phenomenologically similar to peak experiences, and he compares St. Paul's discussion of the fruit of the spirit in Galatians 5 to Maslow's profile of the self-actualized personality.

> Love, joy, peace, patience, kindness, goodness, faithfulness, gentleness, self-control, [are] not terribly different from self-actualization characteristics such as spontaneity, humor, acceptance, democratic character structure, social interest, deep interpersonal relationships, resistance to enculturation, life mission and ethical awareness (Oakland, 1981, p. 162).

Carter (1981, p. 155) draws a parallel between salvation as the renewal of the image of God, and the actualization of personal potential. He claims that Christian maturity equates with the principle of "congruence," the holistic balancing of affect, cognition and behavior. Congruence provides an operational definition of moral integrity (p. 157; see also Hauerwas, 1985).

Predating Maslow, Dimond's (1926) assessment of the effects of Methodist spirituality comes remarkably close to Maslow's findings. Dimond claims that Methodism promoted a progressive, psychological integration that raised the personality to higher level of vitality (p. 204). He implies the principle of congruence when he refers to the unification of character, a "coordination of all mental resources, so that effort and volition provoke no conflict" (p. 204). Methodist conversion led to an increased appreciation of the values of truth, goodness, and beauty. Anticipating Maslow's account of the cognitive content of peak experiences, Dimond refers to the "normal mysticism of the evangelical," a self-transcending sense of continuity with a universe infused with value and order (p. 268). This kind of sensibility spontaneously evokes an attitude of worship and a sense of deep peace (compare Maslow, 1970).

While Oakland's and Carter's claims of a thematic correspondence between sanctification and self-actualization open up a useful line of inquiry, the two terms are not isomorphic. Cohen (1981, p. 145) argues that holiness may become a medium through which neurotic and psychotic pathologies play themselves out. Because holiness can be present without health, only a partial correlation obtains. The distinction has also been phrased psychoanalytically. According to Brierley (1947, p. 47), the "integration of sanctity" involves a "total surrender of ego-direction to super-ego control," and is a variation of the more "inclusive and democratic harmonization of id, ego and super-ego systems." The integration only of holiness more likely leads to conflict and the repression of instinctual needs. Merkur (1996b) reminds us that many mystical traditions "shun love, sex, partnership, parents, children, etc."

On the other hand, the ideas of integration and moral development, so central to the concept of self-actualization, give useful indices of analysis for a psychological examination of Wesley's method and model of long-term spiritual development. His understanding of "Christian freedom" presumes a whole-hearted integration of moral values. Active commitment to Christian ideals results from a "yieldedness," as opposed to "strength" (Deiter et al., 1987, p. 35). In being justified, the love of God is shed abroad in the believer's heart and powerful emotional currents compel the ego to yield, that is, to identify freely and lovingly with its newly acquired ideals. Christian service then flows from an eagerness to fulfill the law, not from a coercive sense of obligation fraught with ambivalence and fear. Phrased psychoanalytically, superego imperatives become more fully accepted by the ego, and internal conflict diminishes.

The rich detail of the historical data obliges us to move beyond simple generalizations about ego-superego integration. Wesley characterized the process of sanctification as a series of standard vicissitudes occurring within successive stages of development. Furthermore, as Methodist autobiographies show, idiosyncratic progressions, regressions, complications and distortions arise due to variations in individual personalities and life circumstances. If we speak of psychological integration, two questions naturally arise: what is integrated, and how do we define the prior state of disintegration? In the following chapter I answer these questions by examining three common traumatogenic experiences that were part of eighteenth century childrearing practices in England.

Two

Trauma and Conflict in Eighteenth Century British Childrearing

Wesley's personal history, the autobiographical accounts of his followers, and the literature on childrearing and social conditions in the eighteenth century reveal three culturally normative phenomena connected to childhood experience. These are forms of autocratic parenting, an inordinately high rate of mortality and childhood bereavement, and precocious ruminations on death, judgment and damnation. The psychological stresses of these phenomena, which in some instances reached traumatic proportions, complicated emotional development and led to disintegrative ruptures between the ego and the "positive superego" (Lederer, 1964). We require some discussion of the latter concept.

The bulk of psychoanalytic literature focuses on the negative and punishing features of the superego inherited from unresolved childhood conflicts. The positive dimensions of the superego that foster non-conflicted ego-motivation, sublimation, self-esteem, and intimacy have been largely overlooked. These are crucial components of a healthy personality. However, several authors, including Sandler (1960), Schafer (1960), Lederer (1964), Schecter (1979) and Josephs (1989) have addressed the topic. Schafer makes a convincing case that Freud already alluded to the construct.

The positive superego has an important protective function in representing the internalization of loving parents or primary objects. It promotes what Saul (1970) refers to as "inner sustainment," the toleration of pain, privation, mistreatment and abandonment. The positive superego is also implicated in the vicissitudes of self-esteem. In living up to one's ideals, the ego experiences relief, satisfaction, self-respect and pride. We gain clarity if we maintain the technical distinction between ego-ideals and the superego as a whole. The former are functions of the latter (Jacobson, 1964; Milrod, 1990). Ego-ideals are abstract and depersonified structures derived from representations of loved and admired qualities of primary objects. Ideals provide a reference point for the ego's achievements in reality (Laplanche & Pontalis, 1988, p. 144) and generate aspirations and direction, along with measures for self-critical evaluation. Because they instill admiration, the ego's ability to both pursue and realize ideal standards is the basis for an on going sense of self-esteem. The superego, as an overarching and autonomous structure, also engages in self-observation and the application of judgments of conscience (Freud, 1933a). Because the positive superego is the locus of values, it is characterized in health by strength and vitality. It promotes sublimation and imbues the personality with a sense of conviction and determination.

Loewald (1962) and Lederer (1964) argue that the superego equips the ego with a decisive vision of the future, a "destiny" (Lederer, 1964, p. 29). Positive superego values promote self-transcendence and concern for others (that is, conscience). Lederer conceives of the superego as an otherness within the self. As internalizations, the superego and its values are "good company." They provide "the ability to be alone" (pp. 38-39). Identifying with the subjectivity of others, empathizing and sharing intimacy depend on the imaginative use of the various object representations that constitute the positive superego (Furer, 1967).

The combined psychological effects of invasive parental authoritarianism, early loss and the morbid preoccupation with divine judgment mutually reinforce each other. Each item impacts negatively on the internalization of ego enhancing representations of parents and primary caretakers. Rage, grief and anxiety promote disintegrative defenses such as splitting and repression, which in turn obstruct the consolidation of the positive superego.

Susanna Wesley's approach to childrearing epitomizes what Greven (1977) calls "evangelical" parenting and what Rubin (1994) refers to as "evangelical nurture." For these authors, evangelical childrearing, a religiously sanctioned practice, seeks to break the toddler's will (p. 48). Autocratic parents make severe demands for impulse control at a time when the child is unable to comply without resorting to disruptive defense mechanisms.

From birth onwards, Susanna's children were "put into a regular method of living" (Greven, 1977, p. 36) that included strictly maintained schedules of dressing, sleeping and feeding. The schedule assured "that the infant's needs and desires would be shaped into conformity with the intentions and plans of the parents" (p. 36). Susanna aimed principally to subdue and conquer the child's self-will. She wished to instill early on a sacrificial attitude necessary to fulfill the will of God and to secure eternal life (Newton, 1968, p. 116). She believed that parents who indulged their child's obstinacy, the inherited residue of Adam's rebellion, aligned themselves with the devil by condemning the child to eternal damnation. The following passage, taken from a letter Susanna sent to her son John, offers advice on the proper method of childrearing:

> In order to form the minds of children, the first thing to be done is to conquer their will and bring them to an obedient temper. To inform the understanding is a work of time, and must with children proceed by slow degrees, as they are unable to bear it; but the subjecting the will is a thing that must be done at once, and the sooner the better; for by neglecting timely correction they will contract a

stubbornness and obstinacy which are hardly ever after conquered, and never without using such severity as would be as painful to me as to the child...When a child is corrected, it must be conquered, and this will be no hard matter to do, if it be not grown headstrong by too much indulgence. And when the will of the child is totally subdued, and it is brought to revere and stand in awe of the parents, then a great many childish follies and inadvertencies may be passed by...no willful transgression ought ever to be forgiven children without chastisement less or more, as the nature of the circumstances of the case may require. I insist on the conquering of the will of children betimes, because this is the only strong and rational foundation of a religious education, without which both precept and example will be ineffectual...then a child is capable of being governed by reason and piety of its parents till its own understanding comes to maturity, and the principles of religion have taken root in the mind (quoted in Greven, 1977, p. 38).

The inculcation of fear as the handmaiden of discipline was essential to the process. Susanna insisted on corporal punishment from an early age, and writes that when her children "turned a year old (and some before) they were taught to fear the rod and to cry softly, by which means they escaped an abundance of correction which they might otherwise have had" (p. 36). As a result, "that most odious noise of the crying of children was rarely heard in the house, but the family usually lived in as much quietness as if there had not been a child among them" (p. 36). Notwithstanding Susanna's zealous concern for the welfare of her children, Greven (1991, p. 20) points to her use of physical punishment in order to enforce control and silence her children by fear of pain.

Wesley's sermons *On the Education of Children* (Wesley, 1984-87, III: pp. 347-360) and *On Obedience to Parents* (III: pp. 361-372) show his full agreement with Susanna's views. In these writings, Wesley surpasses his mother's recommendations with even more urgent and severe rhetoric: "Why, disobedience is as certain a way to damnation as cursing and swearing. Stop him, stop him at first, in the name of God. 'Do not spare the rod and spoil the child'. If you have not the heart of a tiger, do not give up your child to his own will, that is, to the devil" (III: p. 367). Tireless persistence in the breaking of children's wills is necessary to be "clear of their blood" (III: p. 353). Children should be taught that they are "more ignorant, more foolish, and more wicked, than they can possibly conceive" (III: p. 356). Wesley's objection to a parent's expression of warmth and affection—a conviction that he rationalized in the name of compassion—reveals an ambivalence that is presumably the fruit of his own subjection to evangelical nurture.

[Fondness] is usually mistaken for love: but Oh, how widely different from it! It is real hate; and hate of the most mischievous kind,

> tending to destroy both body and soul in hell! O give not way to it any longer, no not for a moment. Fight against it with your might! For the love of God; for the love of your children; for the love of your own soul! (III: p. 369)

Evangelical nurture produces several distinctive psychological effects. Rubin (1994, p. 10) refers to a "culture-bound syndrome" rooted in Protestant ideology. Basic trust and confidence in one's sense of agency and mastery are considerably thwarted. The punishment of willfulness and autonomy interfere with the toddler's gradual movement out of primary identification with an ambivalently perceived parent. Guilt and shame attached to self-assertion create conflicts that grow increasingly evident in the beginning of adolescence and onward into adulthood. Individuals find themselves in painful cycles of defiance and submission. They rebel against parental and religious norms, suffer remorse, repent guiltily, and then rebel once more.

As the child accepts the parent's equation of love and punishment, masochistic qualities begin to shape the pursuit of self-acceptance. Wesley expresses the alliance between love and punishment when he writes, "One of the greatest evidences of God's love to those that love him is to send them afflictions with grace to bear them...we feel pleasure in the midst of the pain, from being afflicted by him who loves us, and whom we love" (Wesley & Wesley, 1981, p. 368).

As a result of the dependency on the parent and the threat of physical retaliation, the infant cannot openly express rage and so turns it inward as guilt. The identification with the punitive parent as an internal censor reinforces unconscious aggression, compelling the individual into endless rounds of submissive expiation. The early crystallization of a harsh superego means that proneness to depression is a defining symptom of evangelical nurture (Greven, 1991, p. 44). In a psycho-historical discussion of the doctrine of predestination, Klauber (1974, p. 254) points out that the introjection of "damaged and revengeful" images of the parents unconsciously legitimates the idea of damnation.

The chronic fear and actuality of punishment in childhood impairs the development of empathy (Greven, 1991, pp. 127-28), the "ability to put oneself in the place of others and to understand how they feel and experience life." Lapses in the empathic imagination impose limitations on the individual's ability to commune and be intimate with others without experiencing conflict and dread. Experiences of inner solitude, emptiness and loneliness intensify.

In sum, the most pathological consequences of evangelical nurture are the splitting of internalized parental representations, the conflicted proscription of autonomy, and the impairment of agency and the will. As we shall see, the psychological themes described above are symbolically repeated in Wesley's writings on repentance, the phase that precedes justification and the new birth.

We know that Wesley's infancy and childhood coincided with the main features of evangelical nurture. The practice traces back to Puritan styles of childrearing (Newton, 1968, p. 107; Pinchbeck and Hewitt, 1969, p. 263; Byman, 1978). Moore (1974, p. 32) states that Susanna's letter provides valuable insights into the childrearing practices of eighteenth century England. He suggests that the popularity of Wesley's message during the early revival may have been due to the way in which it resonated with those who also had the same kind of "over controlling, close-binding mother."

Rack (1989, p. 54-56), however, argues there is no clear evidence to suggest Susanna's approach was normative. Data on European childrearing practices between 1600 and 1800 is sketchy at best. Earle (1989, p. 233) states that apart from fragmentary excerpts, "silence surrounds every aspect of childhood." Amidst inconclusive evidence, a debate has emerged concerning the general attitudes of parents towards their offspring. Stone holds that because high rates of mortality led to parental indifference towards children, they were generally treated in a harsh and unloving manner and frequently beaten. By the second half of the seventeenth century, a shift in attitude among the middle ranks led to a more kind and encouraging relationship. However, the majority of social historians reject Stone's thesis on the basis of "unrepresentative sources and selective quotations" (Earle, 1989, p. 232). They see little change in child-parent relations between the sixteenth and nineteenth centuries. Most parents loved their children, and the fear of losing them only intensified their tenderness. Pollack (1983, p. 120), who sides with this position, questions the common assumption that Puritans, preoccupied with the problem of original sin, sought vigorously to break their children's wills. Earle (1989, p. 232) finds Pollack's views more convincing than Stone's, but he cautions against overgeneralization. Pollack's work relies on extracts from British and American diaries and autobiographies. Although these sources contain clear evidence of benevolent and affectionate attitudes of parents towards children, they do not provide details on childcare, discipline, and early education.

We cannot, therefore, assume that evangelical nurture was a culturally normative mode of childrearing in eighteenth century Britain. Still, sufficient evidence points to an ethos of parental authoritarianism, one that promoted comparable, if not exactly identical, effects in psychic development. Rammage (1967) states that although the period of Puritan political ascendancy came to a close in the previous century, its psycho-social effects continued to reverberate through British culture. Puritan ideology seeped into "social conventions and parental attitudes, and [perpetuated] itself as a slowly diminishing quantity for several generations after its original source had dried up" (p. 200). According to Lorence (1974), parental styles during this period reflect two broad categories. The first is typified by indifference and minimal contact with children, and occurred most commonly among the upper classes and aristocracy. On the other hand, intrusive parents belonging mainly to the middle classes molded and supervised their children, usually for religious reasons. Historians generally hold that economically driven values associated with emergent middle-class domesticity *dovetailed with those derived from Puritan culture.* The list of similarities includes self-control (that is, the government of passions and appetites), obedience, sobriety, and industry. Parents instilled these qualities by exploiting the child's sense of shame (Plumb, 1975, p. 69).

It is significant that a large proportion of Wesley's followers belonged to the "middling ranks" (Dimond, 1926, p. 32; Hempton, 1996, p. 3; Rack, 1989, pp. 9, 22, 173, 440-441). Rack (1989, pp. 438-39) refers to the mistaken assumption that the majority of Methodists were outcasts belonging to the lower orders. Middling ranks of tradesmen, artisans, craftsmen, and industrial workers "were the real target of Methodism and the backbone of its membership" (p. 22).

This sector constituted a rapidly increasing reading public whose sensibilities were shaped by a genre of devotional literature of high Anglican and Puritan piety. These publications constituted a substantial part of total publishing. Ascetic texts such as Jeremy Taylor's *Holy Living* and *Holy Dying*, as well as William Law's *Serious Call to a Devout and Holy Life* emphasized self-control, duty and moral concern. Most books written for parents stressed moral issues—the need to inculcate in the child a fear of God and a respect for parental authority (Earle, 1989, p. 234). Earle's analysis of middle class wills supports this view (p. 235). Fathers conveyed great concern about education and future careers of children, and they sometimes disinherited their sons for disobedience, unfaithfulness and lack of duty. Overall, we see little evidence of pampering and tolerance of disobedience. The expression of filial honor and respect was encoded in a formal discourse of bowing, kneeling or standing in the presence of parents. Earle characterizes middle class homes as "quiet" and "somber," where children were "seen but not heard," and "whisked away" if they became a nuisance (p. 237-238). A parent's desire for respect and obedience "created a more formal relationship than is suggested by some authorities" (p. 239).

Locke's influential 1693 essay on the education of children is believed to have inaugurated a new awareness in child psychology, a more tolerant attitude that replaced the autocratic mindset of the Puritans (Plumb, 1975, p. 65-70). Locke's view of the child differed from the conception that condensed willfulness, wickedness and original sin (Bayne-Powell, 1939, p. 51-52). He claimed optimal educational development occurred in an atmosphere of liberty devoid of "nagging and scolding." A proper facilitating environment and proper education fostered the innate goodness of the child and minimized the propensity for evil. Yet Locke was equally concerned with the virtues of self-control, and his pre-eminence as a "chief educational authority" contributed to conventional middle-class domestic values in the following century. Locke (1964) advocates an ascetic course in childrearing: "[Children] should be hardened against all suffering, especially of the body, and have no tenderness but what arises from an ingenious shame and a quick sense of reputation" (p. 145). He also states, "as the strength of body lies chiefly in being able to endure hardships so also does that of the mind" (p. 40).

The prevailing conviction that parents should "harden" their children to promote self-restraint was physically realized in the custom of infant swaddling, which radically restricted physical movement from birth (Lorence, 1974, pp. 16-17). Plumb (1975, pp. 65-66) sees a direct association between this practice and the cultivation of subservience. Swaddling was rationalized, however, as a way of ensuring the proper growth of the skeletal structure and protecting internal organs (Rendle-Short, 1960, p. 100). Babies were ordinarily swaddled up until the second half of the eighteenth century when, as a result of increasingly vocal criticisms by physicians such as Cadogan and Buchan, the practice gradually subsided. In 1803, Buchan wrote the following:

> There is not any part of my professional labors which I review with greater pleasure, than my exertions in early life to rescue infants from the cruel torture of swaddling, of rolling and of bandages. When I first ventured to take up the subject about half a century ago, it certainly required the ardor, courage and enthusiasm of youth to animate my opposition not only to the prevalence of customs and the stubbornness of old prejudices, but to the doctrines of the Faculty themselves (quoted in Rendle-Short, 1960, p. 105).

As in evangelical nurture, middle class parents encouraged precocity by "catapulting children into adulthood" (Lorence, 1974, p. 18). According to Pinchbeck and Hewitt (1969, pp. 264 ff.) children were regarded and treated as little adults, subject to the same religious pressures and disciplines as their forebears: "Parental anxiety and ignorance of developmental psychology contributed to the idea that childhood was but a brief introduction to the heavy responsibilities of the adult world" (p. 299). Precocity traces back to a prime objective in Puritan childrearing. Parents encouraged their children to acquire a morally independent "inner direction" that opposed "worldly values." Sommerville (1978, p. 131) claims that Puritans recognized and encouraged a degree of intellectual and moral autonomy in children. The danger lay in a potential overestimation of the child's natural capacities, such that other psychological needs in the area of dependency were neglected. Similar to the fact that the Puritans developed a rational children's literature in lieu of folk-

that the Puritans developed a rational children's literature in lieu of folklore (p. 131), we find that between the sixteenth and eighteenth centuries, there were virtually no books written to "divert and entertain children" (Pinchbeck and Hewitt, 1969, p. 299). There was, however, a surfeit of works dedicated to children's moral and religious education.

Davidoff and Hall (1987, p. 22) state that the middle rank's concern with controlled behavior was in part a response to uncertainty created by shifting economic forces, as well as the "depredations of illness" caused by fever, choleric epidemics, and consumption. Survivors of financial ruin and familial devastation depended solely on their labor skills in order to survive. What is more, the commercial activities of the middle class gave impetus to formalize and codify its domestic and vocational realms, thereby reinforcing the ethic of behavioral control (p. 26).

Another factor is specifically religious. In Pollack's (1987, pp. 126-27) sample of autobiographical extracts taken from eighteenth century England, parents grieve the loss of children and anticipate re-union in the hereafter. High infant mortality rates combined with parental separation anxiety reinforced strictness to ensure the child's salvation.

Finally, it is not surprising that parental authoritarianism held sway given that the hierarchical cast of society lent credence to "the idea and practice and mentality of 'dependence'" (Rack, 1989, p. 6).

Evidence also suggests that flogging and other forms of corporal punishment occurred typically in the home, as well as in schools and other educational facilities in the public domain. In an essay on "flogging," published in the *Gentleman's Magazine* in 1735, the author marvels that no writer has yet "treated professedly of the art." A respondent's reply to the essay is telling: "Is not this sort of correction common in almost every family, as well as every school in Great Britain? What great wonder that no learned Dissertator has told us what everyone knows" (quoted in Pinchbeck and Hewitt, 1969, p. 303). Earle (1989, p. 233) refers to the omnipresence of corporal punishment in British life during this period. It was regularly advocated in conduct books and exacted by parents, teachers, vocational trainers and correctional authorities. Even someone as liberal as Locke advocated flogging as a last resort. He believed corporal punishment suited children too young to be persuaded by reason alone (Plumb, 1975, p. 68).

Methodist autobiographical narratives frequently mention parental beatings. Hester Ann Rogers (1832) describes her father, an Anglican minister, as "beset" with the sin of anger (p. 5).

> He was a man of strict morals...of real piety. I was trained up in the observance of all outward duties, and in the fear of those sins, which in these modern times are too often deemed accomplish-

ments. I was not suffered to name God but with the deepest reverence; *and once for telling a lie, I was corrected in such a manner as I never forgot* (emphasis added; p. 3).

Thomas Payne recounts proudly how his father did not spoil his children by sparing the rod: "[He] always remonstrated and then corrected. His well timed corrections seldom failed to leave some good impression upon us" (*Arminian Magazine*, 1781, p. 581). Thomas Rankin was "severely beaten" by his father for fighting with schoolmates (*Arminian Magazine*, 1779, pp. 182-183). For lying, Richard Moss was "whipped severely" by his father, who told him he was "in the way to Hell" (*Arminian Magazine*, 1798, p. 3).

In sum, domestic values associated with the rise of middle class culture in the eighteenth century promoted psychological and behavioral trends akin to those that characterize evangelical nurture. We can assume that the combined impact of parental intrusion, the inculcation of self-control and obedience, psychological and physical "hardening," precocity and corporal punishment created complications in emotional development comparable to those connected with evangelical uprearing.

In the autobiographical narratives published in Wesley's *Arminian Magazine*, childhood bereavement is exceedingly common. The list of names reporting the loss of parents, siblings and other relatives is extensive. In Wesley's own family, only nine of his eighteen siblings survived to reach maturity (Wallace Jr., 1997, p. 8). During his era, life expectancy was thirty-five years, and this was coupled with a markedly high rate of infant mortality (Rack, 1989, p. 8). Families often found themselves devastated by epidemics of small pox, scarlet fever, typhus, malaria, thrush, and tuberculosis (Bayne-Powell, 1939, p. 157; Pollack, 1987, p. 93). John Nelson's (1842, p. 30) autobiography captures the omnipresence of illness and death. In it, he recounts a letter he received informing him of numerous misfortunes. His daughter and father in law were dead. His mother was sick, his son was feared to be dying, and his wife had been lamed by an accident with a horse.

Bowlby (1980, 1988) documents common reactions to early loss. He refers to a "defensive exclusion," or deactivation of the child's attachment needs and behaviors (1980, pp. 46-52; 1988, pp. 70-71). Unresolved mourning or the chronic threat of separation may promote a permanent deactivation, a sealing off of attachment structures that impedes the ability to experience intimacy with others. Bowlby's list of disordered variants of mourning includes features consistent with themes in the Methodist literature. For example, unresolved mourning may generate a hope of reunion expressed as the desire to die in order to join the lost parent (1980, p. 354). At the age of eleven, James Rogers lost his father. For some time, he remained inconsolable and would have gladly given anything to die. Believing he was unprepared for judgment, Rogers begged his brother to tell him what he must do to be saved, convinced that when he was ready, God would take him (*Arminian Magazine*, 1789, pp. 349-350). Moreover, several Methodists describe ecstasies in which rapturous emotions grew so intense that they wish they could die to be fully united with Christ or God the Father in heaven (*Arminian Magazine*, 1781, p. 585; 1784, p. 521). Bowlby (1980, pp. 361-63) also refers to chronic guilt due to a child's egocentric tendency for self-blame and reactive aggression. With respect to rage, Bowlby (1960, p. 24) writes: "There is no experience to which a young child can be subjected more prone to elicit intense and violent hatred for the mother figure than that of separation." In Methodism, these trends generally coincide with the legacy of guilt and the frequency of depression.

Unitive ecstasies (usually occurring at the moment of justification or sanctification) figure prominently in early Methodist experience. Several authors see a link between mystical experience and the loss of significant others (Zales, 1978; Aberbach, 1987; Nixon 1995, 1996a, 1996b). They hold that experiences of mystical unity may in part be motivated by an attempt to resolve grief stemming from incomplete mourning. The lost objects, often parents, are consciously or unconsciously equated with the religious or supernatural object of union. Nixon (1995, pp. 9-10) adds that complications in the mourning process due to guilt reinforce ascetic self-denial in mystical practice.

A third area of pathogenic potential in eighteenth century British childrearing is the early preoccupation with themes of death, divine judgment and damnation. This particular kind of precocity is genealogically linked to Puritanism. (Pinchbeck & Hewitt, 1969, p. 269). In *Grace Abounding to the Chief of Sinners*, perhaps the most distinguished Puritan conversion narrative, Bunyan recalls how the recriminations of his conscience spoiled the pleasure of ordinary play.

> These things, I say, when I was but a child nine or ten years old, did so distress my soul, that when in the midst of my many sports and childish vanities, amidst my vain companions, I was so often much cast down and afflicted in my mind therewith, yet could I not let go my sins. Yea, I was also then so overcome with despair of life and heaven, that I should often wish either that there had been no Hell, or that I had been a devil—supposing they were only tormentors; that if it must needs be that I went thither, I might be rather a tormentor, than be tormented myself (quoted in Delameau, 1990, p. 519).

Delameau (1990) writes, "Excessive feelings of guilt in early childhood, despair, sadistic temptations: Such are the dark vistas opened by this exceptionally loaded text" (p. 519). So much of children's religious literature in the seventeenth and eighteenth century betrays an "inability to appreciate the fundamental differences between the nature of the religious experience of the child and that of the adult" (Pinchbeck & Hewitt, 1969, p. 266). James Janeway's *A Token for Children*, a Puritan text widely distributed well into the nineteenth century, informed children that lying, truancy, Sabbath breaking and neglect of prayer invokes God's insufferable fury. "When they beg and pray in Hell fire, God will not forgive them but there they must lye forever...are you willing to go to Hell and be burned with the Devil and his Angels?...How do you know that you might be the next child to die?" (quoted in Pinchbeck & Hewitt, 1969, p. 266). Wesley (1984-87, III: pp. 39-40) writes in much the same manner: "Is it not *common* to say to a child, 'put your finger into the candle...can you bear it even for one minute? How will you bear Hell fire?" The erasure of psychological differences between child and adult is also evident in Janeway's instructions to young sinners that they retire in private and implore God for his forgiveness.

> Fall upon thy knees and weep and mourn, and tell Christ that thou are afraid that he doth not love thee, but that thou would fain have his love; beg of him to give thee his grace and pardon for thy sins, and that he would make thee his child: tell God that thou dost not care who don't love thee, if God will but love thee; say to him Father, hast thou not a blessing for me, even for me? O give a Christ; O give me a Christ: O let me not be undone for ever (quoted in Pinchbeck & Hewitt, 1969, p. 266).

In English popular literature in the seventeenth and eighteenth centuries, particularly in religious chapbooks and low cost books, visual images of death and final judgment appear more frequently than other types of Christian iconography (Delameau, 1990, p. 510), and up into the nineteenth century, children's works continued to couple moral instruction with morbid themes of damnation. Plumb (1975, p. 83) speaks of a "savage and macabre streak" in attitudes towards children, and cites the "salutary" practice of corpse viewing at Wesley's Kingswood school. In 1770, during a revival, the Kingswood students viewed the body of a dead neighbor. Some of the boys grew so alarmed that they refused to sleep until they had been safely converted (Rack, 1989, p. 359).

Gruesome accounts and visual portrayals of unrepentant deaths and eternal damnation brought considerable nervous strain to tender minds. Children's first-hand exposure to the vagaries of illness and the reality of loss exacerbated their distress. Little wonder that Wesley referred to the prevalence of night terrors:

> I know not whether [Satan] may not have a hand in that unaccountable horror with which many have been seized in the dead of night,

> even to such a degree that all their bodies have shook. Perhaps he has a hand also in those terrifying dreams which many have, even while they are in perfect health (Wesley, 1984-87, III: p. 27).

In Methodist autobiographies, descriptions of night terrors and anxiety dreams accompany recollections of childhood brooding over hell and damnation. Richard Moss, whose narrative is mentioned earlier in connection with physical beatings, writes that, at the age of five, he resolved to stop swearing for fear that it would send him to hell (*Arminian Magazine*, 1798, pp. 3-4). After his father severely whipped him, he became "terrified" for a period of three years. Moss, who lost his mother at the age of three, experienced frightful dreams on a weekly basis. His family was kept up at night as a result of his screaming in his sleep. Resembling the exhaustion common in adults undergoing depressive crises prior to conversion, Moss's night terrors drained him physically. These episodes made him "serious and thoughtful." He no longer took pleasure in play during the final years of his schooling. Here, we see how the effects of early loss and physical punishment orchestrate a religiously inspired dread of conscience. Hester Anne Rogers (1832, pp. 4-5), previously mentioned in the context of corporal punishment, refers to her self-recriminations as a child. On one occasion, "her conscience accused her greatly" because she had neglected her nightly round of prayer. Consequently, she had a vision of Satan appearing at her bedside and shrieked so loudly that her parents were roused. After that, Rogers prayed diligently.

Methodist autobiographies commonly allude to early morbidity and the precocious dread of conscience. Mrs. S.N. found peace with God at the age of three (*Arminian Magazine*, 1789, p. 525-526). In the following years she often wished she had died at that time. At age six, she realized she was a "hell deserved sinner" and lamented that she had ever been born. Because S.N. continually broke and renewed her resolutions to do away with sin, she felt "very uneasy" when by herself. Since her convictions became stronger as she grew older, S.N. devoted herself regularly to hours of prayer and self-examination, and kept a written record of her transgressions that she confessed to God, "sometimes with much brokeness of heart."

Thomas Tennant, whose parents converted to Methodism, remembered having convictions of sin from his childhood. Although able to "get rid" of them as he grew older, he was less successful in "shaking off the fear of death." Prior to the age of fourteen, Tennant experienced an acute panic attack precipitated by guilt over idling on the Sabbath.

> One Sunday afternoon, when I had sauntered up and down St. James's Park, I went into Westminster-Abbey, not for devotion, but to pass away time. I had not been there long before I was struck

> with a horrible dread! My sins were set in array against me! I hastened out of the Church, but did not expect to get home alive. I seemed ready to expire, and was to my own apprehension "Condemn'd the second death to feel, Arrested by the pains of Hell!" I cried to the Lord in an agony of fear, who heard me from his holy place, and came to my deliverance. My dread and horror were in a measure removed; and I resolved never more to spend any part of the Sabbath in merely seeking my own pleasure (*Arminian Magazine*, 1779, pp. 469-470).

In several instances, morbid preoccupations and severe conscience are associated with early loss of primary caretakers and general exposure to death. James Rogers believes the spirit of God strove with him when he was four years old.

> On hearing a passing bell, *or seeing a corpse*, I was very thoughtful, and would often ask my parents pertinent questions about a future state. On seeing lightning, or hearing a loud clap of thunder, my fears were usually alarmed to a high degree; and the more so as an impression always followed me, that it was God speaking from the clouds; and as I generally expected at these times, that he was just descending to judge the world, I would run to the door to see him come! Such ideas as these were much increased and confirmed by several dreams, *which I had from my infancy, about death, judgment, heaven and hell* (emphasis added; *Arminian Magazine*, 1789, pp. 347-348).

When Rogers was ten, he dreamt of an apocalyptic scene in which the earth was set ablaze. "Bad people" and "many of my play-fellows who were accustomed to lie, and cheat, and play on the Sabbath" were "struck with inexpressible horror and consternation." Feeling a "most painful anxiety" for his own safety and "deeply conscious" of his unreadiness for judgment, Rogers's terror roused him from his sleep. The dream left a solemn impression for several weeks and from this time forward, he sought instruction on how to become prepared to "meet [his] judge with comfort."

At some undisclosed period during his early schooling, Charles Hopper describes how his "favorite and only" school teacher succumbed to a religious melancholy, supposedly triggered by his involvement in a card game one week after he had received the sacrament at Ryton church (*Arminian Magazine*, 1781, pp. 25-26). Whether or not this story accurately accounts for the cause of the depression is beside the point. What is significant is Hopper's understanding of the meaning of his teacher's depression, which became increasingly more acute, culminating finally in suicide. Hopper writes: "This melancholy event made my heart tremble, and was a means of bringing some serious thoughts into my mind about *heaven, hell, death, and judgment*" (p. 25). These "impressions" persisted until he fell severely ill for two years. Hopper was reduced to a "mere skeleton" and pronounced incurable by his doctor. The prognosis shocked him into serious preparation for a future life. Later in the narrative, however, he portrays something of his youthful sadism: "I took pleasure in hanging dogs, worrying cats, killing birds and insects, mangling and cutting them to pieces" (p. 26). One evening, Hopper and his friends pelted frogs with stones. Later that night God "requited" him:

> I dreamt I fell into a deep place full of frogs, and they seized on me from head to foot, and begun to eat the flesh off my bones. I was in great terror and found exquisite pain until I awoke, sweating and trembling, and half dead with fear (p. 26).

Hopper immediately adds that his father died of consumption around this time. A rhythm of trauma and response punctuates the account of his childhood. Hopper's "serious" turn to thoughts of death and damnation after the loss of his beloved school teacher point to complications in mourning. His phrasing suggests that the ensuing illness was the natural outcome of his ruminations. The reparative turn to holiness is spoiled by aggression, retaliatory dread, and further loss. Hopper's story conveys a dynamic pattern that is regularly portrayed in Methodist biographies. God's inscrutable wrath and his terrifying arsenal of punishment sharpen the psychological impact of early loss and hinder the working through of sadness and rage. A vicious circle of conflict is set in motion. Rage leads to rebelliousness, and rebelliousness to the fear of punishment. In the end, individuals usually grew helpless and despondent.

Methodist biographies repeatedly depict a pattern that has psychological coherence and is not simply the product of rhetorical flourish (for example, *Arminian Magazine*, 1780, pp. 25-26; 1780, pp. 650-65; 1798, pp. 3-5). A great many of the narratives begin with early bereavements—parents, siblings, friends—followed by the appearance of a bad conscience and ruminations about death and damnation. Anxiety and depression then come to a decisive head in adolescence and early adulthood. The struggle to maintain allegiance to ambivalently held parental and religious norms deepen the stresses of adult autonomy. Early adulthood is characterized by conflict, by oscillations between profane "revelry" and "mirth" (for example, horse races, drinking, card playing, dancing), and resolutions to withstand the temptations of "sin." Since neither of these positions bring any lasting satisfaction, individuals describe themselves as helplessly lacking in resolve, and continually overcome by "evil passions." This period of life is fraught with shame, anxiety, depression and an increasing sense of futility. Because persistent conflicts and unresolved mourning imbue superego directives with unconscious aggression, they are regularly resisted. A resultant need to rebel, to act out the aggression, prompts urges to succumb to temptation.

The repeated portrayals of psychological pain and disturbance are not just a narrative device. *They coincide with the writers' past experiences.* In light of the social-historical factors in the narratives, preconversion depression and conflict in early adulthood line up with the combined effects of harsh parenting, early loss and the culturally sanctioned emphasis on judgment and damnation. The convergence of these elements suggests that depression in Methodist biographies cannot simply be attributed to rhetorical tropes that exaggerate the degree of suffering.

In terms of emotional development and the integration of the positive superego, the psychological effects of these three traumas mutually reinforce each other. For example, evangelical nurture and parental authoritarianism diminish the child's empathy for the parent. This creates *a diffuse sense of loss* even in the living presence of the parent. Bowlby (1960, p. 38) holds that the demise of particular facets of relatedness to caretakers, as for example, the loss of the mother's love, "is in very truth, a bereavement." Moreover, ambivalence towards the authoritarian parent further complicates this "bereavement" if the parent were to actually die. Also, we have already seen how the fear of damnation disrupts mourning. All three of these scenarios affect the consolidation of autonomy. They invoke unmanageable aggression and produce a range of emotional dispositions including anxiety, rage, depression and guilt.

Because of the continuity of these traumas, we may assume that memories and fantasies of a wide range of experiences, all of which shared a common emotional meaning, cohered thematically in the unconscious. Significant moments in early development that contributed directly to the internalization of self and object images became emblematically grouped, or superimposed into organized units of psychic structure (compare Grof, 1976, pp. 46-77; Kernberg, 1976, p. 70; Lichtenberg 1989, pp. 253-293). These groupings, or what Lichtenberg refers to as "model scenes," find expression in cultural narratives and myths. According to Freeman (1981, p. 337), individual myths "contain complex, condensed representations of many of the intrapsychic conflicts and developmental phases encountered by the child during the course of development." Keeping in mind what we know of Wesley's childhood—evangelical nurture and the multiple loss of siblings—we see the condensation of these relational issues in his commentaries on hell and the fall.

In Wesley's view, the horrors of hell are primarily organized around the theme of loss. For the inhabitants of hell, the misery of separation is key:

> They are torn away from their nearest and dearest relations, their wives, husbands, parents, children, and...the friend which was as their own soul. All the pleasure they ever enjoyed in these is lost, gone vanished away. For there is no friendship in Hell (Wesley, 1984-87, III: pp. 34).

The most unendurable loss is banishment from God himself. Since God represents the center of all created spirits, separation from him amounts to an eternity of unrest and destruction (III: p. 35). The pain of separation is made worse by a severe, inconsolable guilt, the "gnawing of a worm" (III: p. 36). Suffering is unrelentingly sadistic: "No sleep accompanies that darkness...And be their suffering ever so extreme, be their pain ever so intense, there is no possibility of their fainting away—no, not for a moment" (III: p. 41).

Wesley's hell depicts a nightmare of severed relationships and tortured absences, "the punishment of loss." His description of those "torn away" from their loved ones employs the language of bereavement. Moreover, loss is connected to willful disobedience, a central theme in the psychology of evangelical nurture. Sin destroys an original intimacy with the parent-deity. In hell, reprobate spirits are deprived of their natural rest in God, for whom they were created. Instead, they are plagued by the burden of intolerable absence and guilt. Several factors intensify the guilt: the awareness of God's wrath, the awareness of one's responsibility for having been banished, and the cruel persistence of the passions and tempers (for example, rage, envy, jealousy, and revenge) that led to the separation.

In this way, hell aptly symbolizes a developmental conflict. Aggression in response to discipline and conditional love diminishes the child's original sense of intimacy with the parent. Unconscious rage and envy directed towards the authoritarian parent cannot permit reparation and the recovery of the original bond. This creates a permanent breach in the quality of relatedness. The central struggle in what Klein (1988) calls the depressive position, the fear that one's aggression will destroy the good object, shows through in Wesley's depiction. Profound longings for divine presence are coupled with the "unholy" passions and tempers responsible for the rupture between the soul and God. Put differently, Wesley's interpretation of hell articulates the "worst fears" of evangelical nurture. Ambivalence due to invasive discipline, conditional acceptance, and the frustration of autonomy culminate in total rejection and the permanent loss of attachment. (I use the expression "worst fears" to imply that not all experiences of loss necessarily involved an underlying psychology of guilt and punishment. Although the cultural scene encouraged a tendency in the direction I have described, we must assume that there were also individuals whose sense of loss was primarily based on love, and whose grief was not inordinately complicated by conflict).

Wesley's (1984-87, II: pp. 189-190) commentary on Adam and the fall points to the same issues. In the beginning, Adam existed in a state of perfection. Because God created him in his image, Adam possessed the love and knowledge of his creator. The undisturbed intimacy and innocence at the start of creation represents an early state of attachment, an unambivalent identification with an all-good parent. However, Adam willfully disobeyed God and ate the forbidden fruit. His infraction severed the bond with the creator. Again, Wesley emphasizes themes of separation and loss: Adam "dies" to his maker, and "loses the life of God." Because of Adam's sin, God deprives him of his favor. Adam for the first time experiences servile fear. Here we see the threat of an angry parent who, in reaction to the child's willfulness, withholds his love and protection. Adam's attempt to hide himself from God symbolizes the child's need to conceal his emotions. Adam's offense "kills" his soul. He becomes steeped in wickedness, corrupt, abominable and wholly unclean (Lindstrom, 1946, p. 22). Here, expressed in the idiom of myth, we see the crystallization of an early superego formed in the wake of parental antagonism and the child's struggle to assert autonomy. Wesley's commentary evinces a developmental line. As the child's motor skills and mental capacities grow, new developments in autonomy—developments greeted by the parents' disapproval—disrupt the placidity of the earlier bond.

THE SPLIT IMAGO

The development of internal representations, or schemas of self and other derived from interpersonal transactions, unfold in a sequence that organizes these materials into higher order psychic structures. These structures contribute directly to reality testing, relatedness to others, and the regulation of drives and affects. According to Blatt et al. (1997, p. 352), the sequence moves from "enactive, affective, and physicalistic to symbolic and abstract." Object representations are crucial ingredients in the development of psychic structure; the depersonification and abstraction of representations consolidate the positive superego. Theorists from several schools of psychoanalysis emphasize the synthesis of polarized parental representations as part of the on-going integration of the psyche (Mahler et al, 1975; Kernberg, 1976; Klein, 1988). Affectively opposed images, or split imagos, produce distortions in superego development. They lead to ambivalence, conflict, and repression, to cycles of idealization and devaluation, elation and depression.

The three traumas of eighteenth century British childrearing encouraged the polarization of self and object representations (Greven, 1991, pp. 141-147). When parental love is based on conditions of absolute obedience, and steeped in threats of punishment, the child resorts to splitting love and rage. As a result of dependency on the parent, rage attached to images of a hostile object and a humiliated self is either isolated or subject to repression. Children lose opportunities to tone down their hostility, to bridge the gap between disparate emotional experiences. Greven argues that the repression of rage in evangelical nurture fosters an enduring ambivalence reflected in "permanent impulses to aggression and destruction" (p. 142), as well as contradictory representations of God as both a loving father and as a fearsome and angry task-master. We observe these trends in Wesley's advice to parents on how to instruct children about the love of God: "Think what he can do! He can do whatever he pleases. *He can strike me or you dead in a moment.* But he loves you; he loves to do you good" (emphasis added; quoted in Maddox, 1994, p. 63). Also, we must keep in mind that oscillations, reconciliations and transformations in these differing representations of the God imago play a central role in Wesley's model of spiritual development.

Because early loss promotes the contradictory emotions of rage, guilt and idealization, it also leads to the splitting of self and object representations. Evidence of split imagos and marked ambivalence appears frequently in Methodist autobiographies. As a child, Sarah Crosby idealized Jesus: "From my childhood I had desires to serve God, and in particular to love Jesus Christ, and often wished I had lived when he was upon the earth, that I might, like Mary, have sat at his feet, and followed him, withersoever he went" (*Arminian Magazine*, 1806, p. 419). However, she also felt a "painful wish" that she "might be as good as anyone was." Funerals led her to fret about her mortality and whether or not she would go to heaven when she died. Crosby concludes the opening paragraph of her narrative by referring to her unmannerly character: "Yet I was extremely rude and heedless, so that some who knew me feared for me" (p. 419). Crosby's summary of her childhood accentuates contradictory emotions. Her idealized view of Jesus and her desire to bask in his loving presence contrast sharply with her fears of God's rejection. Crosby reflects on the perils of dying unprepared for judgment: "When I die what will become of my soul: if I were but sure of going to heaven, I would not care what became of my body" (p. 419). The juxtaposition of love and fear is followed by an allusion to her anger, that is, to her discourteous behavior.

At the age of seventeen, after a period of growing guilt over such worldly "distractions" as singing, dancing and card playing, Crosby's ambivalence climaxed during a panic attack.

> While sitting alone, I was struck, as I thought, with death; being seized with a cold trembling from head to foot, which increasing, I directly fell on my knees, and prayed the Lord to forgive my sins, and save my soul. All that I knew to be sin was then placed before me; so that I had but little hope of mercy. But while I laid myself down to die, my strength came to me again, for which I was very

thankful, and made great promises to live to God; but did not put them in practice till some months after (pp. 419-420).

Ambivalence marks Crosby's entire account. She had a "strong propensity to delight" (p. 419) in profane diversions, although their unholy character left her feeling guilty and unhappy. When she overcame the worry that God would take her life, she expressed her gratitude by making "great promises." Yet she promptly postponed fulfilling her promises for several months.

William Hunter was put to school early and taught to read the scriptures from childhood. His recollections convey two currents of feeling towards God: "I felt a degree of the fear of God when very young, and sweet drawings of love. Sometimes the thoughts of death were dreadful to me, so that I felt very unhappy" (*Arminian Magazine*, 1779, p. 589). Following this admission, Hunter recounts a nightmare: "I once dreamed that Satan came to me, and would have me: when I waked I was full of fear, and prayed much that I might be delivered from him" (p. 589). Given Hunter's apprehension of God along with his thoughts of death, the Satan nightmare can be seen as the negative pole of a split representation of deity. Hunter then reflects on his father, whom he says was "severe" and instilled in him much "dread" (p. 589). Hunter, however, justifies his father's harshness with the claim that his own disobedience warranted such treatment. Here again, conflict and ambivalence organize Hunter's abbreviated account of his childhood: He experiences sweet drawings of love towards God, but fears him when he entertains "dreadful" thoughts of death. At the same time, Hunter also "dreads" his earthly father, but experiences guilt and "[shame] before the Lord" for provoking his father's wrath (p. 590).

When contradictory images of the parent remain separated from one another, the ego's shifting identification with an approving and then rejecting object makes for a series of mood swings between rapturous acceptance and depressive dejection. Widely divergent self and object images prevent constancy in self-esteem.

Long accounts of spiritual struggle and growth in Methodist autobiographies are regularly characterized by vacillations between elation and depression, idealization and devaluation, as well as constant efforts to keep unmanageable hostility in check. Reflecting the style of Puritan and other Protestant conversion narratives, Methodist autobiographies commonly refer to cycles of "rebellion" against God. Individuals rant and blaspheme against the Holy Spirit. Soon after, they sink into despair and, in the extreme, grapple with suicidal impulses (Rubin, 1994, p. 129). Sarah Ryan's narration of her spiritual difficulties illustrates this trend. One evening at a Methodist class meeting, the "power of God overwhelmed [her] soul" (*Arminian Magazine*, 1779, p. 302). Falling into trance, Ryan collapsed in her chair and lost her eye-sight. Immediately, Jesus appeared to her "inward sight" (p. 302). This vision, together with words that were "applied with power" during the following morning, convinced Ryan that God had forgiven her (p. 302). She rejoiced and continued full of "light, happiness and heaven" for six weeks (p. 302). However, introspection of sin, part of the Methodist pursuit of sanctification, led Ryan to doubt whether she really possessed faith and was ultimately forgiven by God. Frustrated by her lack of certainty, Ryan grew more and more hostile and experienced compulsive thoughts that spoiled her efforts to adore God.

> And feeling such enmity against God, I often thought, "Must I always bear this burden? If God *can* deliver me from it, he *shall*. I long to worship him in the beauty of holiness." But all this time I was exceedingly distressed and tempted of the devil. And when I attempted to pray, those thoughts were continually suggested to me, that the Lord Jesus was only an impostor, and the scripture a cunningly devised fable (p. 303).

Ryan's dejection grew worse when she discovered that she harbored an idol in her breast—an abiding attachment to an absent husband. She "continued in great distress and anguish of soul" (p. 303) until an Easter service when she again had words applied during communion and was "filled with light and joy and love" (p. 304). For six weeks, Ryan "went on in glorious light and was taken above temptation" (p. 306). Once more the cycle repeated itself. Her awareness of the evil that remained in her heart, now "more dreadful than ever," triggered a "violent" return of her "old temptation, of denying the divinity of Christ" (p. 304). Ryan's attempts to conscientiously observe her "enmity" against God, a practice essential to spiritual renewal, invoked doubt over divine acceptance and stirred further frustration and aggression. Intermittent episodes of ecstatic communion along with renewed assurances of divine forgiveness provided temporary respite from her worry, leaving her spiritually exhilarated until the introspection of sin deflated her yet again. Ryan's palpable ambivalence led to alternating periods of identification with an idealized, and then devalued and rejecting image of God.

All of the data presented above bear directly on the problem of personality transformation. In the previous chapter, I suggested that a discussion of psychic integration requires an exact definition of what is being integrated. My examination of psychological development and change in early British Methodism hinges on the problem of the split imago, on conflicting self and object representations. Wesley's "method," provided followers with an opportunity to heal the internal splits and to overcome the debilitating effects of infantile ambivalence. Each stage in his model represents an advance in this development, a continual working through of aggression. With every step towards the ideal of sanctification—the eradication of sin—Methodists gained further mastery of their hostility. At the same time, they experienced an increasingly stronger feeling of satisfaction, self-regard, and purpose in genuinely embracing and continually abiding by their ideals.

Three

Wesley's Stages of Spiritual Development

Wesley's lengthiest discussion of sanctification is his 1766 treatise, *A Plain Account of Christian Perfection.* Wesley penned the document in the aftermath of a second Methodist revival that flourished during the early 1760s. Part of Wesley's intention was to offer a reasoned and more tempered definition of sanctification than had been touted by radicals such as Maxfield and Bell (Fraser, 1988, p. 321). Prior to the revival, these men worked as lay preachers for the Methodist cause. Referring to themselves as "The Witnesses" (p. 267), they eventually separated from Wesley's fold to advance an extreme version of infallible perfection. Maxfield's and Bell's schism preached an "absolute perfection" that matched the stature of heavenly angels (p. 283). Among their extreme claims, the Witnesses professed miraculous healings (curing the blind and raising the dead), exemption from death, and an entire renewal that dispensed with any need for self-examination, prayer and participation in the sacraments (Fraser, 1988, pp. 338, 273ff). In the political climate of the era any forms of "enthusiasm" were summarily condemned (Lee, 1931). As a result, Wesley openly criticized the Witnesses for fear that their extravagances would only confirm "the recurring suspicion that Methodism was simply a new version of the wild sects of the Interregnum, or the more recent French Prophets" (Rack, 1989, p. 337).

In developing the views in his 1766 treatise, Wesley relied heavily on the reports of others. The revival fomented a variety of positions on sanctification whose validity he carefully considered. The upsurge of perfectionism allowed Wesley to study the phenomena closely. According to Fraser (1988, p. 318) the revival served as a "laboratory" for testing ideas about the possibilities of grace. Wesley had previously believed that sanctification occurred shortly before death. What he observed during the revival convinced him that it could be sought and expected as a present possibility. Divergent perspectives arose and sparked controversy (pp. 237-336). Were there more than two degrees of regeneration? Was there a third "gift" beyond justification and sanctification? Some claimed that after the heart was cleansed from sin, a person might expect another degree of regeneration, the attainment of the mind of Christ. One's mind would then focus uninterruptedly without any distraction or "wandering thoughts." Did sanctification include an assurance of final perseverance, the impossibility of backsliding? What was the relationship between gradual growth in holiness and the fact that some testified that sanctification was an instantaneous event? Was the eradication of sin absolute, or was it qualified by the contingencies of a mortal body? Did all sanctified believers receive an experimental proof of the Trinity in the form of a vision?

After the flurry of revivalism and radicalism settled, Wesley consolidated his views on these issues. His 1766 treatise provides answers to all of the foregoing problems. As usual, Wesley formulates logically defensible positions with a minimum of ambiguity. Early on in the treatise, he gives a definitive outline of the stages of spiritual development, as well as brief descriptions of their experiential characteristics (Wesley & Wesley, 1981, pp. 312-313). After delineating perhaps the most explicit overview of his model, Wesley remarks that "this is the strongest account [he] ever gave of Christian Perfection," and adds that it is "the same which [he] taught from the beginning" (p. 313). This statement is inconsistent, however, with the evolution of Wesley's thought on spiritual development and sanctification.

Before examining Wesley's 1766 outline of the stages of sanctification, we require some sense of the gradual maturation of his understanding of holiness, and closely related theological notions such as faith, assurance, and salvation (Maddox, 1994, pp. 124-127; Heitzenrater, 1989, pp. 106-149; 1995, pp. 77-95). In the mid 1720s, when Wesley was an Oxford undergraduate, his conception of faith as the assurance of salvation was already influenced by Lockean empiricism. Although his views on other topics evolved, one idea remained constant: the assurance of God's acceptance rested on *certain empirical evidence*. It was the psychological constitution of that evidence, its mode and content, that shifted as time went on. During this early period, Wesley saw faith as an "assent to a proposition on rational grounds" (Heitzenrater, 1989, p. 110). Since divine testimony represented the most reasonable of all evidence, faith was rationally secured by conforming to the conditions ensuring God's promise of acceptance (Maddox, 1994, p. 124). In an exchange of letters, Wesley's parents warned him of the deistic overtones in his thinking. A belief that was predicated on rationality alone was heretical. Wesley accepted the criticism and acknowledged that grace is an assent to God's revelation precisely because God has chosen to reveal it, not because truth derives from reason (Heitzenrater, 1989, p. 111).

At this time, Wesley's definition of holiness focused mainly on "external measures" (p. 111) such as refraining from sin, attending church, saying prayers and participating in the sacraments. From 1725 onwards, he became increasingly concerned with cultivating an inward piety. Influenced by such writers as Jeremy Taylor, William Law, Henry Scougal, and Thomas à Kempis, Wesley's idea of faith began to encompass proper motives and intentions, as well as behavior. He therefore devised a systematic regime for the cultivation of inner holiness. Self-examination and meditation supplemented a rigorous schedule of ascetic regulations that pertained to sleep, diet, study and worship. Wesley's format became the basis of the Oxford "Holy Club," a network of undergraduate students whose conspicuous piety and works of charity attracted attention. They were derisively referred to as "Methodists," a term that Wesley eventually adopted.

During the latter half of the 1720s, Wesley believed that the evidence of assurance resided in the sincerity of one's efforts (pp. 114-116). This position, however, proved somewhat unsatisfactory. Not only were the signs of inward holiness more difficult to gauge than those dictated by external measures, but the very nature of introspection led to a kind of double bind. Wesley's careful examination of sin, a part of the means by which one acquired virtue, cast doubts on the extent to which he possessed sincerity, and hence faith (Gunter, 1989, pp. 102-103, 114-115). Because his uncertainty only made him more scrupulous, his piety became markedly obsessive (Heitzenrater, 1995, p. 53; Rack, 1989, p. 95; Steele, 1994, p. 108). As we shall see, Wesley's mature spirituality resolved this impasse. When self-examination kindled doubt, the experiential sense of God's forgiving presence dispelled depression and anxiety.

Beginning in 1732, Wesley's commitment to inner piety or "holiness of heart" was for a time influenced by mystical writers (Heitzenrater, 1989, p. 116-118). In addition to his familiarity with William Law, Wesley studied the works of Mmes. Bourignon and Guyon, Fenelon, Mons de Renty and others. The mystics emphasized "purgation" and rejected such temporal concerns as rules, discipline and sacramental ritual. Their path to otherworldly union seemed to solve the problem of Wesley's "growing obsession with the rules of holy living" (p. 116). In the end, the mystical approach proved equally problematic. Wesley's personal style was inherently "compulsive, over organized [and] perfectionistic" (Moore, 1974, p. 36). Moore claims that these attributes derived not only from Susanna Wesley's autocratic style of parenting, but also from her belief that John was especially chosen to achieve unique status as a man of God. Wesley's character, his perfectionism and ambition, did not sit well with the passivity of mystical practice. The removal of good works deprived him of the opportunity to gain a sense of assurance through action. Although he based his later rejection of mystical piety on a pragmatic critique of otherworldliness, we should note that the emphasis the mystics placed upon passivity and "blind faith" (Heitzenrater, 1989, p. 118; Tuttle, 1989, pp.106-107) created too much anxiety for one with an obsessive nature.

During his mission to Georgia in the mid 1730s, Wesley first came into contact with the Moravian Brethren (Heitzenrater, 1989, pp. 119-124). In conversations with August Spangenberg and on his later return to England with Peter Bohler, Wesley became convinced that faith was a matter of trust bequeathed by the inner witness of the Holy Spirit. Largely under the influence of Bohler's teachings, Wesley began to understand that the Holy Spirit imparted assurance of salvation in a single moment. Bohler also claimed that faith was not subject to degrees. Weakness of faith was an entirely meaningless concept. Either believers possessed faith fully or they remained unaccepted and unforgiven by God. When it came, the inner workings of the Holy Spirit conveyed both an immediate apprehension of divine pardon and a complete manifestation of the fruits of the spirit: a confidant joy and the freedom from sin, fear and doubt. Any lapse in these subjective criteria of assurance, any residue of anxiety or diminution of joy, was a sure sign of unbelief. During Wesley's own conversion at Aldersgate in May of 1738, his heart "was strangely warmed" (quoted in Whaling, 1981, p. 20). He writes: "I felt I did trust in Christ, Christ alone for my salvation; and an assurance was given to me that he had taken away *my* sins, even *mine*, and saved *me* from the law of sin and death." Even though he had received the assurance of forgiveness and felt that God had removed his sins, he immediately doubted his justification. Adjudicating his experience by Bohler's rigid standards, Wesley believed that he did not possess the full measure of the fruits of the spirit. He experienced peace in God's forgiveness, but he lacked palpable feelings of joy and love for Christ.

Later that same year, Wesley traveled to Germany to meet with Nicholaus von Zinzendorf, the head of a Moravian community in Herrnhut (Heitzenrater, 1989, pp. 124-126). Here Wesley discovered that some of the Brethren professed moderate views of faith that differed from Bohler's either/or stance. The necessity of assurance as a prerequisite of justification was brought into question. Zinzendorf believed that assurance could occur after the actual moment of justification. Speaking in terms more consistent with Wesley's own experience, Zinzendorf stated that peace *may* be evident at justification and that joy was frequently absent (Heitzenrater, 1995, p. 83). Overall, the German Moravians extolled a more differentiated view of the matter. Unlike Bohler, they drew several distinctions that allowed for degrees of faith, an option more attractive to Wesley given his own lack of certainty. The Brethren discriminated theologically and chronologically between justification and assurance, faith and assurance, and the beginning and fullness of salvation (p. 83). Although Wesley never accepted all aspects of Zinzendorf's theological stance, these distinctions found their way into Methodist spirituality.

Because Wesley's sojourn in Germany provided him with an alternate perspective, he grew increasingly dubious of Bohler's absolutist claims. Ultimately, Wesley concluded that Bohler's conception of faith collapsed justification (the forgiveness of sin) and sanctification (the elimination of sin) (Fraser, 1988, pp. 34-41; Heitzenrater, 1995, p. 83; Rack, 1989, pp. 394-397). As is evident in early sermons such as *Salvation by Faith* and *The Almost Christian*, Wesley continued publicly to adhere to the absolutist position. Privately, however, he became more convinced of the difference between faith and full assurance. He also considered the idea that one could be a Christian without being fully so. Moreover, he realized that Bohler's stance had unfavorable psychological implications. Bohler's lofty criteria might easily induce despair in those who had in fact already received some legitimate measure of Christian faith (Maddox, 1994, p. 124).

Wesley returned from Herrnhut in September of 1738. From this time forward, he gradually dismantled Bohler's stark dichotomy between Christians and non-Christians. He began to formulate qualitative distinctions and levels, moving from static perfectionism to degrees of faith. He now held that authentic faith could exist amidst doubt and fear. Yet he by no means abandoned the ideal of perfection that had largely coincided with Bohler's description. Wesley preserved the eradication of sin as an ideal, but he saw it in a more processual light. Freedom from the *reign* of sin, or grace given to overcome temptation and guilt, chronologically preceded freedom from the *remains* of sin (Heitzenrater, 1989, p. 129). In the same way, the assurance of faith, or present pardon, differed from the full assurance of salvation. Wesley tended to view the latter category, the promise of unerring perseverance unto salvation, as exceptional and rare. Faith acquired a dynamic character involving the active co-operation of its recipients (Maddox, 1994, pp. 147, 171-173). One could enhance holiness or neglect it. Because faith became a matter of "daily confidence," Wesley never lost sight of the possibility of backsliding (Heitzenrater, 1995, p. 89).

By 1747, Wesley delineated publicly the essential tenets of his temporal and qualitative modifications of Moravian perfectionism (Maddox, 1994, pp. 126-127). Eventually, Wesley regarded even the fear of God and the reliance on one's own imperfect righteousness—a condition that commonly preceded the perception of divine pardon—as an initial form of justifying faith. The fear of God anticipated the more complete reception of assurance. The notion that faith had various developmental manifestations clearly demonstrates Wesley's willingness to consider subjective and psychological variables.

Already in 1741, applying the biblical allegory of Christian growth as found in St. John's first epistle, Wesley articulated a coherent picture of gradated development (Wesley, 1984-87, II: p. 105). "Babes" acquire peace with God because their sins are forgiven; they are freely justified. To interpolate a more elaborate definition of "babes in Christ," we find that in 1763, Wesley describes them as "partially sanctified." Born in the spirit, they remain partly carnal (I: p. 326-332). These believers are delivered from the power and guilt of sin, but they still feel the remains of the "old man." Even as this power "crucifies" the flesh, they remain aware that it "struggles to break free from the cross." For example, Wesley explains that an individual may experience a strong urge to anger. Yet, the Holy Spirit imparts strength to prevent its actual expression.

"Young men" differ from babes in possessing an *abiding* witness of pardon (I: p. 105). At this level of holiness, doubts and fears as to one's status disappear permanently. Fully sanctified "fathers" no longer experience evil thoughts or tempers. To interpolate once again, in the 1766 treatise on perfection (Wesley & Wesley, 1981, p. 311), Wesley identifies the psychological distinction between babes and fathers. For the former, evil thoughts arise, but babes quell them immediately by "looking up" to Christ. By contrast, because the thoughts of fathers are continually fixed in prayer, evil inclinations have no opportunity to even arise, and therefore subside completely.

Degrees of faith and growth in holiness, here encapsulated in metaphors of lifespan development, are implicit in Wesley's 1766 delineation of spiritual stages leading to sanctification. Because Wesley regarded this statement as his "strongest" account of the process of sanctification, I quote the text at length.

> Indeed, how God *may* work, we cannot tell: but the general manner wherein he *does* work is this: Those once trusted in themselves, that they were righteous, that they were rich, and increased in goods, and had need of nothing, are by the Spirit of God applying his word convinced that they are poor and naked. All the things that they have done are brought to their rememberance, and set in array before them, so that they can see the wrath of God hanging over their heads, and feel that they deserve the damnation of hell. In their trouble they cry unto the Lord, and he shows them that he has taken away their sins, and opens the kingdom of heaven in their hearts, righteousness, and peace and joy in the Holy Ghost. Sorrow and pain are fled away, and sin has no more dominion over them. Knowing they are justified freely through faith in his blood, they have peace with God through Jesus Christ; they rejoice in hope of the glory of God, and the love of God is shed abroad in their hearts.
>
> In this peace they remain for days, or weeks, or months, and commonly suppose that they shall know war any more; 'till some of their old enemies, their bosom sins, or the sin which did most easily beset them (perhaps anger or desire), assault them again, and thrust sore at them that they may fall. Then arises fear that they shall not endure to the end, and often doubt whether God has not forgotten them, or whether they did not deceive themselves in thinking their sins were forgiven. Under these clouds, especially if they reason with the devil, they go mourning all the day long. But it is seldom long before their Lord answers for himself, sending them the Holy Ghost to comfort them, to bear witness continually with their spirits, that they are the children of God. Then they are indeed meek and gentle and teachable, even as a little child. And now first do they see the ground of their heart, which God before would not disclose unto them, lest the soul should fail before him,

and the spirit which he had made. Now they see all the hidden abominations there, the depths of pride, self-will, and hell; yet having the witness in themselves: thou art an heir of God, a joint-heir with Christ; even in the midst of this fiery trial, which continually heightens both the strong sense they then have of their inability to help themselves and the inexpressible hunger they feel after a full renewal in his image, in righteousness and true holiness. Then God is mindful of the desire of them that fear him, and gives them a single eye, and a pure heart. He stamps upon them his own image and superscription; he creates them anew in Christ Jesus; he comes unto them with his Son and Blessed Spirit, and fixing his abode in their souls, brings them into the rest which remains for the people of God (Wesley & Wesley, 1981, pp. 112-113).

OVERVIEW OF PHENOMENOLOGY AND PSYCHODYNAMICS

Because the rest of the chapters in the present study follow the chronology of stages laid out in the preceding extract, the remainder of this chapter provides a brief overview of the basic phenomenology and related psychodynamics.

The first stage, which Wesley elsewhere refers to as "repentance" (Wesley, 1984-87, I: p. 225), may be regarded as a desolation crisis (Laski, 1961, pp. 160-170). Here the solemnity of God's law is forcefully recognized and accompanied by an acute conviction of personal sin and the need for spiritual renewal. Repentant persons feel plagued by the belief that their conduct and vanity warrant damnation. Self-hatred is reinforced by the "sight of the wrath of God hanging over their head." During this phase, religious symbolism exacerbates and magnifies a latent depression derived from the vicissitudes of childhood traumata (see Chapter Two). In other words, a pre-existing neurosis takes shape as a religious crisis. Unconscious ambivalence and guilt stemming originally from conflicted relations with parents now emerge as anxiety over divine judgment. God's wrath symbolizes a punitive superego that tyrannizes and demoralizes a paralyzed ego. Wesley writes: "Those who once trusted in themselves are...by the Spirit of God applying his word convinced that they are poor and naked." This phrasing alludes to an *active* and *voluntary* deepening of the depression, that is, to various practices of ritual mourning. The courage to mourn and then endure the growing intensity of the desolation is paradoxically assured by the promise of God's eventual acceptance. As we shall see, the desire for divine forgiveness, along with the wish for more wholesome and satisfying forms of relatedness to others, mobilizes the crisis and brings it to a head. The individual's ability to sustain a sense of hopefulness, to forge a therapeutic alliance with the positive superego, is key to the resolution of this phase of conflict.

Repentance conforms to what Laski (1961, p. 162) calls a "desolation state." It is distinguished by "feelings of falling, darkness, seeing things as lacking color; the 'mind' felt to be oppressed, the heart dry, hard, cold, dejected; feelings of contraction, of being shut in; general depression; lack of interest or enthusiasm; feelings of isolation" (p. 165). Laski found that features *exactly opposite* to unitive ecstasies characterized desolation experiences: chaos rather than unity; incarceration rather than liberation; anguish and grief rather than joy and peace; abandonment and exile rather than contact; emptiness rather than enlargement (pp. 162-63). Desolation experiences may be treated as religious experiences that are depressive rather than euphoric. Merkur (1999, pp. 120-21) holds that desolation experiences represent a negation of specifically unitive ideas. Desolations are unitive experiences whose compromise with depression results in a manifest sense of exclusion from an otherwise prevailing unity (Merkur, personal communication, 2003). The cognitive-affective contents of desolation experiences may be viewed as the product of a resistance against unitive ideation (Haartman, 2001). Unitive ecstasies symbolically express ego-ideals (Haartman, 1998; Merkur, 1999). Because ego-ideals are developmentally rooted in internal object representations, the inverse relation between desolation experiences and unitive ecstasies connects to psychological conflicts that surround the split imago.

The symbolic conflicts that ensue during the stage of "repentance" mobilize important shifts in the defense structure of the personality. The Methodist desolation crisis allows for a conscious acknowledgment and abreaction of repressed rage and guilt (Rammage, 1967, pp. 193-194). Methodist repentance may reasonably be brought into line with religious practices cross-culturally that use ritual mourning to achieve ecstasies (Merkur, 1989, p. 127). In *The Varieties of Religious Experience*, James (1985) identified melancholy as a basic category of religious experience. Further, he posited *a direct and operative relationship between despair and spiritual awakening*. The conscious contents of religious and existential depressions activate compensatory processes in the subconscious (pp. 166-258). A solution precipitates outside of awareness and then appears, gradually or suddenly, as a jubilant awakening that resolves the depression.

Methodists were aware of the relation between depression and ecstasy. Wesley (1984-87, I: p. 147) speaks of falling into the hands of God, plunging into hell, "sinking into the depths of perdition" and standing "on the brink of the pit." Ostow (1975, p. 402) observes that the onset of depression is "often represented in dreams as falling or sliding uncontrollably down." Conversely, the resolution of descent and darkness that occurs at the moment of justification is portrayed in terms of ascent and illumination.

O may 'the angel of the Lord come upon thee, and the light shine into thy prison'! And mayest thou feel the stroke of an almighty hand raising thee with, 'Arise up quickly, gird thyself, and bind on thy sandals, cast thy garment about thee, and follow me' (Wesley, 1984-87, I: p. 148).

Trajectories of descent and ascent, darkness and illumination, express figuratively the bipolar, depression-to-ecstasy dynamic. Religious melancholy gives way to elation. More specifically, a pre-existing neurosis is deliberately mobilized via religious imagery and exploited as a means to achieve the exhilarating apprehension of God's pardon.

James based his study of melancholy primarily on American Protestant data, but the phenomenon occurs cross-culturally. Zaehner (1957, p. 85), who blended comparative religion with Roman Catholic apologetics, treated Romantic and Transcendentalist nature mysticism as "the manic and depressive poles of what we now call a manic-depressive psychosis." States of "contraction", or "extreme depression" and "utter abandonment" contrast with an "expansion" of the soul (p. 161). Laski (1961, p. 161) objected to Zaehner's unnecessary pathologization. She also argued that Zaehner's correlation of nature mysticism and bi-polar states was too narrow. The phenomenon also occurs in the theistic context of Christian spirituality. Laski cites St. John of the Cross's dark night of the soul (p. 160). St. John's description of a darkness that is eventually dispelled by an illumination represents one instance of a common theme in Christian "affective mysticism" (Moller, 1965). Beginning in the twelfth century with St. Bernard of Clairvaux, affective mysticism emphasized an intensely personal relationship to God. Descriptions of ecstatic union portrayed the "amorous longings of the mystic" (p. 116). Fluctuating passions brought into play by separation from and union with divinity became paradigmatic. For example, during the mystical period of her life, St. Teresa of Avila suffered acute spiritual crises, "states of violently agitated tormenting unrest, doubt, abandonment, anxiety and spiritual anguish, sometimes complete impotence and confusion" (Arbman, 1963, p. 43). These "vehement depressive crises" often ended in ecstasy: "a wonderful, incomparable consolation and elevation, joy, satisfaction, courage and confidence" (p. 43).

Depression has also been noted in connection with Hindu mysticism. Kakar identifies the dark night pattern in Ramakrishna's first ecstatic encounter with the Mother Goddess (1991, p. 11). Ramakrishna's *darshan,* or vision, was preceded by a "full-fledged depression." He suffered restlessness, sleeplessness, loss of appetite, weeping, and suicidal thoughts. Ramakrishna states:

> There was then an intolerable anguish in my heart because I could not have Her vision. Just as a man wrings a towel forcibly to squeeze out all the water from it, I felt as if somebody caught hold

of my heart and mind and was wringing them likewise. Greatly afflicted by the thought that I might not have the mother's vision, I was in great agony. I thought there was no more living in such a life. My eyes suddenly fell upon the sword that was in the Mother's temple. I made up my mind to put an end to my life with it that very moment...suddenly I had the wonderful vision of the Mother, and fell down unconscious. I did not know what happened then in the external world...But in my heart of hearts, there was flowing a current of intense bliss...It was as if the houses, doors, temples, and all other things vanished altogether; as if there was nothing anywhere! And what I saw was a boundless infinite conscious sea of light!...I found a continuous succession of effulgent waves coming forward...Very soon they fell on me and made me sink to the abysmal depths of infinity (quoted in Kakar, 1991, pp. 11-12).

The bi-polar dynamic also occurs in ecstasies induced through psychedelic drug use. Grof (1975) created a phenomenology of standard adverse reactions. He identified three kinds of crises, or negatively toned "psychotomimetic" phenomena, that often occur immediately prior to unitive ecstasies: abandonment depression, life and death struggle, and death-rebirth.

The bi-polar dynamic is *actively* exploited in religious contexts to provoke ecstasies by means of ritual mourning. Merkur (1989, p. 125) shows how Jewish apocalyptists engaged in exaggerated grieving in order to acquire a vision. Merkur claims that grieving was "the crucial psychological element of their technique for inducing an alternate psychic state." Mourning as a means of ecstatic induction traces back at least as far as the fourteenth century BCE in Canaan. The practice was portrayed in the Old Testament in Joshua 7:6-15 and the legend of Elijah's contest with the prophets of Baal. Merkur also argues that the book of Job "can be read as a seer's use of lamentation to induce an ecstasy" (p. 125). In the late antique writings of the Jewish apocalyptists, various references to lamentation, prayer, fasting and weeping in solitude point to ascetic practices connected to ritual mourning. These techniques produced "waking visionary experiences that culminated in positive revelatory material" (p. 126). Merkur draws cross-cultural evidence for the practice of ecstatic mourning by citing early Christian apocalypses and medieval Jewish mysticism, as well as the vision quests of Native American peoples (p. 127).

Religious mourning produces a mood swing from depression to elation. Merkur holds that the elation results from a "versatile bipolar mechanism," an unconscious defense against depression (1989, p. 133). This defense not only occurs in pathological instances (for example, manic-depressive psychoses), but also manifests normally in daily life. Various examples include the shift from "vigilant concern" to "joyous satisfaction" at the completion of a task (p. 133), elation stemming from depressive themes in humor, and the consoling aspects of religion. Merkur emphasizes how religions promote "unnecessary and exaggerated feelings of guilt, shame, doubt and despair...which are unconsciously transformed into the corresponding range of positive affects" (p. 133). He reasons that because depression and elation are tied to the self-critical and self-praising functions of the superego (see: Jacobson, 1964), the emotional shift occurs when conscience applies a "value judgment" (Merkur, 1989, p. 134).

In Methodism, repentance culminates in justification, a unitive ecstasy that is characterized by the apprehension of God's forgiving presence. As the desolation takes its course, religious mourning works in tandem with another psychological process involving the unconscious elaboration of materials initially mulled over consciously. The justification ecstasy may be regarded as the emergence of an inspiration. During repentance, a creative solution crystallizes unconsciously and then manifests as an ego-ideal (Merkur, 1997; 1999). Both James (1989) and Starbuck (1911) accounted for affective and cognitive shifts in conversion by appealing to "subliminal" influences that proceeded beyond the periphery of awareness. Anticipating Wallas's (1926) notion of "incubation," James (1989, pp. 232-233) saw this kind of subconscious creativity as a form of problem solving. The conscious deliberation of a pressing emotional dilemma gave way to mental activity that occurred "subconsciously," in what James called an "extra-marginal" field. In addition, inputs from the external world, be they events or ideas, also contributed to the store of subconscious materials utilized as sources of inspiration (Starbuck, 1911, pp. 106-107). Having provoked resistance during the repentance stage, the newly formulated religious ideal makes its appearance ecstatically. Methodists interpreted the ecstasy theologically as evidence of justification.

Although Methodists regarded justification as a passive event, a divine blessing, they actively prepared for its coming. In his discussion on how to wait for the Holy Spirit, Wesley indicates that the "desire to flee from the wrath to come" (1984-87, I: p. 394) naturally drives one to become immersed in the "order of God" (I: p. 394). One feels impelled to find "a preacher who speaks to the heart," to converse with fellow Christians, and "to [search] the scriptures" and other "serious books" (I: p. 394). Wesley urged his followers to capitalize on this trend, to unashamedly "talk of the things of God," to "pray to him" and partake of his supper. Concentrated exposure to Christian discourse combines with active "meditation" so "that [God's word] may have its full force upon [the] heart" (I: p. 394). The urgent need to get rid of the depression heightens the emotional significance of these experiences—the "day residue"—and sponsors unconscious processes of creative synthesis. Even the idea of a sudden, spontaneous conversion is subject to incubation: "Look then every moment for his appearing!...He is always ready...always willing to save" (I: pp. 395-396).

The importance of the role that unconscious incubation played in the new birth is reflected in the fact that only a minority of instantaneous conversions occurred amidst the "heat" of open air preaching (Albin, 1985, p. 278; Abelove, 1990, p. 90). We cannot attribute conversions solely to the emotional turbulence of these scenes. On the contrary, evidence suggests that Methodist ideas were gradually assimilated over a period of time coinciding with the tribulations of the repentance phase. Based on a statistical analysis of spiritual narratives published in the *Arminian Magazine,* Albin (1985, p. 278) concludes that the new birth occurred most frequently in the privacy of the home. He writes: "This fact suggests that Evangelical conversion in early Methodism was a slow process involving significant thought and reflection."

The experiential characteristics of justification, the second stage, interrelate thematically and psychologically. The justified become aware of God's pardoning love and feel blissfully enraptured. This, in turn, eradicates guilt, anxiety and the sense of condemnation. Forgiveness is witnessed directly by conscience. Divine acceptance temporarily resolves the existential dilemma of repentance and restores self-regard. The justified feel an intense devotion to God. This devotion leads to an empathic unitive love for all mankind. Central to justification is a metamorphosis of the conception and experience of deity, a transformation of the God imago (Rizzuto, 1979; Meissner, 1984).

God is no longer the projection of a punitive superego, exacting obedience out of fear. He is now an indulgent father compelling obedience out of love. During the repentance phase, intense depression and anxiety reach a critical threshold. Here a powerful abreaction results in a spontaneous alternate state of consciousness. The unitive ecstasy is the vehicle through which an idealized imago enters consciousness and replaces its persecutory counterpart.

The third stage in the process involves a psychological inflation that eventually collapses into a depression. Wesley states that justified believers remain in peace "for days, or weeks, or months, and commonly suppose that they shall not know war any more; 'till some of their old enemies, their bosoms sins...assault them again." The justification ecstasy brings with it a joy that is often tinged with manic overtones. Methodists regularly describe a loss of both appetite and the desire for sleep (for example, *Arminian Magazine*, 1779, p. 189). This initial infatuation and relief causes many to believe the process of sanctification has already been completed. In time, various "unholy" impulses, which had been put to rest for a period, resurface and promote another depression. For Methodists in this phase, the sense of failure in being unable to sustain their joy, in feeling as though they were falling back into the grips of sin, leads them to doubt their status. Have they been "forgotten" or abandoned by God? Was their justification authentic? After a time the Holy Spirit returns to comfort them and take away their depression. At this juncture, the sense of assurance is portrayed as *permanent*: now the Holy Ghost bears "witness continually with their spirits."

Despite justification and the gains made during repentance, unconscious aggression has not actually been worked through. Split off anger accounts for the manic overestimation of personal holiness. Eventually, currents of unconscious aggression are stirred and return in the form of doubt. This "dark night" (Fauteux, 1994, pp. 63-82) provides an important opportunity for the active working through of neurotic depression. The feeling of abandonment by an absent God is a fantasy that rationalizes aggression and "immorality." It recapitulates a childhood dilemma. Aggression towards the parent is projected and then experienced as rejection. Now individuals actively draw on the memory of their recent acceptance by and love for God. The memory of the ecstasy serves as a motivational wellspring, allowing believers to withstand the temptation to act on their rage and to sustain their hope in the resiliency of the bond. Tolerating frustration without blacksliding builds up psychic structures in the ego. Individuals acquire greater impulse control and consolidate further an internal object representation whose goodness survives the pressures of rage and ambivalence. The successful completion of this developmental task is met by the revival of assurance, a renewed bestowal of the superego's approval and love that endures. What the superego initially inspired in ecstasy, the ego begins to actualize in practice. This intrapsychic work involves processes that parallel the achievement of libidinal object constancy (McDevitt & Mahler, 1989).

During the fourth stage of Wesley's model, Methodists systematically examined their "sinfulness." They used a meditative technique that is indispensable to sanctification, or "righteousness and true holiness," "a single eye and a pure heart." The technique of introspection commences at a point when the witness of pardon abides permanently, for then children of God are "*meek and gentle* and teachable." The persistence of the witness, on the one hand, and introspection and self-knowledge, on the other, combine with one another synergistically. Here Wesley reveals his implicit understanding of the unconscious. For the first time, believers "see the ground of their heart, which God before would not disclose unto them." They see "hidden abominations," "the depths of pride and self-will and hell." Yet, in undergoing the "fiery trial" of introspection, in examining their carnal wickedness, they continue to feel God's pardoning acceptance. In short, a sound therapeutic alliance with the God imago strengthens the ego. Herein lies the psychotherapeutic genius of Wesley's method. An abiding sense of forgiveness provides the courage to explore closely the very impulses, thoughts, feelings and intentions that starkly contradict the will of God and incite his wrath. Previously, these impulses may have created anxiety or depression; one may have acted upon them or unsuccessfully suppressed them. In principle, Methodists can now systematically examine their inner lives without reacting neurotically. The persistence of divine acceptance mitigates depressive anxiety, while identification with religious ideals, the "inexpressible hunger" after full renewal, ensures that temptation will remain a fantasy and not translate into action. The stable representation of a benign deity, the equivalent of libidinal object constancy, allows for this integration to occur. As a result, aggression that was initially split-off during justification can now be more substantially resolved.

We must keep in mind that Wesley's identification of discrete phases is an abstraction. His strict chronological description of the stages is in part determined by the need to classify observations in accordance with his scriptural standards, such as St. John's metaphors of lifespan development (that is, "babes," "young men" and "fathers"). Certainly, the formulation of coherent distinctions has heuristic worth both theologically and pastorally. On the other hand, Methodist autobiographical narratives reveal a great deal of idiosyncratic variety in terms of spiritual progress. Few individuals progressed through the stages in an unencumbered, linear way. Hauerwas (1985, p. 253) points out that Wesley's scheme is "too neat." The model's sequential "exactness" obscures actual patterns of human experience because it fails to account for regressions and the fact that the stages overlap.

A final observation is necessary. In classical psychoanalysis, the modus operandi of the "recovery," the overcoming of defenses and the working through of psychic pain, resides in the transference. Freud (1923 [1922], p. 247) writes, "In the hands of the physician, [the transference] becomes the most powerful therapeutic instrument and it plays a part scarcely to be overestimated in the dynamics of the process of cure." The notion that the patient displaces on to the analyst the essential patterns of object relatedness established primarily in childhood remains axiomatic in post-classical development of psychoanalytic thought. The therapeutic action of analysis resides in the working through of conflict within the transference itself (Rycroft, 1973, p.169). In classical terms, the conditions of the clinical encounter—lying prone on the couch, verbalizing the free flow of one's thoughts, experiencing the intimacy of sustained personal disclosure—summon the transference into being and amplify the patient's neurosis in direct relation to the analyst. According to this view, *the transference relationship necessarily exacerbates and facilitates the neurosis towards a therapeutic end.* Thwarted love and rage, rigidly embedded forms of interpersonal expectations such as the anticipation of seduction or rejection, feelings of envy, hostility and affection—all these must emerge in the immediacy of the encounter in order for change to occur.

This view of the remedial effect of psychoanalysis illuminates the psychology of transformation in Wesleyan spirituality. In Methodism, a crucial transference plays out in the realm of religious symbolism, primarily in relation to individuals' culturally mediated perceptions of God. In Wesley's model, the exacerbation of the neurosis first occurs in the desolation phase. The "transferential" dread of divine condemnation intensifies a pre-existing depression. An equally powerful wish to unite with a "good" object, reinforced by the promise of Christ's unconditional acceptance, is activated and later realized during the moment of justification. The unprecedented access to a positive imago, *whose actuality is heightened by the cognitive and affective features of the ecstasy*, provides the opportunity for an enduring transformation comparable to positive outcome expectations in contemporary clinical psychoanalysis. The sense of God's benign presence, rooted in the memory of the justification ecstasy, offers a form of self-object containment, a holding space that grants Methodists the confidence to lay bare the "depths" that previously remained "hidden" from view. Wesley, an astute depth psychologist as well as theologian, combines the two chief paradigms in current psychoanalysis: the supportive-empathic approach and the insight-uncovering approach.

Four

Repentance

Repentance, the first phase in Wesley's *ordo salutis,* referred not only to a state of mind, but also to a technique that promoted an ecstatic apprehension of the Holy Spirit. Emotionally charged symbolism tapped into and enhanced a pre-existing depression, such that grief, abandonment anxiety and guilt were consciously magnified. Wesley believed that his followers needed to draw out and maximize their sorrow. He instructed his followers to know their corruption; grieving itself led the way to the kingdom (1984-87, I: p. 225). Wesley's depiction of repentance is both a description *and* an inductive technique. His sermons functioned as instruction manuals on how to receive the spirit. While Wesley viewed the resolution of the depression as an act of grace, he also paradoxically believed that active mourning orchestrated the new birth since contrition appealed to God's mercy.

Deliberate grieving galvanized latent conflicts, which, when brought closer to consciousness, manifested as a transference neurosis onto God. As the transference developed, individuals grew increasingly aware of their ambivalence and guilt. Theologically, Wesley held that in order to receive pardon, one had to be fully cognizant of sin. Only through this form of immediate self-knowledge, coupled with authentic remorse and the desire to be saved, could one hope to be justified. The goal of the first step in spiritual renewal was to achieve an intimate awareness of one's anger towards God. Psychologically, the transference neurosis, couched in religious imagery, promoted a conscious acknowledgment of unconscious ambivalence, and created the potential for a therapeutic shift in the relationship between the ego and the positive superego.

Finally, although the transference neurosis was unconsciously framed by the various traumata of infancy and childhood, it was ultimately triggered by Wesley's invitation to accept Christ. The promise of unconditional acceptance, love and spiritual satisfaction acted as a potent incentive. Yet it also inevitably stirred resistance and fueled the conflict of repentance. The prospect of Christ's forgiveness served as a prevailing source of hope, the object of a therapeutic alliance that permitted individuals to endure the stresses of desolation.

WESLEY ON REPENTANCE

The depressive themes of Methodist repentance represent one variation of a larger historical lineage, the discourse of melancholia (Rubin, 1994, p. 5).

Hippocratic writers of the fifth century BCE first conceptualized melancholy as a humoral imbalance. Its effects were the result of an excess of black bile produced by the spleen. Melancholics suffered fear, sadness, loss of appetite and sleep, and despondency. Galen systematized humoral medicine in the 2nd century and established melancholy as a "clinical standard" for the next 2000 years (p. 5). The Elizabethans regarded melancholy not so much as a disease, but as a virtue that signified exceptionality and genius. Puritans inherited this view. They regarded melancholy as a "special chastisement" by God, a sign of his favor (p. 5). Trials of estrangement and conviction of sin ensured spiritual maturation. By the late sixteenth century, the humoral imbalance motif acquired a further distinction. Puritan conversion and its preoccupation with discerning the signs of election created a "pathological discourse" (King, 1983, p. 15) focusing on what, in modern parlance, we call obsessionality. In his *Treatise of Melancholia*, Timothy Bright referred to a "salvation panic" (Rubin, 1994, p. 5) associated with pietistic Puritans. Oppressed by conscience and overwhelmed by the sense of sin, individuals became terrified of God's wrath and the prospect of eternal damnation. In 1621, Robert Burton first identified religious melancholy proper in his *Anatomy of Melancholy*. Basing his observations on "Schismatics" or "Separatists" (King, 1983, p. 24), he identified three features: innate depravity and sin; the crisis of spiritual passage and conversion (feeling forsaken by God and dread of the law); and extreme guilt (Rubin, 1994, p. 5). Puritans depicted the melancholic temperament in a series of metaphors that epitomized their spiritual crises: "solitude, dryness, wilderness, desert; slime, mud, foulness, slough; sorrow, fear, darkness, despair; doubt, weariness, exhaustion, strain" (King, 1983, p. 24).

Burton highlighted the obsessive character of Puritan piety in his treatise. The search for unequivocal signs of election led to an uneasy hypervigilance that spread to all personal actions and external events. A surfeit of interpretations and speculations about one's status vis à vis God—the constant questioning of intention and the discerning of signs in the daily flow of events—led to misgivings, indecision and hesitancy. Individuals became perfectionistic, weighed down by a laborious attention to detail. Puritans tried to ensure that "any small business or circumstance [not] be omitted" (p. 26). The absence of certainty only magnified and refined their circumspection. To add to their misery, Puritans found themselves "possessed" by demonic infusions or "fiery darts" (p. 27). They felt vexed by irresistible compulsions in the form of fixed ideas. Blasphemous devaluations of Christ, hostile impulses and verbal obscenities—these urges overcame them in private prayer and public worship. For Puritans, such hardships preceded and accentuated the exhilaration of divine acceptance.

Because Puritanism played an important role in Wesley's ancestral heritage, melancholic themes made their way into Methodist repentance. Although subject to theological modification (Wesley adamantly rejected predestination), the dread of having "passed the day of grace" (*Arminian Magazine*, 1778, p. 180), that is, the crippling suspicion that one's wickedness created a permanent alienation from God, was, as in Puritanism, the proper route to salvation. The stark opposition between salvation and damnation, between true Christians and "almost Christians," is particularly apparent in Wesley's early sermons (Holland, 1973-74) while he was still under the sway of Moravian absolutism. During the early years of the revival, Wesley encouraged feelings of anxiety and futility in those who had not yet received the assurance of pardon (Maddox, 1994, p. 160). He writes, "It is my endeavor to drive all I can, into what you may term [a] species of madness...and which I term *repentance* and *conviction*" (quoted in Holland 1973-74, p. 77). Various hysterical phenomena occurred frequently during the early revival: individuals roaring aloud and dropping down as if dead, bodily convulsions, and contortions. Holland argues that these effects stemmed from Wesley's uncompromising view of faith. Wesley told his followers they were damned until faith appeared passively through grace. Despite their "longing to be reconciled to God," faith could not be "voluntarily exercised" (p. 80). Mounting anxiety in the face of helplessness induced panic attacks and dissociative reactions. Holland claims that Wesley's later modification of the either/or stance, his revised conviction that those who waited earnestly for faith were already accepted, radically diminished the depressive and hysterical reactions (pp. 83-84; see also Outler, 1984c, pp. 200-202).

Even so, the depressive character of repentance, along with the hysterical outbreaks, remained conspicuous in Methodist circles throughout the eighteenth century (Gunther, 1989, pp. 150-151; Rack, 1989, pp. 195-197). The emotional mayhem of the early revival may have subsided in the mid-1740s, but it by no means became obsolete. Methodist autobiographies consistently depict prolonged depressions, panic attacks and dissociative phenomena. Even in the 1780s, Wesley documents instances of "mass hysteria" in his journal (Thompson, 1963, p. 418). Moreover, such reactions were regularly observed by Methodist itinerant preachers (Gunther, 1989, p. 150), many of whom were perceived as "hell fire" preachers (for example, *Arminian Magazine*, 1780, pp. 98, 309). Also, as late as 1760, rhetorical "scare tactics" continue to appear in Wesley's printed sermons. In discussing the new birth, he states that the unholy "will all drop into the pit together" and lie in "the lake of fire burning with brimstone" (Wesley, 1984-87, II: p. 195). Commenting on the persistence of convulsive reactions, Rack states that many of these responses resulted from a cultural predisposition that operated independently of cues given by hell fire preachers: "What is common to all of them is often a strong sense of hell, and this seems to be induced...by the subjects own innate belief and conscience which appear to have required little to arouse them. They created their own hell" (Rack, 1989, p. 197).

Wesley regarded repentance as an "awakening." Prevenient grace, or God-given conscience, which has hitherto been suppressed, now manifests consciously as "convincing grace" (Lindstrom, 1950, pp. 114-115). Repentance promotes self-knowledge of one's spiritual decrepitude (Wesley, 1984-87, I: p. 225). This self-knowledge, in turn, promotes feelings of futility, loss, and guilt.

Themes of abandonment and separation are encapsulated in the idea of being spiritually "lost" while "mourning for God" (I: p. 151). The soul is viewed as "dead" both to itself and to divinity.

> But before any dead soul can live, he 'hears (hearkens to) the voice of the Son of God': he is made sensible of his lost estate, and receives the sentence of death in himself. He knows himself to be 'dead while he liveth', dead to God and all the things of God; having no more power to perform the actions of a living Christian than a dead body to perform the functions of a living man (I: p. 145).

Those who realize they are "dead to God" find themselves encompassed by "clouds of ignorance" and the "shadow of death." All this flows from a "perverse and distorted" will (I: p. 226). The knowledge of absolute "corruption" (I: p. 225) breeds self-hatred. Repentance is "neither more or less than a deep sense of the want of all good, and the presence of all evil" (I: p. 194), the "inbred corruption of the heart" (I: p. 226).

> All thy passions, both thy desires and aversions, thy joys and sorrows, thy hopes and fears, are out of frame, are either undue in their degree, or placed on undue objects. So that there is no soundness in thy soul, but 'from the crown of the head to the soul of the foot'...there are only 'wounds, and bruises, and petrifying sores" (I: p. 226).

Corruption is an "evil root" from which "springs unbelief, ever departing from the living God" (I: p. 226). It fosters "independence" from God, "affecting to be like the most High" (I: 226).

> From this evil fountain flow forth the bitter streams of vanity, thirst of praise, ambition, covetousness, the lust of the flesh, the lust of the eye, and pride of life. From this arise anger, hatred, malice, revenge, envy, jealousy, evil surmisings; from this all the foolish and hurtful lusts that now 'pierce thee through with many sorrows', and

if not timely prevented will at length 'drown the soul in everlasting perdition' (I: pp. 226-227).

Wesley's formulation matches the psychology of evangelical nurture. Inbred corruption symbolizes the effects of an unresolved fixation. The child's struggle for autonomy in face of the parent's disapproval produces adversarial conflict. To compensate for feelings of humiliation and envy, the child identifies with the parent's power, that is, "affecting to be like the most High". The narcissistic defense, expressed here as "pride," is cast as the fruit of corruption. Narcissistic wounds and their exaggerated compensations generate rage—"anger, hatred, malice"—and the fear of punishment. Conflict stemming from early object relations is here transcribed as a spiritual crisis. A struggle focusing on themes of "rebellion" and "independence" generates a horrible sense of separation from God and fear of his wrath. The latent content of the separation symbolism refers to the child's desire to be at one with the parent, a wish that is continually spoiled by danger, antagonism and dread of retaliation.

Self-knowledge of sin and contrition flow from this dynamic. For Wesley, this knowledge lies at the core of repentance. Methodist desolation is marked by a terrible guilt that is magnified to an extreme pitch.

> These 'who are sick', the 'burden of whose sins is intolerable', are they that 'need a physician'; these who are guilty, who groan under the wrath of God, are they that need a pardon. These who are 'condemned already', not only by God but also their own conscience, *as by a thousand witnesses*, of all their ungodliness, both in thought, and word, and work, cry aloud for him that 'justifieth the ungodly' (emphasis added; I: p. 192).

The stalemate of ambivalence and the burden of overwhelming guilt creates passivity, helplessness, and a pervasive sense of futility. As mentioned, Wesley's inculcation of despair is particularly apparent in his early sermons, while he still adhered to Moravian standards. The doctrine of the law rationalized this position. Wesley preached that until justification and the new birth, one remains subject to the old "covenant of works" (I: p. 210). This pact, which exacts unremitting perfection in both deed and intention, originally coincided with Adam's divine status prior to the fall. At that time, Adam's spiritual faculties bore the imprint of the *imago Dei*. Created in God's image, Adam was "righteous, merciful, true and pure," completely devoid of sin (Lindstrom, 1946, p. 25). Adam's divine nature enabled him to fully comply with the dictates of the law. After his transgression, God deprived Adam of the very faculties that ensured his perfection. Adam's loss of the *imago Dei* and his descent into abject carnality was subsequently passed on to the rest of humanity. As a result of original sin, the covenant of works necessarily devolved into a doctrine of unattainable ideals. Now, the total poverty of righteousness leads to "despair over works." Wesley writes:

> Alas, thou canst do nothing...If thou couldst now do all things well, if from this very hour, till thy soul should return to God, thou couldst perform perfect, uninterrupted obedience, even this would not atone for what is past...Yea, the present and future obedience of all the men upon the earth, and all the angels in heaven, would never make satisfaction to the Justice of God for one single sin (1984-87, I: p. 228).

We find perhaps the most graphic and systematic depiction of the repentance desolation in Wesley's 1746 sermon, *The Spirit of Bondage and Adoption*. Wesley begins his discussion by describing repentance as a horrid awakening into fear of an omnipotent, vengeful deity.

> He is terribly shaken out of his sleep, and awakes into a consciousness of his danger...Horrid light breaks in upon his soul; such light as may be conceived to gleam from the bottomless pit...He at last sees the loving, the merciful God is also a 'consuming fire'; that he is a just God and a terrible rendering to every man according to his works, entering into judgment with the ungodly for every idle word, yea and for the imaginations of the heart. He now clearly perceives...that he is an avenger of everyone who rebelleth against him, and repayeth the wicked to his face; and that 'it is a fearful thing to fall into the hands of the living God' (I: p. 255).

The knowledge of God's awesome fury brings with it an acute awareness of the infallible righteousness and omnipresence of his law. This leads to an exaggerated sense of self-reproach.

> The inward spiritual meaning of the law of God now begins to glare upon him. He perceives the 'commandment is exceeding broad', and 'there is nothing hid from the light thereof'. He is convinced that every part of it relates not barely to outward sin or obedience, but to what passes in the secret recesses of the soul, which no eye but God's can penetrate. If he now hears, 'Though shalt not kill', God speaks in thunder, 'He that hateth his brother is a murderer...If the law say, 'Thou shalt not commit adultery', the voice of the Lord sounds in his ears, 'He that looketh on a woman to lust after her hath committed adultery with her already in his heart' (I: pp. 257-258).

The conviction that one has "trodden under foot the Son of God" (I: p. 256) creates overwhelming guilt and further augments the negative sense of self.

> So he sees himself naked, stripped of all the fig-leaves which he had sewed together, of all his poor pretenses to religion or virtue, and his wretched excuses for sinning against God...His heart is bare, and he sees it is all sin, 'deceitful above all things, desperately wicked; that it is altogether corrupt and abominable, more than it is possible for tongue to express; that there dwelleth there no good thing, but unrighteousness and ungodliness only; every motion thereof, every temper and thought, being only evil continually (I: p. 256).

Self-hatred strengthens the conviction that one truly deserves eternal damnation.

> And he not only sees, but feels in himself, by an emotion of soul which he cannot describe...[that] he deserves to be cast into the 'the fire that never shall be quenched'. He feels that 'the wages', the just reward, 'of sin', of his sin above all 'is death;' even the second death, the death which dieth not, the destruction of the body and soul in hell (I: p. 256).

In turn, the anticipation of death and damnation triggers persecutory anxiety.

> He feels...fear of death, as being to him the gate of hell, the entrance of death eternal; fear of the devil, the executioner of the wrath and righteous vengeance of God; fear of men, who if they were able to kill his body, would thereby plunge both body and soul into hell; fear, sometimes arising to such a height that the poor, sinful, guilty soul is terrified with everything, with nothing, with shades, with a leaf shaken of the wind. Yea, sometimes it may even border on distraction, making a man 'drunken, though not with wine', suspending the exercise of the memory, of the understanding, of all the natural faculties. Sometimes it may approach to the very brink of despair; so that he who trembles at the name of death may yet be ready to plunge into it every moment, to 'choose strangling rather than life' (I: p. 257).

Finally, desperate attempts to do away with sin meet with failure. Cycles of active reformation and sin lead to hopelessness. In short, the covenant of works drives home the futility of personal righteousness.

> Now he truly desires to break loose from sin, and begins to struggle with it. But though he strive with all his might he cannot conquer; sin is mightier than he. He would fain escape, but he is so fast in prison he cannot get forth...The more he strives, wishes, labours to be free, the more does he feel his chains, the grievous chains of sin, wherewith Satan binds and 'leads him captive at his will'...He is still in bondage and fear by reason of sin: generally of some outward sin...but always of some inward sin, some evil temper or unholy affection. And the more he frets against it, the more it prevails; he may bite, but cannot break his chain. Thus he toils without end...repenting and sinning again, till at length the poor sinful, helpless wretch is even at his wit's end, and can barely groan, 'O wretched man that I am, who shall deliver me from the body of this death?'...[he] is being hurried away by a force [he] cannot resist (I: pp. 258-260).

As mentioned, the religious symbolism of repentance repeats a conflict of ambivalence that stems from early interactions with the parent. *Wesley's description of repentance is a religious interpretation of neurosis.* The awakening into conviction involves the mobilization of a latent conflict, the emergence of a transference focused on a negative representation of deity.

Hostility is captured in the symbolism of corruption. The allure of carnal desire, the very essence and fruit of this condition, is the source of the soul's alienation from God. Corruption, by definition, breeds willful opposition to the law. For this reason, Wesley highlights the terminology of *rebellion*; he speaks of independence and an adversarial pride modeled on divine self-sufficiency. He refers to an innate "enmity against God" (IV: p. 155), and the wickedness of men's hearts (IV: p. 152). Rebellious pride leads to hatred, malice, and envy. The doctrinal notion of corruption promotes a conscious recognition of these feelings, and serves as a symbolic medium for coherent reflection. *The provision of this culturally congenial metaphor suspends the chronic denial of rage, so that rage overcomes self-deceptive barriers and is consciously acknowledged.* I stress this point because the integrative potential of Wesley's method depends on the awareness of aggression.

The problem of hatred towards God is a common theme in Protestant experience. Luther describes how his rage "as a sinner who could not find forgiveness in the sight of an angry and righteous God" (Rubin, 1994, p. 21) only quickened his already disturbed conscience. According to Jonathan Edwards, Christians regularly harbor wishes to dethrone God (p. 42). Because these wishes inspire fear, they remain hidden as a result of denial. Edward's notion, typified by the theme of rebellion, reminds us of Wesley's use of the phrase, "affecting to be like the most High." Similarly, intimations of revolt, envy and robbery inform Wesley's discussion of divine providence. In describing God's omnipresence, Wesley cautions against usurpation: "Walk humbly: for if you in any wise rob God of his honour, if you ascribe anything to yourself ...[it will be] 'an occasion of falling'...It is as long as you do this you are under the peculiar care of your Father which is in Heaven" (1984-87, II: p. 549).

Fantasies of usurpation relate directly to the authoritarian psychology of evangelical nurture. Klein (1988, p. 351) holds that reparation is spoiled by the child's wish to reverse the power structure of the child-parent relationship. This idea fits well with the sheer debility of personal righteousness. All attempts at reparation are, by definition, rendered useless by inbred wickedness. In a religious idiom, Wesley articulates the stalemate of love "corrupted" by hostility and resentment. Even sincere contrition and desire for forgiveness fail to provide consistent motives for action. The need to assert one's thwarted autonomy unconsciously fuels opposing impulses to reject the law. Under these conditions, personal righteousness remains inalienably tainted. Hence the disempowering cycle of repentance and transgression, of doing and undoing. The frustrated desire for autonomy repeatedly and irresistibly compels one back into sin. Psychologically, backsliding is akin to acting out. Wesley masterfully transposes the impairment of the will into religious language.

Wesley's discourse deftly portrays neurotic conflict. Consider the following passage:

> He is indeed a 'sinner that goeth two ways'—one step forward and another backward. He is continually building up with one hand and pulling down with the other. He loves sin, and he hates it: he is always seeking, and yet always fleeing from God. He would and he would not...He is a motley mixture of all sorts of contraries; a heap of contradictions jumbled in one. Oh, be consistent with thyself, one way or the other (Wesley, 1984-87, I: p. 638).

"Compulsive anti-moral" behavior was overdetermined by a further cultural variable that dovetailed with the infantile source of fixated rage. Rammage (1967) holds that Methodists influenced by Calvinistic conceptions of God revolted inwardly against an inscrutable tyrant who "saved or damned by arbitrary decree" (p. 203).

The obsessive thoughts reported by Puritans such as John Bunyan, Cotton Mather and Benjamin Colman were similarly viewed as proof of innate enmity (Rubin, 1994, pp. 53-54). Rack points out that doubt and the temptation to blaspheme are "familiar experiences" in the Methodist conversion literature and "part of the psychology of this type of convert" (1989, p. 425). Here, anger manifests consciously but is typically disavowed and displaced. Compulsive blaspheming was seen as the work of the devil (p. 425; King, 1983, p. 27). Wesley speaks of "evil angels" who darken the heart with infusions of rage and envy (1984-87, III: p. 22).

In line with the basic logic of neurotic conflict, the fear of retaliation accompanied the awareness of hostility. Now that the projection of aggression largely determines one's perception of God, the negative pole of the split imago comes menacingly to the fore. The angry deity of the old covenant is the displaced representation of a parental introject that condemns and demoralizes a paralyzed ego. Wesley portrays this God as uncompromisingly furious. He is a "consuming fire," an "avenger." His fierce displeasure is an "earthquake," a "mighty tempest" (I: p. 147). He vindictively casts unrepentant sinners to the bottomless pit, into the "jaws of everlasting destruction" (I: p. 147). The omnipotence of God's anger complements his piercing omniscience. Sinners see how the law is "exceeding broad" and that "there is nothing hid from the light thereof." The dread of retribution is coupled with scrupulously thorough self-condemnations, an index of the enormous scope of the original conflict and repression. We here observe a classic manifestation of neurotic guilt. Every idle word and every imagination of the heart are condemned. Thoughts are equivalent to deeds. Hatred and lust are equivalent to actual murder and adultery.

Profound self-blame inspires the belief that one is worthy of eternal damnation, and the anticipation of one's just deserts inspires persecutory anxiety. Wesley alludes to sado-masochistic fantasies of attack, the "fear of men, who if they were able to kill his body, would thereby plunge both body and soul into hell." Anxiety generalizes indiscriminately to all facets of perception: the "guilty soul is terrified with everything, with nothing, with shades, with a leaf shaken of the wind."

We have already considered how the covenant of works metaphorically portrays a conflict of ambivalence. Unresolved aggression, symbolized as the inherited residue of original sin, defiles personal righteousness. All forms of expiation remain ineffective by the taint of corruption. Not only does the religious symbolism of the covenant aptly characterize a psychological reality, but Wesley's preaching of the doctrine was specifically designed to instill hopelessness and despair. It exacerbated conflict and produced the equivalent of learned helplessness, a veritable "no-win" situation. Cohen's (1986) analysis of the effects of the covenant in Puritan spirituality also applies to Methodism. He speaks of a "theological noose," a contradictory "double-bind" (p. 62) that commands obedience while stipulating, in the same breath, its very impossibility. Echoing Holland's claim that Wesley's inculcation of passivity led to hysterical panic, Cohen writes, "Unveiling the Covenant of Works exposed congregations to conflicting signals...preachers fully expected the covenant to agitate their hearers, inducing affections of fear, enmity and fright" (p. 62). Cohen explicitly claims that the covenant encouraged neurotic behavior.

Here again, we find a subtext that both allegorizes and repeats a modal child-parent scenario. In the authoritarian style of uprearing, children develop a sense of inadequacy, futility and guilt when rigorous demands for impulse control supersede their developmental abilities to comply. Preaching the covenant of works induced neurotic reactions because it resonated unconsciously. It was an all too familiar story that activated an archaic and irresistible force not easily stilled.

To summarize, Wesley's depiction of repentance eloquently portrays a neurosis. Repentance includes the vicissitudes of aggression (corruption as innate wickedness, compulsive blaspheming, the deadlock of contrition versus rebellion); the punitive parental introject manifesting as the angry deity; aggravated conscience and pervasive guilt; persecutory anxiety; and agitated conflict leading to despair.

Methodist autobiographical accounts substantiate Wesley's account and my interpretation of it. Joseph Jones describes the disappointment he felt in his father, who brought "numerous troubles both on himself and his family, which ended in extreme poverty" (*Arminian Magazine*, 1789, p. 234). Jones laments that his father failed to apprentice him in his trade. At length, a kindly blacksmith, a distant relative of Jones, provided him with an opportunity to be trained. Although he was treated well, Jones "ran away" from his employer to find work in another town (p. 235). Later, he returned and the blacksmith graciously took him back. Then, after fleeing a second time, Jones found himself seized with fever and financially destitute. These circumstances catalyzed his repentance: "In this affliction I was brought to a sight of my sins, when I cried heartily to God for the pardon of them" (p. 236). Yearning for the Savior's forgiveness, and realizing that "reformation was necessary," he "became a diligent attendant on the means of grace, and was very regular in the performance of all the outward duties of religion" (p. 236). To his dismay, Jones soon discovered he was unable to follow through on his resolutions.

> But after a while I fell again into my old sin of drunkenness...I was more like a fiend than a man...for I cursed and swore, and altogether like one newly come from the bottomless pit. When I came to myself, I knew not where to hide my guilty head; and was greatly tempted to put an end to my wretched existence. As I now gave up all hopes of mercy...[I] tremblingly looked for all the fierceness of the Divine displeasure! Thus finding myself under

> the frowns of the Almighty, and my parents not suffering me to come near them, I was driven to almost everything that was desperate: and why I did not destroy myself no one but God can tell...the most horrid, terrifying and blasphemous thoughts that can be conceived had possession of my mind (p. 236).

Based on the information that Jones discloses in his narrative, I suggest that unresolved resentment towards his father played a key role in the conflict that shaped Jones's repentance crisis. He dealt with his resentment by identifying with his father, whom Jones regarded as neglectful and irresponsible. As if in prelude, he displaces his anger onto the "kindly" blacksmith, who, on two occasions, Jones rudely leaves in the lurch. After his illness, Jones finds another beneficent father figure in God, whose mercy "melts" Jones's heart. Ambivalence sets in again, however, and he abandons God by succumbing to drunkenness and verbal profanity. His guilt-ridden behavior instills anxiety, and his parent's refusal to have anything to do with him seemingly confirms "the fierceness of the Divine Displeasure." A feedback loop of aggression and bad conscience spirals towards hopelessness. Jones's fear further exacerbates his rage: "Thus finding myself under the frowns of the Almighty...I was driven to almost everything that was desperate." Aggression rebounds back and forth between self and object. Suicidal temptations blend with blasphemous thoughts; for example, "Thousands of temptations I had to curse the Father, Son and Holy Ghost" (p. 237). Jones's text affirms how sin is motivated by hostility and defiance, forms of acting out behavior.

> I was indeed as a vagabond upon the earth, and continually expecting when the wrath of the Almighty would visibly break forth! At length I grew so hardened, and insensible, as to dare the Almighty to do his worst! and as I had no hope of mercy, I gave the reigns to my lusts, and determined to have all the pleasure I could in this world (p. 237).

Jones's writing illustrates the psychological effects of the belief that divine acceptance depends conditionally on good works. The autobiographies also attest to the incapacitating effects of persecutory anxiety. Wesley by no means exaggerates when he refers to a mounting terror that "may even border on distraction," "suspending the exercise of the memory, of the understanding, of all the natural faculties" (1984-87, I: p. 257). Ruth Hall writes that during her crisis of repentance,

> My convictions grew deeper and deeper, till I was scarce fit for any business. I hardly had any natural understanding left, and no memory at all; so that if I went out to fetch anything, I had forgot it be-

fore I was half way down the street. I then, by the advice of my parents, who were afraid I should be quite distracted, removed to York (*Arminian Magazine*, 1781, p. 477).

REPENTANCE ATTACKS

We can identify hysterical attacks not only by obvious descriptions of extraordinary behavior and subjective experiences, but also by references to their specific duration. Because hysterical crises bring to climax issues that remain central throughout the entire desolation phase, Methodists regularly highlight the length of time in which the attacks transpired. In 1739, Wesley noted in his journal that while he preached, approximately eight individuals "dropped down as if dead" (quoted in Rammage, 1967, p. 147). They underwent "violent agonies," what Wesley calls the "the snares of death" (p. 147). While, for one individual, the "strong pain" lasted an hour, several others remained in this way for three days (p. 147).

Zechariah Yewdall provides a description of his brother's experience.

> One evening while in prayer with the family, the Lord visited him in an extra-ordinary manner. The heinousness of his crimes was presented to the eye of his mind; he saw the righteous displeasure of the almighty, the curse of the broken law, and the horrors of a guilty conscience: To his apprehension, Hell was moved from beneath to meet him. *His soul and body were in dreadful agony for two hours together*, and he cried aloud for mercy. We were even afraid the whole neighborhood would be alarmed. In the midst of this distress, the Lord was pleased to visit him in love (emphasis added; *Arminian Magazine*, 1795, p. 113).

Here the "extra-ordinary" character of the attack is, amongst other things, indicated by reference to its duration.

Hysterical somatizations and irregular motor behaviors, or "abnormal physical attacks" (Dimond, 1926, p. 126), commonly occurred during these crises. Surveying a wide variety of Methodist sources, Dimond provides a comprehensive set of symptomatic manifestations (pp. 277-279). I single out what appear to be the most salient items and reduce them to two general headings. The first heading, "general bodily disturbances," includes such items as: cold perspiration; muscle tremors and rigidity (p. 277); bodily paralysis (p. 278), for example, the "dropping down as dead" phenomena, currently referred to in certain evangelical circles as being "slain in the spirit" or "resting in the spirit" (see MacNutt, 1990); diffuse convulsions (Dimond, 1926, p. 279); heaving breasts (p. 279); and frantic bodily efforts representing "instinctive flight" (p. 278). The second heading, "oral-respiratory disturbances," a sub-grouping of the first, includes: labored breathing, suffocation and strangulation (p. 277); gasping, gulping and convulsive motions of the lips (p. 277); dry mouth (p. 278); loss of voice or conversely, loud roars and bellowing (p. 278); and oral aggressive behavior such as the gnashing of teeth and impulses to bite. Certain types of oral disturbances are associated with feelings of "repulsion and disgust" (pp. 143, 279): spitting; oral expulsion; and sensory hallucinations of noxious or evil tasting substances (p. 279).

Bodily disturbances frequently linked up with particular forms of ideation, often hallucinatory in nature (pp. 136-137), and precipitated a death crisis. At Gateshead Fell, Wesley asked those who cried aloud to describe their experiences. He writes, "Some said they felt as if a sword was running through them; others, that they thought a great weight lay upon them, as if it would squeeze them to the earth...and others...as if their whole body, was tearing to pieces" (quoted in Dimond, 1926, p. 131). Wesley also made inquiries about such phenomena at Newcastle.

> A few gave a more intelligible account of the piercing sense they had of their sins, both inward and outward, which were set in array against them roundabout; of the dread they were in the wrath of God and the punishment they had deserved, into which they seemed to be falling, without any way of escape. One of them told me, "It was as if I was just falling down from the highest place I have ever seen. I thought the devil was pushing me off and that God had forsaken me." Another said, " I felt the very fire of hell already kindled in my breast; and all my body was in as much pain as if I had been in a burning fiery furnace" (quoted in Dimond, 1926, p. 147).

The physical and mental upheavals of the death struggle all too easily invoked comparisons to labor. The metaphor seemed logical given that the ordeal so often climaxed with the new birth. Wesley recorded the following account in his journal.

> As my mother bore me with great pain, so did I feel great pain in my soul in being born of God. Indeed I thought the pains of death were upon me, and that my soul was taking leave of the body. I thought I was going to Him whom I saw with strong faith standing ready to receive me. In this violent agony I continued about four hours; and then I began to feel the 'Spirit of God bearing witness with my spirit that I was born of God'. Because I was a child of God, He 'sent forth the spirit of His Son into me, crying, Abba, Father'. For that is the cry of every new-born soul. O mighty, powerful, happy change! I who had nothing but devils ready to drag me to hell, now found I had angels to guard me to my reconciled Fa-

ther; and my Judge, who just before was ready to condemn me, was now become my righteousness (quoted in Lee, 1936, p. 285).

Furthermore, like real labor, mental anguish and convulsions took their toll on the body. Recipients of the attacks were left physically drained and exhausted (compare *Arminian Magazine*, 1779, pp. 32-33). Sarah Crosby states that her body felt "as though it had been beaten" (*Arminian Magazine*, 1806, p. 471).

Finally, in another variation of the attack, individuals presented as manifestly possessed by and consciously identified, to varying degrees, with demonic forces. Here repressed hostility erupted in the most undisguised manner. Individuals railed at God, as well as at preachers and other intermediaries who tried to exorcise the intruder and deliver their souls. Wesley noted the phenomenon in his journal.

> I was sent for to one in Bristol, who was taken ill the evening before. She lay on the ground furiously gnashing her teeth, and after a while roared aloud. It was not easy for three or four persons to hold her, especially when the name of Jesus was named. We prayed; the violence of her symptoms ceased, though without complete deliverance. In the evening I was sent for to her again. She began screaming before I came into the room; then broke out into a horrid laughter, mixed with blasphemy. One, who apprehended a preternatural agent to be concerned in this, asking, "How didst thou dare to enter into a Christian?" was answered, "She is not a Christian—she is mine." This was followed by fresh trembling, cursing, and blaspheming. My brother coming in, she cried out, "Preacher! Field preacher! I don't love field preaching." This was repeated two hours together, with spitting, and all expressions of strong aversion. We left her at twelve, and called again at noon the next day. And now it was, that God showed He heareth prayer. All her pangs ceased in a moment; she was filled with peace, and knew that the son of wickedness was parted from her (quoted in Dimond, 1926, pp. 152-153).

John Cennick provides a dramatic account of a hysterical outbreak amongst a crowd who gathered to hear him preach on the forgiveness of sins. The event occurred during a violent thunderstorm. He writes, "indeed, it seemed that the Devil, and much of the powers of darkness, were come among us" (*Arminian Magazine*, 1778, p. 180).

> Large Flashes of Lightning, and loud claps of Thunder, Mixed with the Screams of frightened Parents, and the Exclamations of nine distressed Souls!...many raving up and down, crying, "The Devil

will have me! I am his Servant! I am damned! My Sins can never be pardoned! I am gone, gone for ever!" A young man (in such Horrors, that seven or eight could not hold him) still roared, like a Dragon, "Ten thousand Devils, millions, millions of Devils are about me!" This continued three hours. One cried out, "That fearful Thunder is raised by the Devil: in this Storm he will bear me to Hell!" O what a power reigned amongst us! Some cried out with a hollow voice, "Mr. Cennick! Bring Mr. Cennick!" I came to all that desired me. *They then spurned with all their strength, grinding their teeth, and expressing all the Fury, that heart can conceive. Indeed, their staring eyes, and swelled faces, so amazed others, that they cried out as loud, as they who were tormented. I have visited several since, who told me, their Senses were taken away; but when I drew near, they said, they felt fresh Rage, longing to tear me to pieces!* (emphasis added; pp. 180-181).

Even for those manifestly possessed, their expressions of rage were displaced through dissociation. They attributed their malevolence to an external source, to a demonic infusion. However, we find some variability in the extent to which individuals remained detachedly aware of a foreign presence responsible for their actions. In Wesley's report, he depicts the woman as fully identified with her tormentor. Cases in which the capacity for self-reflection was entirely repressed presumably reflected hysterical or hypnotic dissociation. Cennick's account provides even further evidence of dissociation. Here intervals of fugue punctuated possession. Several claimed their senses were taken away when they were not in Cennick's immediate presence.

For many, however, the identification with evil was not exclusive. Despite their fury, those in Cennick's group simultaneously retained the ability to plead for assistance. In fact, possessions sometimes proceeded in an *entirely* ego-alien fashion. Although they experienced convulsions known to be the result of demonic intrusion, certain persons disidentified from the presence and the behaviors it provoked. In undergoing a possession attack, John Haydon beat himself against the ground while three men subdued him. At the same time, he remained sufficiently lucid and self-possessed to pass judgment on himself as a former skeptic. According to Wesley, during Haydon's seizure, he proclaimed, "Let all come and see the judgment of God...I said it was a delusion, I was wrong...O devil, O legion of devils. Christ will cast thee out. I know his work is begun. Tear me to pieces if thou wilt; but thou canst not hurt me" (Rammage, 1967, p. 150). The capacity to maintain self-reflection during dissociation is variable; it is termed "psychic depth" in the context of hypnosis (Schilder & Kauders, 1956; Shor, 1972b). In Methodism, self-reflection often remained active even in the midst of violent struggles. For the most part, throughout the attacks, be they acute abandonment desolations, convulsive death struggles, or demonic possessions, individuals retained the ability to appeal for divine assistance, and to confidently glorify God.

In explaining how the attacks were induced, several authors have advanced views that rely exclusively on external variables and neglect the role of predisposing personality factors. Dimond (1926) argues that attacks were precipitated by hypnotic dissociation due to the effects of a "crowd mentality" (pp. 133-135). Dimond's explanation fails, however, because the attacks were not limited to public gatherings. Southey (1820) and Sargant (1959; 1976) emphasize the inculcation of terror. They suggested that Wesley's great skill as an orator, his impassioned admonishments of sin and terrifying threats of damnation, instilled a terror that led to hysterical outbursts. However, Holland (1973-74) challenges the portrayal of Wesley as a "heated" hellfire preacher. He shows that Wesley was "calmly logical as an orator" and did not frequently deal with the subject of hell in his sermons (pp. 80-81). Holland attributes the hysterical attacks to a sense of helplessness rather than to fear alone. "To become hysterical, people must feel not only threatened but also to some extent trapped or helpless in the face of that threat" (p. 80). Holland claims that the attacks that occurred in Wesley's early ministry resulted from a combination of two factors: his then current view that without the full measure of faith one was still damned, and his conception of faith as passively received. This argument also falls short, because it fails to account for the persistence of hysterical attacks beyond the early period.

Picking up on Holland's lead, I suggest that the sense of helplessness and the violent behavior that it created derived primarily from internal conflict and the anxiety attendant upon gradually overcoming resistances to painful materials. Both Wesley himself and some of his cohorts resorted to a conflict model to make sense of the attacks. They believed that demonic resistance produced the convulsive episodes. Cennick, in fact, held that diabolic opposition was stirred even before the convulsions erupted. He claimed that the preceding dread of abandonment already reflected a demonic antagonism hastened by the invitation to accept Christ.

> Now, after the word of the Most High has touched the heart...the Serpent is seeking to root it up...but as the Spirit of God has gained entrance, he rageth with all his might...[and] troubleth the soul with the Justice of God, with Fear of having passed the Day of Grace, or having sinned too greatly to be forgiven, in order to make them despair. Hence ariseth a fierce combat in the inward parts, so that he weaker part of man, the Body, is overcome, and those Cries and Convulsions follow (*Arminian Magazine*, 1778, p. 180).

Wesley's position was less straightforward given his uncertainty (Rack, 1989, pp. 196-197). He was aware of naturalistic explanations such as epilepsy and hysteria, but believed that the physical agonies he observed had a supernatural origin. Wesley wavered between viewing the attacks as the work of the devil "tearing" individuals as they came to Christ (quoted in Rammage, 1967, p. 173) and as the result of the Holy Spirit applying the conviction of sin. In his final pronouncement, Wesley stated that either of these causes could be operative (Rammage, 1967, p. 174).

Demonic resistance theory posits a dynamic interruption of the relationship to Christ. More specifically, *Christ's offer of love and pardon elicits stringent opposition*. Empirical observation gave credence to this observation. In contrast to theories that place a premium on damnation fear as the cause of the attacks, Wesley observed that most of his converts were "cut to the heart while he was inculcating the doctrine that Christ died to save sinners" (Gunther, 1989, p. 148).

This trend has not gone unnoticed by scholars (Rack, 1989, p. 228; Rammage, 1967, pp. 149, 158-59, 160-161, 206). For Rammage (1967), this observation provides the key for comprehending the core psychodynamics of the repentance attacks. He stresses that although Wesley emphasized the "sin and hopelessness" of natural man, this was essentially a "preamble" to his real message: the infinite mercy of God (p. 124-125). Rammage argues that in rejecting the doctrine of predestination and "abolishing the arbitrariness of God's justice and the uncertainty of his mercy" (p. 131), Wesley radically undermined the authoritarian conception of God. The promise of unconditional acceptance struck a profound chord in the "love starved hearts" (p. 221) of his listeners. The deprivations of childhood left their emotional lives impoverished. The ongoing repression of hatred and resentment exacted a heavy price. In being persuaded by Wesley of God's benevolent intentions, an archaic wish to embrace the good parent was reawakened and effectively set in motion. However, images of the positive imago were inextricably bound to their opposite, to the painfully fixated representations of the bad parent. In order to access the former, a wedge had to be driven through the layer of repressed feelings and fantasies associated with parental trauma. The desire to surrender lovingly to Christ aroused fears of a traumatic repetition. The anticipation of rejection prompted fresh eruptions or rage, which only intensified separation anxiety (compare: Fauteux, 1994, p. 68). Given the threat of retraumatization, now expressed in terms of divine wrath and demonic assault, resistance understandably intensified. Yet, in so many instances, longstanding defenses were eventually let go. Rammage (1967) holds that Wesley's benign portrayal of God offered a haven of safety (p. 202). Unconscious materials could now be delivered up, explored, and, in the case of the attacks, dramatically abreacted and worked through.

Rammage also draws a clinical analogy. He singles out the analyst's unconditional acceptance of the patient's hatred and destructiveness. He writes, "Only in a relationship where the expression of his feelings will no longer be a threat to his safety can the patient acknowledge them" (p. 234). For Rammage, convulsive crises were healing abreactions of "primitive and powerful emotions of hatred" (p. 188).

During the desolation phase, the problem of the split imago takes center stage. From an intrapsychic point of view, we may say that, while trying to negotiate their salvation, individuals remained precariously suspended between the contrasting poles of a split representation of Deity. We can best conceptualize the resistance encountered in surrendering to Christ as a failure of trust. Inasmuch as one continues to rage against God, one can never be certain of his mercy. Trust is perpetually spoiled by projective fantasies of retaliation. *Stated differently, resistance is born of a dread that during the moment of surrender the good object will transform into its abandoning and persecutory opposite.*

Ambivalence leading to the projective oscillation and confusion of internal object representations generates resistance to unitive ecstasies (Fauteux, 1994, p. 71). In commenting on the vicissitudes of ecstatic merger states, Modell (1968) states: "when there is an intense fear of merging with the 'bad' object the subject may fear a loss of identity, a dread of being influenced, and ultimately, [the subject] may fear complete annihilation" (p. 37). In a related context outside of the discussion of religious ecstasy, Klein (1988) refers to the way in which aggression can promote a paranoid confusion of good and bad internal objects. In her view, persecutory anxiety depletes one's trust in the good object. Consider the following case vignette:

> The night after his mother's funeral, D dreamt that X (a father-figure) and another person (who stood for me) were trying to help him, but actually he had to fight for his life against us; as he put it: 'Death was claiming me'...I interpreted that he felt the helpful external parents to be at the same time the fighting disintegrating parents, who would attack and destroy him...and that I myself and analysis had come to stand for the dangerous people and happenings inside himself (p. 366).

The unconscious fear that aggression will obliterate the good object finds symbolic expression in Methodism in the fear of taking the sacrament. Autobiographical reports continually make mention of this phenomenon (for example, *Arminian Magazine* 1779, p. 186, p. 471; 1789, p. 415; 1798, p. 5). The belief that "unprepared and careless" ingestion of the Lord's body and blood was a dangerous undertaking traces back to New Testament times

(Rack, 1989, p. 20). The dread of "eating and drinking one's own damnation" (*Arminian Magazine* 1798, p. 5), a notion already given credence by the authority of scripture, was so common that John Wesley felt moved to address the problem in one of his sermons. He reminded supplicants that communion appeals to God's mercy, not his wrath. Through it, God offers not damnation, but pardon (1984-87, III: pp. 433-34). In eating the holy sacrament, and communing with the purified body of divinity, individuals feared their own corruption would rob the host of its inherent goodness, and that such sacrilege would provoke retaliation. This dynamic also played out in the attacks that preceded the equally sacramental moment of justification.

In the midst of their attacks, Methodists typically preserved the good object by displacing persecutory dread onto the devil. The shift, effected through a change of symbolism, maintained the integrity of the good object and safeguards the therapeutic alliance. Protective displacement also proceeded by deflecting anger against the self, for example, as convulsive outbursts. This view correlates with Fenichel's explanation of "hystero-epilepsy."

> Very intense destructive and sadistic drives which have been repressed for a long time...find an explosive discharge in the seizure. The repression of destructive drives [through their containment in convulsions] is due to an intense fear of retaliation (quoted in Merkur, 1998, p. 39).

However, something more than displacement must occur in order for the attacks to work as "healing abreactions." In ideal circumstances, the experiential sign of God's acceptance successfully curtailed the attacks. At this juncture, Methodists achieved a partial working through of primitive anxieties, as well as the conscious acknowledgment and tolerance of rage. As a result of mastery, made possible through symbolic means, individuals experienced a high degree of self-esteem, a feeling represented by divine pardon. Sarah Crosby offers a description of a desolation attack that demonstrates the conscious working through of conflict stemming from parental authoritarianism.

> And now the fiery hour came...I was in such agony of body and soul, as it is not easy to conceive. In an hour and a half, I had hardly life left in me...but for several days, my body was as though it had been beaten...God had shut out my spirit from his presence *for ever*; compared to which misery, I thought, had ministers trampled me under their feet, it would have been as nothing. Satan now suggested, "Will you ever exalt Christ again? Will you dare to say, God is Love?" I answered, in my heart, "I will exalt Jesus Christ; I

will say *God is Love,* while I have breath." Then said he, "Where is now his love to let you suffer thus?"

In the midst of these exercises, however, the Lord lifted up my head, and often enabled me to say, in faith, "Although the fig-tree do not blossom, and there be no fruit on the vine, or heard in the stall, &c. yet will I rejoice in the Lord, and joy in the God of my salvation; for when he has tried me, I shall come forth as gold."

I now perceived God had restrained the tempter, and began to inquire, "What condemnation is there in my soul?" There is no condemnation for those that are in Jesus Christ. How is it, that, in all I have suffered for these three years past, I have not felt the least inclination to turn back from the path of life, or entertained one hard thought of God?" I then appealed to him: Lord, dost thou not know that all my aims and intentions are upright before thee?" And I felt a witness in myself it was so...I now felt my soul fully cast on the Lord Jesus, and found a rest, which before I had not known, while peace and love filled my heart (*Arminian Magazine*, 1806, pp. 471-472).

At the beginning of her attack, Crosby deals with rage by turning it against herself. She refers to an anguish that left her feeling for several days afterward as though she had been beaten up. She also displaces her hostility towards God by reversing and then projecting her rage: she speaks of ministers trampling her underfoot. Her anger leads to separation anxiety and the conviction that God has permanently deprived her of his presence. Here we see the symbolic repetition of the object relational drama between the child and the authoritarian parent. Because hostility signals the threat of abandonment, it must be defensively controlled. In this case, Crosby's concern that she has been forsaken is a disguised acknowledgment of her rage. Furthermore, the very nub of the infantile conflict is summed up in the devil's suggestion: "Where is now his love to let you suffer thus?" In the context of evangelical nurture, this question expresses the unthinkable and unanswerable predicament that the child must, at all cost, repress. While she is tempted to disbelieve, that is, to resist Christ as a bad object, Crosby simultaneously "exercises" her commitment to the Lord. Even during the height of her attack, she proclaims her "faith," her confidence that she will "come forth as gold." In demonstrating her allegiance to her ideal, she overcomes anxiety and the masochistic distortions of the bad parental introject. Under the sway of a newly emerging ego-ideal, Crosby for the first time evaluates herself in a positive light. She perceives that the tempter is "restrained"; no longer "condemned," she re-assesses her conduct in the previous three years and rationally deduces that she is an "upright" Christian. The ego-ideal reinforces this evaluation through a symbolic conferral of acceptance: "And I felt a witness in myself it was so."

RITUAL MOURNING

Whether individuals were overtly depressed prior to their contact with Methodism, or subsequently brought into depression on hearing Wesley's message, they were encouraged to voluntarily heighten their sadness and anxiety through practices of ritual mourning. Methodist biographies describe a variety of mourning practices, including fasting, sleep deprivation, lamentation, and solitude. Wesley knew the process well. He recognized it in scripture. Quoting the New Testament, Wesley states that those who "receive the spirit of fear" (compare: Romans 8: 15; 2: Timothy 1:7) should view it as a "gift of God" (I: p. 250): "And thus is the scripture fulfilled: 'Blessed are they that mourn, for they shall be comforted'" (Matthew 5: 4; I: p. 424). Backed by divine decree, Wesley literally *commands* his followers to know their corruption. He enjoins sinners to actively enhance their guilt and voluntarily deepen their depression.

> For he that cometh unto God by this faith must fix his eye singly on his own wickedness, on his guilt and helplessness, without having the least regard to any supposed good in himself, to any virtue or righteousness whatsoever. He must come as a *mere sinner* inwardly and outwardly, self-destroyed and self-condemned, bringing nothing to God but ungodliness only, pleading nothing of his own but sin and misery. Thus it is, and thus alone, when his 'mouth is stopped', and he stands utterly 'guilty before God', that he can 'look unto Jesus' as the whole and sole 'propitiation for his sins'. Thus only can he be 'found in him' and receive the 'righteousness which is of God by faith'...Go as altogether ungodly, guilty, lost, destroyed, deserving and dropping into hell, and thou shalt then find favor in his sight (1984-87, I: p. 198).

To escape God's judgments, one should "cast [one]self into them. 'Judge thyself', and thou shalt 'not be Judged of the Lord'" (I: p. 147). Deliberate self-condemnation combines with grieving. Sinners must earnestly "cry aloud" to receive forgiveness: "Now weep for your sins, and mourn after God till he turns your heaviness into joy. And even then weep with them that weep, and for them that weep not for themselves" (I: p. 696).

We find further evidence of ritual mourning in Wesley's discussion of fasting. Wesley saw a definite link between fasting and melancholy. Citing instances from scripture, he points out that "strong emotions of mind," "any vehement passion such as sorrow or fear," deprive individuals of their desire to eat (I: p. 597). Depressive affect is the "natural ground of fasting": "One who is under the deep affliction, overwhelmed with sorrow for sin, and a strong apprehension of the wrath of God [naturally abstains]...not only from pleasant, but even from needful food" (I: p. 598). Deliberate fasting expiates sin and "weans" the soul from the "indulgences of the inferior appetites which naturally tend to chain it down to earth" (I: p. 600). It is "a means of averting God's wrath" (I: p. 601). Wesley disapproved of self-abusive asceticism: self-flagellation, mutilation, starvation, and the neglect of proper clothing (I: pp. 594-595, 609). However, he stipulated the necessity of self-sacrifice. Those who "desire to walk humbly and closely with God will find frequent occasion for private seasons of thus afflicting their souls before their Father which is in secret" (I: p. 597). Intimately tied to the induction of religious melancholy, fasting acted as an "outward" means by which one received grace (I: p. 605).

> But let us take care to afflict our souls as well as bodies. Let every season, either of public and private fasting, be a season of exercising all those holy affections which are implied in a broken and contrite heart. Let it be a season of devout mourning, of Godly sorrow for sin...'For godly sorrow', the sorrow which is according to God, which is a precious gift of his Spirit, lifting the soul to God from whom it flows, 'worketh repentance to salvation, not to be repented of' (I: pp. 609-610).

For Wesley, fasting helped one to attain faith (I: p. 60). He furnishes his text with biblical examples in which fasting is clearly tied to ecstatic modes of revelation in prophecy, dreams and visions (I: pp. 602-603).

Methodist autobiographies document the use of various forms of ritual mourning. I single out three kinds of data that appear frequently. These are fasting, grieving in solitude, and, more generally, the psychological paradox inherent in the use of depression inducing techniques. Let us consider each of these items in turn.

Fasting

In many of the narratives, fasting was "added to all the other means of grace" (*Arminian Magazine*, 1780, p. 480) during desolation. Even though Wesley proscribed harmful forms of mourning, the autobiographical evidence suggests that his followers frequently disregarded the rule. John Nelson (1842, p. 18) writes, "I would neither eat nor drink, till I had found the Kingdom of God." For three weeks, John Atlay did not sleep or eat, "but just enough to keep life" (*Arminian Magazine*, 1778, p. 578). Four days after his justification, Richard

Moss found himself in darkness (*Arminian Magazine*, 1798, p. 53-54). The comforting sense of God's presence had vanished abruptly. He consequently "tried every means of recovering the Light," but to no avail. Doubting whether his sins had really been taken away, Moss resorted to fasting.

> I never eat a full meal, so that I was hungry from the beginning of the week to the end. From Thursday noon till Saturday noon, I tasted no food at all. Insomuch, that I was quite worn away, and grown weak, that I could scarcely walk...I wished I had never been born or, that my soul and body might die together. I was weary of life, and would have starved myself to death; only for offending God (pp. 53-54).

We know that excessive fasting often played a role in Christian asceticism prior to Protestantism. Menninger (1938, pp. 77-126) and Mounteer (1981, p. 160) argue that the deliberate starvation of Christian martyrs, practiced, for example, by the early Desert Fathers, expressed buried feelings of hatred and revenge towards parents. These feelings, which, according to both authors, lead to cannibalistic urges to devour and destroy, are penitentially turned against the self. Starvation represents a primitive compromise formation. It both denies and displaces rage. Similarly, Rubin holds that in Protestant tradition, excessive fasting is a culture-bound syndrome that connects to evangelical nurture (1994, pp. 82-87). "Evangelical anorexia nervosa" (p. 82), as he refers to it, was one of several forms of "humiliation" and "self-maceration" that individuals used to assuage guilt and gain acceptance (p. 87). The features that characterized this syndrome included starvation, anxiety, sleep disorders, and obsessive-compulsive ceremonials. Because self-interest also pertained to the satisfaction of the body's natural appetites, conflicts focusing on autonomy made their way into the domain of orality. Fasting, taken to a symptomatic extreme, arose out of a deadlock in which the hope of receiving forgiveness was offset by the pessimistic conviction that one was destined for damnation.

Wesley designated fasting as a means to avert God's wrath (1984-87, I: p. 601). This suggests that eating was unconsciously permeated with aggressive meanings. In the autobiographies, images of the demonic, of greed, malice and persecution, often related to orality. For example, Richard Moss, who fasted until he could hardly walk, refused to take the Lord's Supper for fear that if he sinned afterwards, he would "eat and drink his own damnation" (*Arminian Magazine*, 1798, p. 5). While fasting, a "strange horror" disrupted his prayers: "It seemed as if the enemy were just by me, *ready to swallow me up*" (emphasis added; p. 54). J.B. of St. Hellier expresses both the divine and the demonic in terms of oral aggression. She begins her memoir with a standard trope: "I was one day deeply troubled. It seemed Hell was just ready to devour me, for the sins I had committed" (*Arminian Magazine*, 1788, p. 71). Further on she describes an eidetic image (perhaps a vision) in which the Lord revealed to her how he had destroyed "the man of sin": "I beheld sin as a horrible monster, which the Lord *dismembered*, till the whole appeared lifeless and *torn in pieces*" (emphasis added; p. 183). In his writings, Wesley employed biblical images that relied on oral metaphors. He refers to Hell as the "jaws of everlasting destruction" and portrays sinners as "swallowed up" and "consumed" by sin (2 Thessalonians 1:9). He speaks of idolatry as swallowing up the unawakened (I: p. 113). Elsewhere he explains how sins "have gashed and mangled us all over. They are diseases that drink up our blood and spirits" (I: p. 586). Similarly, the hysterical panic attacks of repentance included oral aggressive fantasies of mutilation and dismemberment, as well as behaviors such as gnashed teeth, choking, suffocation, and spitting (Rammage, 1967, pp. 131, 152-153).

All this suggests that fasting, as a form of atonement, was a reaction formation, a passive denial of rage. Those who abstained from food humbled themselves sacrificially. The unholy vicissitudes of oral sadism—greed, envy, voraciousness, and destruction—are diabolical hallmarks of carnality. They constitute the repressed underside of evangelical nurture. Extreme fasting, emaciation and exhaustion, served as demonstrative submissions, as palpable proofs that one had really forsaken willfulness in exchange for grace. The masochistic character of fasting dovetails with an object-relational pattern internalized by children weaned on evangelical authoritarianism. They learned that parents bestowed their love on condition of pain. Early on, children developed a modal fantasy that parental acceptance hinged on suffering and deprivation. Oral sadism was masochistically reversed. Through ritual fasting and, in the extreme, starvation and physical depletion, Methodists hoped to assuage God's anger and finally receive his forgiveness.

Solitude

In seeking the proper way to conversion, many Methodists consulted several of the old practical Puritan works by authors such as Alleine, Baxter and Bunyan (Rack, 1989, p. 176). Like Wesley's writings, these texts served as instruction manuals, just as they did in their own cultural setting during the previous century. King (1983, p. 40) states that prominent spiritual narratives functioned in Puritanism like oral traditions in that "conventions of writing became a force capable of fashioning a person's reality...the Puritan autobiographer offers his soul's anguish as an exemplum or as an affliction for emulation." Methodists readily inherited this tradition.

In his autobiography, Silas Told (1954), who was separated from his mother at an early age and "sent to nurse at Kingswood" (p. 12), explains that during childhood he felt only bliss in comprehending God. He portrays his early spiritual experiences in an exuberant, if not rapturous, light. While he was still in petticoats, he was often "transported in such a measure with heavenly bliss, that whether in the body or out of the body [he] could not tell" (p. 16). He found peace "meditating on things divine." Church services were "a heaven upon earth." He "drank deep into the bliss of ever blessed and adorable Jesus" (pp. 57-58). At the age of ten, when Told began to "read pious books, especially Pilgrim's Progress," we see a decisive shift in his religious sensibilities. The suggestive force of Bunyon's text clearly stimulated his repentance at the age of twelve.

> Sitting one day, reading the Pilgrim's Progress, I suddenly laid down the book, leaned my right elbow on my knee, with my hand supporting my head, and meditated in the most solemn manner upon the awfulness of eternity. Suddenly I was struck as with a hand on the top of my head, which affected my whole frame; the blow was immediately followed by a voice, with these words, "Dark! dark! dark!" and although it alarmed me prodigiously, yet upon the recovery from so sudden a motion, I found myself broad awake in the world of sin. Notwithstanding all my former happiness, I now found nothing could give me satisfaction; nor could I ever rest satisfied about my salvation, as temptations from the world, the flesh, and the devil were ever besetting me (pp. 58-59).

In his thirties, Told endured a long period of depression that conforms to religious melancholy. Told's depiction of his depression borrows the language of Bunyan's own spiritual narrative, *Grace Abounding to the Chief of Sinners*. Told takes long solitary walks in fields, "roaring for the very disquietude of [his] soul" (p. 75). Begrudging the placid ignorance of the beasts, he chooses "strangling rather than life," believing that suicide will "afford him the greatest happiness" (p. 75).

Methodism inherited the practice of solitude and withdrawal from Puritanism. The Puritan motif of the self-exiled sinner searching for God in the wilderness was literally enacted as a technique. Methodists commonly mourned in the solitude of fields, woods, barns and private chambers. As we have just seen, Silas Told took this approach. One Sabbath-day during John Pawson's desolation, he attended preaching but, as he puts it, "could not break through" (*Arminian Magazine*, 1779, p. 27).

> When it was over, I walked into the garden and wept bitterly. From thence I went into a solitary place and, where no one might see me,

> bemoaned myself before the Lord. O, the anguish I then felt. I was scarcely able to look up (pp. 27-28).

John Hanby explains that he spent much time "praying in the fields, woods, and barns."

> Any place, and every place, was now a closet to my mourning soul, who longed for the Day-Star to arise in my poor benighted heart. And it pleased infinite mercy, while I was praying in a dark place (greatly terrified for fear I should see the devil), that the Lord set my weary soul at liberty...[with an] extasy of joy (*Arminian Magazine*, 1780, pp. 511-512).

Hanby spent much time "in the fields, praying and meditating" (p. 513). He refers to these practices as his "method." William Carvosso (1835), whose mind was "greatly distressed" because he had yet to receive the blessing of sanctification, "turned into a lonely barn to wrestle with God in secret prayer" (p. 42). He writes, "While kneeling on the threshing-floor, agonizing for the great salvation, this promise was applied to my mind, 'Thou art fair, My love; there is no spot in thee'" (p. 42).

Several narratives refer to childhood convictions that are similarly coupled with the practice of solitude. Mrs. A.B. reports that somewhere around the age of ten, she experienced "great distress" over her "lost estate" (*Arminian Magazine*, 1789, pp. 414-415).

> I wandered in the woods. I did not communicate my feelings to any person, nor had I indeed anyone to whom I could open my mind, or could be of use to me. At length, one day as I was wrestling in prayer in a wood, I found a measure of that rest which I sought: I found love and joy in my heart, and retained a degree of it till I was fifteen years of age (p. 415).

Being "much afflicted" from her infancy, S. Mallit began to seek God when she was nine years old (*Arminian Magazine*, 1788, p. 130). The question of who God was, and why she had been brought into the world "troubled her."

> My trouble so increased, that I was deprived of my sleep, and often passed the night in weeping. I was frequently weeping in the day too; so that some thought I was going melancholy. One night *as I was mourning by myself*, the Lord took pity and revealed himself to me. In a moment all my sorrow was turned into joy, and I knew I was made to love and serve God (emphasis added; p. 130).

Albin (1985) provides further evidence of the importance of isolation as a facet of ritual mourning. In his sample, Methodists were alone in slightly less than half of the reported cases of conversion (42.8%; p. 278). This was also the case for those who were instantaneously sanctified (45.6%; p. 279).

Solitude fostered sensory deprivation. Individuals actively sought secluded low stimulus settings such as private chambers, stables and barns, and many recount mourning alone under the cover of night. Recall that John Hanby's soul was set at liberty while praying alone "in a dark place." Experimental research on sensory deprivation shows that it can induce alternate states of consciousness whose contents range from simple eidetic images, extended dreamlike sequences, and unitive experiences (Bexton et al, 1954; Lilly, 1956; Heron et al, 1956; Merkur, 1993). Merkur demonstrates how sensory deprivation evokes visionary experiences in religious contexts such as Inuit shamanism and initiation (1992), Jewish apocalypticism (1989), where it is combined with darkness, solitude, fasting and sleep deprivation, and Hellenistic Gnosticism (1993).

Self-Reflective Grieving

In examining Methodists' descriptions of mourning, not only do we see them deliberately applying techniques designed to deepen their convictions, we also see an intriguing pattern that is best described as a psychological paradox. In these descriptions, one sector of the personality feels authentically and deeply distressed, while another self-consciously applies a technique, assesses its effects and anticipates the joyous arrival of the spirit. Put differently, *part of the ego remains relatively detached from the process in order to engage in self-reflection and to make "executive decisions" with respect to actions that intensify the depression.* The characteristics ascribed to this self-observing function stem from an intra-psychic "therapeutic alliance" between the ego and the positive superego. Ideally, the alliance creates a safe holding space in which the transference neurosis onto God can develop. As a result, painful materials that fuel the depression are permitted to emerge and be managed until dispelled by the justification ecstasy.

We find a good example of this fascinating "dual-consciousness" in John Pawson's narrative (*Arminian Magazine*, 1779, pp. 29-32). He describes a difficult struggle with his father who strenuously objected to his son's involvement with the Methodists. After continual threats of disinheritance, Pawson finally convinced his father to attend a number of Methodist services, whereupon Pawson senior became amenable and "began to pray that the Lord would shew him the way of Salvation" (pp. 29-30).

> A little later after [Pawson senior] went...into the stable, where he thought no-body could hear or see him, and prayed earnestly to the Lord. Here it was that the light of the Holy Spirit broke in upon him: he now had a clear sight of his sinful and lost condition, and was brought into such distress, that...he roared for the very disquietness of his soul. He was now ashamed and confounded, and could hardly hope for mercy. This was a day of glad tidings to me...(p. 30).

Once the conflict with his father subsided, Pawson turned to the state of his own soul. He writes, "Though I knew myself to be without God in the world, I was dull and unaffected" (p. 30). Having assessed himself in this manner, he begins to cultivate his own repentance.

> It was my continual prayer, that the Lord would take away my heart of stone, and give me a heart of flesh. I cried day and night unto him, that he would give me a broken and a contrite heart, and it was not long ere he inclined his ear. I went to hear the word at a neighboring village, when, in the beginning of the service, the power of God came mightily upon me and many others. All of a sudden my heart was like melting wax, and my soul was distressed above measure, I cried with an exceeding bitter cry; the trouble and anguish of spirit that I labored under far exceeding all description. The arrows of the Almighty struck fast in my flesh, and the poison of them drank up my spirits; yet in the height of my distress I could thank the Lord, that he had granted me what I had so long sought for. I now sought the Lord with my whole heart, and neglected no opportunity of hearing his word, or of waiting upon him in every means of grace; yet many times did I not hear one half of the sermon, my distress being so exceedingly great. I had such a clear sight and deep sense of my exceeding sinfulness, that I was humbled in the dust...The things of this world became quite bitter to me...my mind being so occupied with grief for my past sins, and with my desire to be delivered from them. My business became a burden to me: I was quite confused and brought very low... I was on the very brink of despair (pp. 30-31).

One morning, while walking in the fields, Pawson was tempted to believe that it was "all in vain...to expect any mercy" (p. 31). The Lord then revived his "drooping heart" with the word, "O tarry thou the Lord's leisure: be strong and he shall comfort thy heart" (p. 31). This enabled him "both to hope and quietly wait for the salvation of God" (p. 31). Next, Pawson describes feeling discouraged by news of an acquaintance "who had only heard about three sermons" but was "brought to enjoy a clear sense of the love of God" (p. 32).

> I returned home, and immediately retired into my chamber; but here I had no sufficient opportunity to give vent to my grief: I therefore walked into the barn, where I thought no one could see or hear me. Here I prayed and wept, and roared aloud, my distress being greater than I was able to bear: yet, I was not quite without hope, but expected, vile as I was, that the Lord would at last be gracious unto me (p. 32).

Pawson's narrative provides a clear account of deliberate mourning and the paradoxes of induced depression. He explains how his father, after asking the Lord to show him the way to salvation, withdrew into a stable to pray and consequently received a clear sight of his sins. Pawson junior rejoiced over his father's good fortune in becoming afflicted: "This was a day of glad tidings to me." Influenced by example, Pawson observed his own state of unaffectedness, and began to mourn by crying unto the Lord and petitioning for a "broken and contrite heart." His entreaties incubated unconsciously and later found incentive to manifest during a public service. Pawson's heart promptly "melted like wax." His soul "was distressed beyond measure" and he bitterly cried aloud. Here we see how auto-suggestive incubation plays a central role in the amplification of religious melancholy. In some instances, suggestive incubation led to panic attacks. For example, in a separate narrative, Zechariah Yewdall states that he would do and suffer anything "to find the blessing and peace of God" (*Arminian Magazine*, 1792, p.164). He beseeched God to "shake him over the mouth of Hell" (p. 164). Shortly thereafter, he attended a prayer meeting and, in contemplating his hypocrisy, discovered the wrath of God hanging over his head. Frightened of "dropping into Hell" (p. 164), Yewdall, along with several others, wailed for two hours, while friends stood by and prayed over them.

Returning to Pawson's account, we see that, despite his anguish, he remains encouraged: "yet in the height of my distress I could bless the Lord, that he had granted me that which I had so long sought for" (p. 31). Sentiments of this nature—the dread of damnation that is paradoxically welcomed as a sign of hope, as evidence that one is on the right path—appear frequently in the Methodist narratives (*Arminian Magazine*, 1780, p. 127, p. 480; 1881, p. 2; 1798, p. 8). They aptly illustrate the dual-consciousness of deliberate mourning. Even as his convictions worsen, Pawson partially extracts himself from the depression to observe and comprehend it as a reassuring sign of progress. His detached evaluation does not impede his ability to genuinely grieve. His life becomes a burden, he is "confused" and "brought very low": "I was on the brink of despair." The authenticity of his condition finds further confirmation in the account of his state of mind just prior to his justification. He writes: "I heard very little of the Sermon, but continued kneeling all the time of service; and after it was ended, I still continued trembling, weeping and crying aloud for mercy...my bodily strength was quite exhausted" (pp. 32-33).

Following the onset of his repentance convictions, Pawson continues to nurture his depression. He explains that he walked in the fields, "bemoaning himself" (p. 31). At the moment that he decides that he was beyond the reach of mercy, he is comforted by the word, "Be strong and he shall comfort thine heart." In effect, Pawson reminds himself that his despair, although difficult to endure, is key to his salvation. If he simply musters the strength to bear the pain, God will forgive and redeem him. These reflections enable him to become calm and hopeful. The intensification of grief initiates a symbolic self-reflection, the "comfortable word," which keeps him mindful of the salvific purpose of his exertions. In this way, Pawson's verbal inspiration, a product of the therapeutic alliance, gives him the courage to sustain the basic intensity of the mood.

When Pawson learns about an acquaintance who is justified in a very short time, he feels "confounded" and returns home to exploit his distress. He retires to his chamber to mourn but decides that he requires greater privacy to cry aloud and "vent his grief." He then goes into the barn where "no one will see or hear [him]" and aggravates his sorrow in solitude. Once again, real anguish is contained by the self-consciousness of his actions, and the awareness of their sanction by God. He writes, "my distress [was] greater than I was able to bear: yet I was not quite without hope, but expected, vile as I was, that the Lord would at last be gracious unto me."

The psychological paradox of ritual mourning in Methodism, the "dual-consciousness" of grief management, bears on an important methodological issue. In his study of religious melancholy in British and American Puritanism, King (1983, pp. 47-48) criticizes naive psychohistorical approaches that uncritically assume that textual depictions of melancholy can be taken at face value and therefore convey the real intentionality of the authors. Opting instead for a post-modern definition of writing, King stresses that we can infer nothing outside of textual discourse itself. To adduce a phenomenology of the writer's actual intentionality and inner experience is to impose an alternate discourse that is, by definition, absent in the original source. Viable scholarship confines itself to the systematic examination of conventional tropes and turns of phrases. King's stance is uncompromisingly unilateral; discourse alone determines consciousness and identity. He allows for the retroactive reconstruction of individual's experiences through the use of culturally selected metaphors, but he rejects the idea that the syntax actually "articulated the sensations they felt and wanted to exclaim" (Cohen, p. 20). In rejecting a middle ground between formalized rhetoric and psychological interiority, King reifies discourse. For example, there is a current consensus in cognitive linguistics that the tropes of everyday speech convey the actual ideas with which we think, and through which we experience the world (Lakoff & Johnson, 1980; Ortony, 1993). Methodists spoke and wrote the way they did because their metaphors expressed the terms of their experience.

King's (1983) critique is at least partially valid. He rightly challenges the view that "temptation to suicide [is] an actual expression of American cultural pathology" (p. 51). He writes, "When Puritan ministers warned of self-murder, their words did involve an irony, for an authority's admonition became the suggestion that one should in fact think of suicide" (p. 51). King's use of the term "irony" deconstructs the literal authenticity of suicidal intentions. The intervening variable of suggestion implies that they would not spontaneously appear otherwise. His critique easily applies to Methodism given that Wesley and many of his followers refer to suicidal temptations. On the other hand, we can more adequately understand the irony of suggestion as the dual-consciousness of ritual mourning. In delineating the psychodynamics of authoritarian parenting, I have argued that the varieties of preconversion suffering should not be dismissed as mere narrative devices (see Chapter Two). Their characteristics coincide with object-relational precursors. The suggestive force inherent in the expectation of suicidal temptations was given real emotional force by predisposing factors in the personality (for example, unconscious aggression and guilt). In the main, when this kind of ideation emerged it was experienced in an emotionally compelling manner. At the same time, Methodists safely tolerated these feelings because they signified the coming of the spirit. The voluntary use of culturally sanctioned mourning techniques, along with the provision of linguistic images already symbolically attuned to the practitioner's inner world, allowed for the manageable emergence of a genuinely intense set of negative emotions.

SUMMARY

Wesley called the first phase of spiritual regeneration "repentance." Theologically, sinners awaken abruptly from sleep. They can no longer rely on self-deception now that the piercing convictions of prevenient grace frighteningly alter their perceptions of themselves. Wesley understood repentance as a form of self-knowledge brought to bear by the judgments of a formerly suppressed conscience.

The massive shifts in self-perception are brought on by the activation of repressed materials now making their way into consciousness. The traumatic consequences of parental authoritarianism, loss and bereavement find expression through appropriate analogies conveyed in a religious idiom. Wesley's doctrine of repentance promotes a transference neurosis through which ambivalence towards the parent emerges as enmity towards God. All of the standard psychic disturbances originally instilled by culturally modal complications in childhood development are given thematic representation. Rage is frameworked by the idea of innate corruption and rebellion. Parental punishment finds expression in God's intractable wrath. Loss and actual bereavement are encoded in terms of alienation, spiritual deadness and mourning after God. Wesley's provision of deeply reverberating symbolism magnetizes unconscious memories, feelings and fantasies. They are both drawn into consciousness and given a coherent medium for thoughtful elaboration beyond the limited and rigid meanings assigned by the infantile source (compare: Obeysekere, 1990, pp. 12-13).

The transference neurosis onto God is deliberately amplified through techniques of religious mourning that include fasting, weeping and grieving in solitude. Although these practices occur cross-culturally, they have a particularly striking psychological resonance in the Methodist context. Like the religious imagery of repentance, the techniques used to heighten convictions are themselves fraught with meanings that interlace with pre-existing unconscious themes. For example, fasting is an especially effective form of atonement given the many allusions to oral aggression in Wesley's writings and the autobiographical literature. Moreover, solitude re-enacts feelings of separation and abandonment, while weeping gives individuals opportunities to vent grief over previous losses, the circumstances of which may have prevented them from doing so originally.

Ritual mourning created an ideal circumstance for the maximal production of unconscious creativity. The wish to resolve the depression provided ample motivation for psychic work, both within and outside of awareness. Moreover, depression favors introversion and an increased focus on the self and the internal world. Wesley states that convictions dampen one's natural attraction to "idolatry," a term which not only refers to irreverent affections such as pride and ambition, but also to the whole realm of sensual gratifications and worldly pleasure. One therefore instinctively disengages from the world: "When once you are possessed of this genuine conviction, all your idols will lose their charms. And you will wonder how you could so long lean upon those broken reeds" (1984-87, I: p. 113). Methodists undergoing repentance deliberately sought personal seclusion and isolation as part of their mourning technique. In this regard, the Committee on Psychiatry and Religion (1976) posits a connection between mystical ecstasy, solitude and creativity. They hold that both mystics and "creators" seek solitude because only in this state "can the mind work out the new mental configuration it seeks" (p. 795).

The transference neurosis is not facilitated by negative doctrinal imagery and ritual mourning alone. Individuals allow themselves to undergo the miseries of repentance precisely because they feel enticed by the promise of

Christ's unconditional love and acceptance. Consider, for example, the following extracts from narratives written by Thomas Rankin and William Carvosso, who appear to have willingly induced hysterical attacks through ritual mourning. The narratives both contain typical themes, images and sequences that exemplify repentance in all its major features.

Rankin's repentance commenced when he was seventeen. He suggests that it was, at least in part, precipitated by the recent death of his father (*Arminian Magazine*, 1779, p. 184). Rankin was left "all on a sudden as dark as midnight," and went on in a "wretched" state for over six months (p. 186). As the time for the sacrament grew near, he was "filled with horror," fearing that his participation, as a reviled sinner, would "crucify the Son of God afresh" (p. 186). In the end, he approached the table "in confidence," but accidentally spilt some of the wine (p. 187). Inexpressibly distressed, Rankin felt tempted to interpret the mishap as a sign that Christ's blood was also spilt in vain for him. Later, God removed "the violence of the temptation" and gave him "a dawn of hope" (p. 187). Rankin, now actively mourning, fought for his salvation "from the ground of his being" (p. 187). He wept, prayed and searched the scripture. After hearing Whitefield preach in Edinburgh, Rankin realized that only unbelief stood between his soul and Christ. Two days before he found "peace" (p. 187), his convictions climaxed.

> I arose in the morning greatly distressed, went out into the garden, and mourned over my deplorable state. All at once, I had such a view of the wrath of God, that my soul sunk down into despair. I felt a taste of that misery, which the damned in hell feel. I had not the least glimpse of hope...I was strongly tempted to lay violent hands upon myself. I said, *Strangling is better than life: why do I tarry any longer?* At that instant, these words darted into my mind, *How can I do this great evil; and Sin against God?* I stood amazed and confounded...I went into my chamber, and cast myself down upon my face on the bed...Soon after, I was deprived of my senses, and seemingly fell into a trance. It appeared to me, that I was lying in the bed, and my soul near entering into the world of spirits. To die, I thought, was but a trifle; but to go to hell-fire was dreadful: yet, after a while, I was willing to go to hell, if God could not otherwise be glorified. I saw the justice of God demanded it; and cried out, *Thy will be done.* I looked to the foot, the sides, and the head of my bed, and thought I beheld it surrounded (as thick as they could stand) with fiends of the most horrible aspects, ready to convey my soul to eternal flames. They seemed to look upon me with a hellish triumph, which words cannot describe. I had, at that time, such a view of eternity as I never had before or since; and also of the soul's immortality. I had also such a view of the holiness and justice of God, as was unspeakable. Just as my soul seemed wait-

ing for her separation from the body, this thought darted into my mind, "O! where is the sinner's friend? Where is the Lord Jesus Christ?" In speaking these words, I lifted up my eyes to heaven; and, I thought, I beheld the heavens open; and there appeared a most glorious person, who looked upon me and smiled. I cried out, "That is the Lord Jesus Christ! That is the Lamb of God, who taketh away the sins of the world!" I gazed upon him a considerable time: and then looked for my hellish attendants; but they were gone, and I saw them no more. I was then restored to the use of my senses, and arose from the bed. All my misery and despair were gone (pp. 187-188).

Before the attack begins, Rankin struggles with his ambivalence. Mixed feelings appear to have been stirred up by the death of his father and the obligation to assume his father's responsibilities to oversee family worship and to assist his mother in business (p. 184). Clearly, the metaphors he chooses to convey his fear of communion betray hints of destructiveness. Rankin believes he has "trampled on the blood of the cross" and crucified Christ afresh (p. 186). He expresses his ambivalence in a "slip," when he accidentally spills the wine during communion. Rankin is aware of his resistance: all that stands between himself and Christ is his own "unbelief." The imaginative content of the actual panic attack makes his aggression even more apparent. When it begins, Rankin is given an unprecedented view of the wrath of God. Rankin feels convinced he is without hope of mercy, that he is guilty of "quenching the light" previously given him. He feels abandoned by an indignant God, rages against himself and momentarily contemplates suicide.

In the second phase of the attack, an ecstatic interlude characterized by demonic persecution and death struggle augment themes of abandonment, guilt, despair, and suicide. Lying in bed, Rankin loses his outward senses and experiences a vision. When the vision begins, Rankin believes he is dying. His soul separates from his body and enters into the world of spirits. Although he considers death to be a "trifle," he is admittedly terrified by the thought of hellfire. Nevertheless, Rankin overcomes his fear and decides to completely surrender himself to the experience: "yet, after a while, I was willing to go to hell, if God could not otherwise be glorified." In consenting to his punishment by offering his soul for the greater glory of God, he gains the reassuring approval of an ego-ideal. The reparative gesture, in turn, grants him the courage to let go and to allow the vision to unfold. In other words, Rankin makes active use of the therapeutic alliance. Further unconscious materials emerge in symbolic form, and the vision proceeds in terms of discrete episodes, as is the case with narrative sequences in dreams. Rankin beholds a legion of fiendish devils "ready to convey [his] soul to eternal flames." When he is about to be permanently separated from his body, Rankin cries for mercy: "O! Where is the sinner's friend?" The appeal serves as an auto-suggestion and initiates a salvific vision of Jesus. This image, which effectively resolves the death struggle, symbolizes the ego's awareness of its active allegiance to the ego-ideal. It comes in response to Rankin's decision to relinquish control and suffer demonic persecution in the name of the God. When Christ appears, Rankin lovingly gazes upon the lamb until he realizes that the "hellish attendants" have vanished and that he has been graciously delivered. Here, the ecstatic vision comes to an end: "I was then restored to the use of my senses, and arose from the bed."

Rankin's account contains a series of features frequently represented in the descriptions of hysterical attacks. During these experiences, the repentance motifs of guilt, abandonment despair, suicidal temptations, persecutory anxiety and the fear of death erupt with unparalleled intensity. If they are accompanied by an alternate state of consciousness, as with Rankin, these items undergo symbolic elaboration in visual form. They may then culminate in a death crisis that is followed by a salvific outcome, usually in the form of an eidetic image of Christ, or a non-visual sense of Christ's presence.

Rankin's extract also exemplifies typical psychodynamic trends. Firstly, his resistance or "unbelief" is a product of unconscious ambivalence, the derivatives of which appear in both the events that lead up to the attack and the content of the vision. We see further evidence of resistance in the fact that after his saving vision of Christ, Rankin, although relieved of his heavy load, has no palpable testimony of pardon. The following morning, after wrestling with God in prayer, he finally receives the full blessing. His language, however, indicates that aggression continues to interfere with the manifestation of the ideal: "I was so overwhelmed with the love of God, *that I thought I should then have died*" (p. 189). Secondly, Rankin manages his rage by using symbolic displacements; he turns aggression against himself or projects it into God and the demons. He also actively appeals to his ego-ideal. A sense of protection afforded by the alliance with the positive superego allows the experience to completely run its course.

Let us turn to Carvosso's account. After attending a Methodist sermon given by Thomas Hanson, Carvosso (1835) states that the "word quickly reached [his] heart": "the scales fell off my eyes; and I saw and felt I was in the gall of bitterness, and in the bond of iniquity" (p. 36).

> I had such a sight of the damning nature of sin, and of what I had done against God, that I was afraid the earth would open up and swallow me up. I then made a solemn promise to the Lord, that if he would spare me I would serve him all my days. I now gave up my sins and all my old companions...That night I had a hard struggle with Satan, about praying before I went to bed. It appeared as

> if he was by me, and labored to terrify me with his presence, and the cross of the duty; but the Lord helped me against the temptation by applying that portion of Scripture, "let your light so shine before men that they may see your good works...Satan instantly fled and I fell on my knees...I suffered much for many days; but about the space of eight hours before I received the pardon of sin, I might say with David, "The pains of hell gat hold upon me"; and the adversary of my soul harassed me with this temptation, "The day of grace is past; it is now too late." I had no one to instruct or encourage me, no one to point me to Christ...in the midst of the conflict I said, in answer to the powerful suggestions of the devil, "I am determined, whether I am saved or lost, that, while I have breath, I will never cease crying for mercy." The very moment I formed this resolution in my heart, Christ appeared within, and God pardoned all my sins, and set my soul at liberty. The spirit itself now bore witness with my spirit that I was a child of God (pp. 37-38).

Carvosso's repentance begins during Hanson's preaching. For Carvosso, the shift from desolation to justification occurs quickly. He is saved only a few days after the onset of his convictions. When they arise, he immediately resolves to repent and find salvation: "I now gave up my sins, and all my old companions." Carvosso's unequivocal resolve, his speedy conversion, and the fact that his attack is not as lurid as the likes of Rankin and others, suggests that Carvosso's ambivalence was not excessive. Even so, his writing reveals some degree of conflict and resistance. For example, after making a "solemn promise to the Lord," Carvosso's efforts to pray in the evening are disrupted. Resistance manifests symbolically as an intellectual vision of the presence of Satan: "It appeared as if he was by me, and labored to terrify me with his presence." Through a creative inspiration in which a portion of scripture is "applied," Carvosso re-establishes the rapport with his ideal and recovers his equilibrium. The actual full-blown attack, the "pains of hell," lasted eight hours. Although he makes no explicit mention of a death struggle, Carvosso experiences an acute abandonment desolation: "The day of grace is past; it is now too late." His statement that he was alone, without any guidance or encouragement from others, reinforces the theme of abandonment. That Carvosso's attack centered primarily on abandonment is likely due to his early history. After his father left the family while Carvosso was still very young (p. 35), Carvosso resided with his mother and five siblings until the age of ten. At this time he was requested to go and live with a farmer who attended the same parish. When Carvosso claims that he "cheerfully consented" (p. 35), we may infer a denial of grief and the possibility of unresolved mourning. The theme of separation anxiety figures conspicuously in Carvosso's writing. For example, much later in his memoir, he describes how he was devastated to learn that his son was considering entering on a foreign mission.

> At reading [his letter] I was greatly affected; indeed I was for some time overwhelmed, and incapable of giving him any answer...I could not bear to entertain the thought, and therefore begged him not to think of anything of the kind till I should be removed hence...The subject was a burden to my mind indescribable (p. 104).

Carvosso's memoir reveals that he found partings and farewells especially difficult moments (compare: p. 166).

During his attack, Carvosso viewed his fear of abandonment as a diabolical "temptation." This suggests that ambivalence due to separation trauma initially served as a resistance to Christ. However, as in Rankin's narrative, Carvosso overcomes the resistance by appealing to his ideal. He answers "the powerful suggestions of the devil" by declaring he "will never cease crying for mercy." His verbalized resolve to persevere through the crisis of doubt clinches his justification. The moment is punctuated by a sense of divine presence: "Christ appeared within, and God pardoned all my sins, and set my soul at liberty."

Finally, another aspect of Carvosso's experience matches with that of Rankin's. Following his conversion, Carvosso continues to experience some degree of ambivalence. For several days he labors under the "delusion" that he must not speak of his salvation (p. 38).

> From experience I now knew well that Satan was a "roaring lion"; but I was not yet aware of his being able to transform himself into an "an angel of light." He now told me, I must not declare what I had experienced; that if I did, I should at once fall into condemnation...without the least hesitation I said, "Then I will take care not to mention it." (p. 38).

The combination of involuntary depressiveness and hysterical attacks with the voluntary activity of ritual mourning introduced psychodynamics that are atypical of neurotic suffering alone. By converting passive into active, depressiveness was augmented with mourning, bringing both poles of the split imago into simultaneous operation. By forming a conscious therapeutic alliance with a merciful deity (the ego-ideal), individuals muster the courage to examine their repressed ambivalence while tolerating the dread of punishment (the bad parental introject). Even so, longstanding anxieties produce considerable resistance. Inasmuch as individuals long to "believe" or surrender themselves to Christ, persistent unconscious aggression means that they are never certain that they can relinquish their defenses, lest they surrender to an annihilating God who would damn them eternally.

During repentance, a comprehensive series of religious ideas and ideals attaching to the theme of reconciliation with God are subject to long-term consideration. What begins as a voluntary reflection on God's acceptance through faith, his merciful omnipresence, and the moral rationality of his commandments is assimilated unconsciously and worked through in a way that engages all levels of the self. Ideally, a cognitive-affective synthesis of new religious ideals and identity structures crystallizes in response to conflict, and manifests during the ecstatic moment of justification.

The initial working through of the transference neurosis during desolation is ensured by the ability to maintain trust in the intrapsychic therapeutic alliance between the ego and the ego-ideal. As individuals' despair deepens or climaxes during repentance attacks, they continually voice their allegiance to God, thereby gaining a sense of approval from the ideal. This approval fosters hope and courage that allow them to apprehend greater and greater intensities of ambivalence. We recall Merkur's (1989, p. 134) claim that the bi-polar affective shift from depression to elation is the rational result of a superego value judgment (See Chapter Three). The Methodist data permit us to conclude that the value judgment commences at a point when one has achieved a relatively durable tolerance of primitive anxieties and hostility. As unconscious ambivalence is mastered symbolically in consciousness by way of the alliance, the emotional influence of the negative parental imago vanishes temporarily. No longer under the sway of conflict and guilt, the ego adopts its ideal without further inhibition. A sense of divine pardon results from the ecstatic sense of acceptance by or "union" with the ideal. Individuals then acquire an insight that relates to self-esteem and expresses itself theologically: "I am loved by God even despite my sinfulness."

Five

Justification and the New Birth

In several works written in tandem with the rise of psychedelic culture in the 1960s, Maslow clarified the defining features of spontaneously occurring unitive ecstasies. He deliberately side-stepped religious terminologies in order to avoid their doctrinal biases. Maslow coined the secular term "peak experience" to refer to transcendent moments of "highest happiness and fulfillment" (1968, p.73). Several authors have found the concept useful in illuminating facets of Methodist spirituality (Outler 1981, p. xiii; Oakland, 1981; Maas, 1990). The comparison is not unfounded. For Maslow (1970, p. 32), peak experiences are characterized by a "unitive consciousness" whose psychological components, or "beta-cognition," reflect ultimate values of "being." Most importantly, the ecstasy is organized by an abstraction through which the particularities of the cosmos are beheld as an integrated unity (pp. 59-68, 91-96). Individuals feel as though they inhabit a new world that is singularly redolent with meaning. The abstract perception of an underlying unity and one's immediate participation in it lead to further alterations of consciousness. During the intervals in which they occur, peak experiences accentuate empathy and promote an increased ability to adopt the subject's point of view. An intensification of healthy conscience is coupled with a decrease of narcissism and materialistic values. Charity, humility, joyfulness and calm override conflict, depression, anxiety and, ultimately, the fear of death. Exhilaration and relief foster spontaneous expressions of worship and praise.

In much the same way, Wesley explains that justification opens up a new world in which one intuits the presence of God in and through all things. Believers who undergo a second birth receive an entirely distinct set of supernatural faculties. "Spiritual senses" supplement the sensory capacities of the physical body by offering a view of the "eternal world," "the invisible things of God" (Wesley, 1984-87, II: p. 161). This gift, which Wesley regarded as the condition of faith, makes it possible for believers to see directly how God's love imbues and sustains all facets of creation (III: pp. 89-95). As in Maslow's formulation, the sense of an all-encompassing unity, the omnipresence of God, leads to a series of dramatic psychological changes that affect the entire personality. By receiving "the spirit of adoption" (I: p. 22), believers experience a feeling of acceptance and inclusion as children belonging to the universal family of God. The spirit of adoption presupposes divine forgiveness. In overcoming the dread of judgment, individuals experience a "joy which surpasses all understanding." Faith eradicates guilt and anxiety over sin. It also promotes a good conscience that lays the basis for the justifying sense of pardon (I: p. 274). God's love is reciprocated and extended to all creatures united in the same spirit (I: p. 274). The view of the "eternal world" (II: p. 161) overcomes the fear of death (II: p. 481). The justified also undergo an irresistible shift in their values. They develop a distaste for vain and materialistic pursuits and prefer instead to glorifying God in all things (Steele, 1994, p. 133).

As a form of ecstasy, peak experiences occur during an alternate state of consciousness that transforms the conditions and content of normal perception. Maslow (1971, pp. 251-59) highlights a shift not only in affect but also in cognition. Here I need to specify my use of the term "ecstasy." Merkur (1993, p. 11) employs the term as a synonym for "religiously interpreted alternate state experiences." He offers a definition that singles out a psychological variable operative in all varieties of religious ecstasy. Merkur's approach provides a corrective to previous conceptualizations that are biased by the ideologies of particular religious traditions. He opts for a psychological explanation that emphasizes the "autonomous" nature of ecstasy.

> It is characteristic of all ecstasies that they involve at least some autonomous phenomena—what Catholic tradition terms "contemplation" and contrasts with "meditation." Autonomous psychic materials seem subjectively to the ecstatic to be independent of control by will (p. 12).

In highlighting the concept of autonomy, Merkur offers a formulation that applies cross-culturally.

> I define ecstasy as *any state of involuntary belief in the reality of the numinous*. Like sense perception during normal waking sobriety and dream hallucinations during sleep, the autonomous contents of an ecstasy have a compelling psychic reality for at least the duration of their occurrence. The ecstatic is then convinced that the numinous is real—as real or more than the perceptible world. In contrast with sober faith in the numinous, which requires an act of will, ecstatic belief in the reality of the numinous is involuntary. Whether or not the occurrence of ecstasy was voluntarily sought, once the experience is underway, faith in the reality of the numinous is not subject to volition. Doubt can be entertained, but it cannot be sustained for the duration of the experience (pp. 12-13).

Ecstasies are unique among the varieties of religious experience because they "have the power not only to confirm religious faith that already exists, but also to produce conversions from unbelief to belief" (p. 13).

Merkur distinguishes between two generic types of alternate states—trance and reverie. The terms correspond to the distinction between hypnosis and hypnagogia, respectively. During hypnotic trance, symbolic fantasies become reified due to the repression of ego-functions that normally engage in reality testing (p. 34; compare: Shor, 1972a; 1972b). As a result, the content of a vision may be apprehended as an objectively real event, at least for the duration of the ecstasy. Conversely, during reveries states, in which ego functions are "relaxed" as opposed to repressed, fantasies are for the most part "known subjectively to be intrapsychic" (Merkur, 1993. p. 34). In other words, while in a reverie state, the individual remains aware of the imaginative nature of the experience, although "[psychic materials] may be interpreted variously...as imaginations, extrasensory perceptions, or divine revelations" (p. 34). Most peak experiences, along with psychedelic and sensory deprivation experiences, are instances of reverie. The variable that distinguishes reverie as a discrete class of ecstasy is the relatively unencumbered activity of conscious and preconscious ego functions. Unlike the mental conditions that hold sway during hypnotic trance, reverie preserves self-conscious awareness so that one can engage to varying degrees in rational forms of reflection and symbolic interpretation.

Merkur's model of alternate state experience, his definition of ecstasy as involuntary belief in the numinous, and his identification of reverie as distinct from trance prove useful in examining Methodist justification. Wesley's theological description of the instantaneous and passive reception of faith coincides with the category of ecstatic reverie. To begin, the reformed conception of faith as received through grace clearly shaped Wesley's understanding of justification. The objective evidence (Maddox, 1994, p. 173) or "experimental knowledge" (Wesley & Wesley, 1984-87, I: p. 154) of pardon proceeds in an entirely autonomous, involuntary fashion. Quoting St. Paul, Wesley writes,

> [He] strongly insists...that the terms of pardon and acceptance must depend, not 'on us, but on him that calleth us'; that there is no 'unrighteousness with God' in fixing his own terms, not according to ours, but his own good pleasure: who may justly say, "I will have mercy', namely, on him who believeth in Jesus. 'So then it is not of him that willeth, nor of him that runneth', to choose the condition on which he shall find acceptance, 'but of God that showeth mercy' (I: p. 197).

Faith does not flow from a deliberate, reasoned deduction. "It is not barely a speculative, rational thing, a cold lifeless assent, a train of ideas in the head" (I: p. 120). On the contrary, "God both opens and enlightens the eyes of our understanding...And we then see, not by a chain of *reasoning*, but by a kind of *intuition*, by a direct view, that 'God was in Christ, reconciling the world to himself'" (II: p. 481). Wesley appropriated the Moravian view of justification which placed special emphasis on the witness of the spirit, that is, on the immediate sense of pardon and the manifestation of the fruits of the spirit. As a result, Wesley came to advance a doctrine of "perceptible inspiration" and linked the reformed view of justification with "a more positive spiritual sensation that [he] described in terms of a new birth" (Whaling, 1981, p. 44). For Whaling, this linkage attests to Wesley's theological "originality" (p. 44). Using scriptural language that emphasizes passive apprehension, Wesley speaks of being "sensibly" inspired by the Holy Ghost. One literally "feels" it and is "moved" by it (Wesley, 1984-87, I: p. 155). The experiential nature of this innovation regularly drew accusations of enthusiasm. Anglican critics held that Wesley's portrayal of the new birth, as both instantaneous and inwardly felt, presupposed "extraordinary communications" that seditiously bypassed the ordinary doctrinal assurances of divine presence (Lee, 1931, p. 132).

Relying on scriptural precedent, Wesley states that the witness consists of two components. The testimony of God's spirit "is an inward impression on the soul, whereby the spirit of God directly 'witnesses to my spirit that I am a child of God'; that Jesus Christ hath loved me, and given himself for me; that all my sins are blotted out, and I...am reconciled to God" (Wesley, 1984-87, I: p. 274). God's testimony is subsequently greeted by the testimony of one's own spirit—the affirmation of conscience. The undeniable feeling of good will towards God, a sentiment ensured by his pardon, brings with it holy tempers, or the fruits of the spirit. These fruits represent a further dimension of the second witness:

> Even a loving heart toward God and toward all mankind, hanging with childlike confidence on God our Father, desiring nothing but him, casting all our care upon him, and embracing every child of man with earnest, tender affection, so as to be ready to lay down our life for our brother, as Christ laid down his life for us—a consciousness that we are inwardly conformed by the Spirit of God to the image of his Son, and that we walk before him in justice, mercy and truth; doing the things which are pleasing in his sight (I: p. 274).

Wesley insists that the conscious effects of the two witnesses are anything but obscure. The drawings of the spirit are unequivocally apparent to its recipients. "That divine consciousness, that 'witness of God'...is more and greater than ten thousand human witnesses" (I: p. 146).

Furthermore, Wesley's delineation of faith coincides with alternate state experience because he depicts faith as something that transcends normal sensory modalities. It is "not discoverable by the bodily senses" (I: p. 194), yet it remains entirely experiential. The perceptual abstraction of the invisible world was attributed to an altogether different register of spiritual senses. Wesley's assertion that the witness of the spirit cannot be explained to those who do not possess it (I: p. 283) *phenomenologically* resembles what Hollenback (1996) refers to as the "trans-sensory" character of mystical consciousness: "I am observing that the mystic seems to perceive the objects of his or her visions and locutions by means of some faculty other than the five physical senses" (p. 43).

Justification coincides with Merkur's definition of ecstasy because grace is instantaneously given and belief in Christ proceeds independently of volition. But in what sense does justification also conform to the category of reverie? Here we must recall Dimond's (1926) and Rack's (1989) assertions that Wesley effectively synthesized rationalism and supernatural enthusiasm. Lockean empiricism informed his epistemological stance (Dryer, 1983, pp. 21ff; Mathews, 1985, pp. 411-412; Heitzenrater, 1989, p. 145; Rack, 1989, pp. 384-386). Like Locke, Wesley rejected the notion of innate ideas and held that all knowledge built on the senses. Since knowledge of the things of God was not discernible by the sensory capacities of the flesh, Wesley extended the empirical premise into the idea of spiritual senses. With divine sentience, one could access the "data" of the eternal realm and engage in the same series of sequential steps that Locke identified as the basis of reasoning: apprehension, judgment and discourse. Contrary to the philosophy of the Deists, Wesley knew that reason *alone* could not discover the verities of the spirit and therefore was an inadequate basis for faith. However, when faith was granted at justification, one discerned the things of God. Believers then applied the reasoning process to divine perception in exactly the same manner as they did in the context of profane perception. In other words, Wesley's view of faith allowed for lucid self-reflection to proceed in tandem with ecstatic perception. In agreement with the character of peak experiences, the apprehension of God's eternality and omnipresence was inextricably bound up with the temporal world. Methodists beheld the creator directly in his creation.

Phenomenologically, Wesley may be compared with the intellectual mystics of late antiquity and the middle ages, who employed rational, discursive meditations in connection with reverie states (Merkur, 2001a). Wesley's knowledge of faith was rational because the ecstasies involved reveries that did not preclude the ego's ability to engage in reality testing. Consider, for example, Marg Jenkins's account of her justification ecstasy. She received the full assurance of pardon during a sermon.

> I was surprised with the glory of the Lord that shone around me: it shone, indeed, in a way that is unutterable. It was as bright and as

discernible as the natural sun at noon day. I thought my body as well as my soul was changed, and I seemed as if I was lost to this world, and yet my understanding was never clearer. The lord spoke loudly unto my soul, "This day salvation is come to thy house, I will never leave thee or forsake thee." I felt myself clean every whit; nor could I make myself sensible that ever I had sinned...I knew I was born of God, and felt I was brought to an innumerable company of angels, and Spirits of just men made perfect to Jesus the Mediator of the New Covenant...I opened my eyes (for they were shut) and I thought, all things around me were holiness unto the Lord (*Arminian Magazine*, 1778, pp. 228-230).

Jenkins's light vision signifies both pardon and renewal. Note how she insists that in the midst of her ecstasy her "understanding was never clearer." This clarity dovetails with her non-reified use of language: she "seemed" as if she was lost to the world and "felt" she was brought into a company of angels. These qualifications attest to an ongoing rational assessment of her subjective state, her appreciation that, although it is divinely bestowed, the vision occurs in her mind. Even though initially she seems lost to the world, when later she opens her eyes, the sense of presence first encapsulated in the image of purifying light now merges with the objects of external sense perception and manifests as a symbolic abstraction: "all things around me were holiness unto the Lord."

FAITH AS THE MEDIUM OF ECSTATIC PERCEPTION

Wesley abides by the scriptural notion of justification as pardon (Lindstrom, 1946, p. 74). Tainted by inbred corruption and the lack of righteousness, men cannot placate God's wrath. Forgiveness is granted only through faith in Christ, whose death vicariously propitiated the sins of humankind. Pardon, in turn, presupposes acceptance by and reconciliation with God. When freed from the "spirit of bondage," believers receive the "spirit of adoption" (I: p. 122). They no longer see God as a "severe master," but as an "indulgent father." "The Spirit itself bears witness with their spirit, that they are children of God" (I: p. 22). The spirit of adoption signifies a deliverance from guilt. The witness is subjectively verified by a good conscience. Having passed through the crucible of repentance into merciful pardon, the justified find that "the love of God is shed abroad in their hearts." They feel persuaded "that neither death, nor life, nor things present, nor things to come, nor height, nor depth, nor any other creature, shall be able to separate them from the love of God, which is in Christ Jesus our Lord" (I: p. 123). Justification implies an intimate communion. "These, who 'have redemption through his blood', are properly said to be 'in him', for *they* 'dwell in Christ and Christ in them'. They are 'joined unto the Lord in one Spirit'" (I: p. 235).

Faith constitutes the sole condition of justification and its renewing effects (I: p. 195). Faith is, as it were, the medium through which the testimony of the spirit, the assurance of pardon, is conveyed (I: pp. 237-238). Mathews (1985) shows that, over time, Wesley worked with three different conceptions of faith. The development of his thought gradually condensed these particular definitions. In 1725, Wesley defined faith primarily on rational grounds (pp. 406-407). It meant "fides," an assent to propositional truth afforded by divine testimony. "Faith must necessarily at length be resolved into reason." By 1738, Bohler convinced Wesley that his rationalist leanings were inadequate as a source of assurance; and Wesley's persistent lack of confidence, his "profound emotional and spiritual depression," lent credibility to Bohler's argument (p. 407). Consequently, Wesley embraced the Moravian conception of faith as "fiducia," "a trusting confidence in God's grace and mercy" (pp. 407-408). In the early 1740s, however, Wesley settled on what would be his final definition: a spiritual experience guaranteed by the provision of supernatural senses. Wesley writes:

> [Faith is] the demonstrative evidence of things unseen, the supernatural evidence of things invisible, not perceivable by eyes of flesh, or by any of our natural senses or faculties. Faith is that divine evidence whereby the spiritual man discerneth God and the things of God. It is with regard to the spiritual world what sense is with regard to the natural. It is the spiritual sensation of every soul that is born of God (quoted in Mathews, 1985, p. 408).

Faith as spiritual discernment was, by far, the most inclusive definition, because it integrated the previously irreconcilable meanings of fides and fiducia. Even with the comprehensive notion of supernatural sight, Wesley maintained the importance of a "trusting confidence," the assurance of pardon (1984-87, II: pp. 109-110). However, the emphasis on sensory experience, with its empirical overtones, also implied that "faith is always consistent with reason" (II: p. 414). Mathews (1985, p. 414) writes, "The knowledge of God to which we come through religious experience, by 'seeing with the eyes of faith', is not one whit less 'reasonable', according to Wesley, than the knowledge of the natural world around us to which we come through physical sensory experience."

For Christian thinkers such as Origen, who "invented" the doctrine of the "five spiritual senses," onwards through Bonaventure and Loyola, the concept of spiritual senses explained how mystical visions of God, angels, and the heavenly realms were mediated to the soul (p. 409). Mystics regarded the soul's senses as *literally sensory*. The soul saw spiritual sights, heard spiritual sounds, felt spiritual touches, smelled spiritual odors, and tasted spiritual foods. The doctrine of the soul's senses traditionally accounted for experiences of spiritual phenomena that were not apprehensible by the abstract conceptual powers of the mind (Ruth, 1975; Rahner, 1979). Wesley's usage differed. He referred to spiritual senses in a metaphoric sense that pertained to apprehensions by the mind of conceptual phenomena. In this way, Wesley "wedded" spiritual experience to the notion of faith as "a divine evidence or conviction of things not seen" (p. 409).

Wesley held that when believers acquired spiritual senses during justification, they were "regenerated" (Dryer, 1983, p.18) or born anew by the power of the Holy Ghost (Lindstrom, 1946, pp. 83-84). Although Wesley distinguished between justification and sanctification, he stipulated that both transpired at the same point in time. Justification was a singular event while sanctification commenced at justification but proceeded gradually, culminating eventually in entire sanctification. In one sense, Wesley continued to adhere to a strictly reformed view of justification as implying only "the forgiveness of sins and the acceptance incident to it" (p. 84; see also Abelove, 1990, p. 89). However, a new birth, the beginning of sanctification, occurred alongside justification. The new birth implied the impartation of a "real, inherent righteousness" (Lindstrom, 1946, 84). In being pardoned, believers embarked on a journey towards full spiritual renewal. Inasmuch as they were already sanctified in some measure, they were regarded as "babes in Christ" (Wesley, 1984-87, I: pp. 326-332). By delineating a sanctifying process that was theologically distinct but temporally inseparable from forgiveness, Wesley supplemented the Lutheran conception of justification (Lindstrom, 1946, p. 92). Justification alone entailed a "relative" change whereby God "does something for us" by restoring individuals to his favor and taking away their sins (Wesley, 1984-87, I: pp. 431-32). By contrast, the new birth effected a "real" change in which God "does something in us." The image of God is inwardly restored and the power of sin is eliminated. Both of these categories are subsumed under and therefore linked to the idea of spiritual senses. Because faith removes the veil between the temporal and the eternal world, faith secured both the witness of assurance and one's renewal through the Holy Ghost.

The application of the sensory metaphor to faith compelled Wesley to articulate a further set of distinctions. He claimed that in a *particular* sense, faith referred to the assurance of pardon and divine acceptance (II: pp. 160-161). In a *general* sense, however, the term pertained to supernatural sight and the divine evidence and conviction of things not seen:

> [Faith implies] a kind of supernatural *light* exhibited to the soul, and a supernatural *sight* or perception thereof...We have a prospect

of the invisible things of God. We see the *spiritual world,* which is all round about us, and yet no more discerned by our natural faculties than if it had no being; and we see the *eternal world*, piercing through the veil which hangs between time and eternity (II: pp. 160-161).

The particular meaning of faith, the sense of pardon, emphasizes an entirely affective experience of gratitude and love. But Wesley augmented the Moravian conception of faith as fiducia by introducing an empirical slant. In reconciling reason and affect by insisting on the active involvement of a sensory mode, Wesley points to a *cognitive* dimension that is clearly implied by the believer's altered view of the cosmos: "We see the *spiritual world*, which is all round about us." The combination of invisibility, omnipresence and eternality suggests that the cognitive component is a unitive abstraction.

Wesley's sermon on *Spiritual Worship* shows how the unitive knowledge of God's imminence in creation plays a crucial role in Christian life. Here Wesley delineates the various facets of God's relationship to creation. He is at once the "Supporter," "Preserver," "Redeemer" and "Governor" of the cosmos (III: pp. 89-95). Since God's presence continually creates, animates and sustains all that he has brought into existence, all things are imbued by and participate in his being. Wesley reasons that awakened Christians apprehend God's immanence primarily through an inward communion with Christ. They are thereby "filled with him," and made "complete."

> When we dwell in Christ, and Christ in us, we are one with Christ, and Christ with us; then we are completely happy; then we live all 'the life that is hid with Christ in God'. Then, and only then, we properly experience what the word meaneth, 'God is love; and whosoever dwelleth in love, dwelleth in God, and God in him' (III: pp. 96-97).

The "knowledge" of God is rooted in the union of the believer's spirit with the "Father of spirits" (III: p. 101). However, this inner union of spirits necessarily furnishes the believer with an additional view of God's immanent presence in the external world:

> He is 'about your bed'! He is 'about your path'. He 'besets you behind and before'. He 'lays his hand upon you'. Lo! God is here! Not afar off! Now, believe and feel him near! May he now reveal himself in your heart! Now him! Love him! And you are happy" (III: pp. 102-103).

Wesley points to a "near resemblance between the circumstances of the natural birth and of the spiritual birth" (I: p. 432). His elaboration of the analogy further underscores the unitive perceptions of faith in terms of external sense perception. While in the womb, a child has no awareness of the "visible world" that in actuality "surrounds him on every side" (I: p. 433). When the child is delivered into the world, "all the bodily senses [are] now awakened" and he "exists in quite a different manner" (I: p. 433).

> He now *feels* the air with which he is surrounded, and which pours into him from every side...His eyes are now open to see the light, which silently flowing in upon them discovers not only itself but an infinite variety of things which before he was wholly unacquainted. His ears are unclosed, and sounds rush in with endless diversity. Every sense is employed upon such objects as are peculiarly suitable to it. And by these inlets the soul...acquires more and more knowledge of sensible things (I: p. 433).

Similarly, one who is spiritually unawakened "seeth not the things of God, the eyes of his understanding being closed" (I: p. 434).

> Hence he has scarce any knowledge of the invisible world...Not that it is far off. No; he is in the midst of it: it encompasses him round about...[It] is not far from every one of us. It is above, and beneath, and on every side...But when he is born of God, born of the Spirit, how is the manner of his existence changed! His whole soul is now sensible of God, and he can say by sure experience, "Thou art above my bed, and about my path;' I feel thee in 'all my ways'. 'Thou besettest me behind and before, and layest thy hand upon me'. The spirit or breath of God is immediately inspired, breathed into the new-born soul; and the same breath which comes from, returns to God...And by this new kind of spiritual respiration, spiritual life is not only sustained but increased day by day, together with spiritual strength and motion and sensation; all the senses of the soul being now awake, and capable of 'discerning' spiritual 'good and evil' (I: pp. 434-435).

In this excerpt, the sense of divine presence is expressed by the unitive metaphor of respiration. Inhalations and exhalations of the spirit-breath circulate between God and the newborn soul. Elsewhere, Wesley expresses the experience of God's omnipresence in terms of sight.

> And 'blessed' are they who are thus 'pure in heart'; for they shall see God...He will bless them with the clearest communications of his Spirit...He will cause his presence to go continually before

> them, and the light of his countenance to shine upon them...They now see him by faith (the veil of the flesh being made, as it were, transparent) even in these his lowest works, in all that surrounds them, in all that God has created and made. They see him in the height above, and in the depth beneath; they see him filling all in all...They see him in the firmament of heaven, in the moon walking in brightness, in the sun when he rejoiceth as a giant to run his course. They see him 'making the clouds his chariots, and walking upon the wings of the wind'. They see him 'preparing for the earth', 'and blessing the increase of it'; 'giving grass for the cattle, and green herb for the use of man'. They see the creator of all wisely governing all, and 'upholding all things by the word of his power' (I: pp. 513-514).

Because the sight of divine presence "in all, and over all," renders events in the cosmos as personal and purposeful, faith is inseparable from providence.

> In all his providences relating to themselves, to their souls or bodies, the pure in heart do particularly see God. They see his hand ever over them for good; giving them all things in weight, and measure, numbering the hairs of their head, making a head round about them and all they have, and disposing all the circumstances of their life according to the depth both of his wisdom and mercy (I: p. 514).

Again, Wesley's description of the sense of God's presence coincides with his Lockean convictions. He rejected out of hand any speculative knowledge of God: "The invisible things of God are known from things that are made...from what he hath written in all his works" (quoted in Dryer, 1983, p. 23). Seeing the "invisible" things of God involves a cognitive dimension in which the abstract significance of concrete perceptions are imaginatively reconfigured by an ideal. For example, following his justification, Thomas Olivers felt rejuvenated by a passionate commitment to serve the Lord. Through public preachings and exhortations, his conscience grew "abundantly tender" such that "in [his] actions, [he] could not do an act of injustice, no, not to the value of a pin" (*Arminian Magazine*, 1779, p 86). All of his "thoughts, intentions and desires" (p. 87) focused on the glorification of God. He writes, "Upon the whole I lived by faith. I saw God in everything: the heavens, the earth, and all therein, showed me something of him; yea even from a drop of water, a blade of grass, or a grain of sand, I often received instruction" (p. 87).

Olivers's description of faith presupposes a mindset that is both affective and cognitive. The devotional standards that inform his behavior also determine his view of nature as an expression of divine presence. Creation consists of an infinite series of revelatory signifiers that attest to the transcendent unity of God. Interestingly, even when theologians discuss Wesley's understanding of faith as a spiritual sensation, they tend to ignore the cognitive dimension inherent in the unitive perception of divine presence. They emphasize what Wesley calls the particular meaning of faith, the affective sense of acceptance and love (for example, Whaling, 1981, p. 44-45; Lovin, 1985; Mathews, 1985, p. 414; Clapper, 1989, pp. 56-58; Maddox, 1994, p. 173; Steele, 1994, pp. x-xi). In *On the Discoveries of Faith*, a sermon written in 1788, Wesley's enumeration of the various objects of spiritual knowledge reveals the extent to which his conception of faith involves more than an affective experience of pardon. Here faith not only gives evidence of one's own "immortal spirit," it also allows one to become aware of other discrete presences or "orders of spirits."

> These I term *angels*, and I believe part of them are holy and happy, and the other part wicked and miserable. I believe the former of these, the good angels, are continually sent of God 'to minister to the heirs of salvation'; who will be 'equal to angels' by and by, although they are now a little inferior to them. I believe the latter, the evil angels, called in Scripture, 'devils', united under one head (termed in Scripture 'Satan', emphatically, the 'enemy', the 'adversary' both of God and man) either range the upper regions, whence they are called 'princes of the power of the air'; or like him 'walk about the earth as roaring lions, seeking whom they may devour' (Wesley, 1984-87, IV: p. 31).

It may be argued that the discernment of such presences was an entirely metaphorical interpretation of ordinary life circumstances, directed either by providence or demonic influence. We must not exclude the possibility, however, that Wesley also referred to moments of ecstatic perception. In previous chapters, I have cited instances of both intellectual and imaginal visions of Satan and his host of demons. We also find similar accounts of angels (for example, *Arminian Magazine*, 1778, p. 228; 1784, p. 307; 1788, pp. 128-129; Carvosso, 1835, p. 255; Told, 1954, pp. 60-62).

Mathews's (1985, p. 414) and Dryer's (1983, p. 15) insistence that Wesley did not regard "visions and voices" (p. 15) as a constituent of religious knowledge is too simplistic. Although wary of enthusiastic extravagances, he was also more cautiously accepting of "extraordinary communications" than these authors suggest. Gunter (1989) states that Wesley "often encouraged" enthusiastic practices in local Methodist societies and "let them go for some time before he applied a correcting hand": "One wonders if Wesley was not only tolerant, but perhaps even pleased that at times there was more 'heat than light' in the Methodist Societies" (p. 137). Wesley believed that the work of the spirit was not simply confined to the past, and he gave more credit to these experiences than he would openly admit to in apologetic contexts. We must also bear in mind how Wesley's views were largely shaped by careful observation of others' experiences (Gunter, 1989, pp. 40, 209-211; Rack, 1989, pp. 157, 548-550). Since various kinds of ecstatic experiences are richly documented in the autobiographical narratives that Wesley edited and published, we can hardly assume that he did not take them into serious consideration. An example of Wesley's open-mindedness appears in his commentary on the "voice of God" (1984-87, I: p. 282-283). He writes, "Meantime, let it be observed, I do not mean hereby that the Spirit of God testifies by any outward voice; no, nor always by an inward voice, although he may do this sometimes" (I: p. 287). Given the frequency of written reports that document the occurrence of an imaginal voice, an audible pseudo-hallucination that functions as a witness of pardon (for example, *Arminian Magazine*, 1778, p. 579; 1779, p. 418; 1784, p. 521), Wesley here appears to grant some degree of leeway for such phenomena.

Returning to the 1788 sermon on faith, Wesley claims that faith provides a view of the "eternal world" that includes eschatology and judgment.

> And here again faith supplies the place of sense, and gives us a view of things to come...Faith discovers to us the souls of the righteous, immediately received by the holy angels, and carried by those ministering spirits into Abraham's bosom; into the delights of paradise, the garden of God...It discovers likewise the souls of unholy men, seized the moment they depart from the quivering lips by those ministers of vengeance, the evil angels, and dragged away to their own place...Moreover faith opens another scene in the eternal world, namely the coming of our Lord in the clouds of heaven to 'judge both the quick and the dead'. It enables us to see the 'great white throne coming down from heaven, and him that sitteth thereon...We see 'the dead, small and great, stand before God'. We see 'the books opened...and the dead judged, according to the things that are written in the books'. We see 'the earth and the sea giving up their dead, and hell' (that is, the invisible world) 'giving up the dead that were therein, and everyone judged according to his works' (IV: pp. 32-34).

Faith allowed for the perception of these eschatological scenes. They were likely inspired by the ecstatic visions of judgment that were commonly reported amongst Methodists (Rack, 1987, p. 38). According to Rack, Judgment visions typically convinced individuals "of their risk of hell" or assured them that "their names were (literally in some cases) 'written in the book of Life'" (p. 42).

Finally, Wesley states that the faith of "fathers," meaning those who are perfected, allows them to know the "eternal Three-one God" (1984-87, IV: p. 37). He writes, "One of these [The Marquis de Renty] expresses himself thus, 'I bear about with me an experimental verity and a plenitude of the presence of the ever-blessed Trinity" (p. 37). In this excerpt, Wesley refers unequivocally to a specific type of ecstatic encounter. From the late 1770s onwards, a particular form of visionary experience, a revelation of the separate persons of the Trinity, became associated with a select group of individuals who underwent spiritual crises related to entire sanctification (Rack, 1987, pp. 39ff). During the early years of this decade, Wesley believed that Trinitarian visions were regularly given to those who had been perfected (p. 43; see also Fraser, 1988, p. 189).

Rack (1987) holds that the most frequently documented vision in early Methodism is that of Christ crucified, an interior image "commonly associated with some crucial phase in a conversion crisis" (p. 38). He provides an excerpt from Thomas Taylor's autobiography.

> While I was calling upon the Lord, He appeared in a wonderful manner, as with his vesture dripped in blood. I saw him with the eye of faith, hanging on the cross: and the sight caused such love to flow into my soul, that I believed that moment, and never since gave up my confidence (quoted in Rack, 1987, p. 38).

Similarly, Dimond points out how justification and the new birth often occur in tandem with "imaginal" visions (1926, pp. 180-185; see also Rack, 1987, p. 40). These experiences occur during states of reverie. Subjects remain aware that their imaginations have "furnished the material for the vision" (Dimond, 1926, p. 184-85). They are able to "indicate the subjective character of the hallucination" while simultaneously entertaining its reality. The sense of subjectivity "does not disprove the sensory character of the experience" or its religious significance. Taylor beheld his vision by the "eye of faith." In many Methodist narratives, individuals understood that interior visions were mediated by a supernatural sense, a visual faculty explicitly correlated with faith. For Charles Perronet, faith refers to what he calls an "external vision." "It is an impression upon the mind. While the soul is under the power of faith, the person of Christ is often presented to the imagination" (*Arminian Magazine*, 1779, p. 204). James Rogers writes that during his justification, "all the sufferings of Christ came to my mind" (*Arminian Magazine*, 1789, p. 462).

> By the eye of faith I had as real a view of his sufferings on Calvary as ever I had of any object by the eye of sense. I saw his hands and

his feet nailed to the cross; his head crowned with thorns; and his side pierced with a soldier's spear: with innumerable drops of blood falling from the different parts of his body (p. 462).

J. B. of St. Hellier's had been in prayer for three hours when she "saw by faith the Lord Jesus on the cross, and the blood streaming from his side" (*Arminian Magazine*, 1788, p. 72). Immediately her "load dropped off," and she believed her sins were "blotted out" (p. 72).

Bearing in mind that Wesley's description of faith includes a view of God's omnipresence, we find that, along with the imaginal or eidetic vision, the intellectual vision of presence also occurred commonly. The latter entails an abstract yet compelling feeling of God's immediate proximity (compare James, 1985, pp. 53-77). The following excerpts are exemplary:

> I had such a calm peace, and such an inward Communion with the Lord, that when I sat down to work, I seemed to be compassed about with the immediate presence of God: so that I sometimes cried out, "I am a child of a hundred years old!...The Lord now taught me many things and led me by a way I had not known (Marg Jenkins, *Arminian Magazine*, 1778, p. 229).

> O how does the Lord deal with such an unworthy worm! Such an effusion of his divine love and presence, that all within and without seems nothing but God! I feel that my whole body, soul and spirit, is a sacrifice to him (Bathsheba Hall, *Arminian Magazine*, 1781, p. 196).

> I had several times such drawings of the Father (though I knew not then what they were) as made me seem to be out of the body; and I could scarce cast my eyes on anything, but I saw God in it: nor had I any fear of his wrath, but always saw him as a loving Father (Sarah Ryan, *Arminian Magazine*, 1778, p. 298).

The standard doctrinal view of "faith" in early Methodism prioritizes the affective sense of pardon and acceptance but does not fully encompass the phenomena that Wesley and his followers designated by that name. Theologically, pardon is prioritized since reconciliation with God is the necessary condition for spiritual renewal. *However, as a supernatural faculty, faith was clearly understood to provide a further set of experiences whose cognitive content corresponds to typical patterns of ecstatic perception, namely, imaginary pseudo-hallucinations. These include eidetic images as well as the abstract or intellectual sense of God's unitive presence.* Why then has theological scholarship given precedence to the affective dimension and generally ignored the cognitive components?

I suggest that the scholarly neglect of the unitive dimension of faith, the abstract perception of presence, is a consequence of Wesley's *ostensible* rejection of mysticism. In 1736, he wrote a letter to his brother, which scholars and theologians often cite as evidence for the demise of Wesley's early interest in mysticism (Tuttle, 1989, p. 85). In the letter he declares, "I think the rock on which I had made the nearest shipwreck of the faith was on the writings of the mystics: under which term I comprehend all, and only those, who slight any of the means of grace" (quoted in Tuttle, 1989, p. 85). What appears to be a critique of mysticism per se is on closer examination a rejection of Quietist forms of piety. We must not forget that there was much in the mystical literature that Wesley not only admired but saw fit to disseminate amongst his followers. Whaling (1981), who challenges the notion that Wesley "suddenly repudiated the mystical influences on his development" (p. 10), points out that during the height of the revival, he published the works of such spiritual masters as Scupoli, Fenelon, de Renty, Mme. Bourignon, Mme. Guyon, Molinos and others. Tuttle (1989) goes as far as to claim that Wesley's ambivalent attitude towards mysticism was "psychoneurotic." He was both "disillusioned" by *and* "irresistably drawn" to the mystics" (p. 43). Wesley admired several mystical themes: the necessity of crucifixion; the perfection of love; and the achievement of a direct and unbroken communion with God via the practice of the presence (Rack, 1989, pp.102-103, 401; Tuttle, 1989, pp. 42, 149-150). However, Wesley also believed that the antinomianism, passivity and otherwordliness that epitomized Quietism, destroyed the dignity and "value of the human personality" (Dimond, 1926, p. 85).

Molther advocated an extreme form of "stillness." He encouraged individuals to do away with communion, prayer, communication, and, in effect, all forms of action. This undermining of the instituted means of grace and the Quietists' preference for seclusion flew in the face of Wesley's "volitional and practical predilections" as well as his pronounced "social sentiment" (Dimond, 1926, p. 85). Wesley promoted an active "social holiness," rather than "private virtue" (Steele, 1994, p. 140). He "visualized a state of perfection to be achieved by a sizable body of dedicated people in the world rather than a few in solitude or the monastery" (Rack, 1989, p. 401). Furthermore, Quietist spiritual practice cultivated a passive resignation or "indifference" to one's own salvation. Fenelon, for example, defined perfection as a self-less love for "what God *is*, not for what he *grants*" (Tuttle, 1989, p. 40). In order to overcome self-love, the will had to be annihilated. One acquired indifference by divesting the mind of any representational content that kindled the desire of the senses. All forms of discursive meditation that employed mental imagery were renounced (Chadwick, 1975, p. 219; Dupré, 1989, p. 133; Tuttle, 1989, pp. 37-38). As both an empiricist and an ardent reformer, Wesley could not accept a practice that sought to eliminate sensory experience.

> Many eminent men...have advised us 'to cease from all outward actions'; wholly to withdraw from the world; to leave the body behind us; to abstract ourselves from all sensible things—to have no concern at all about outward religion, but to 'work all virtues in the will', as the far more excellent way, more perfective of the soul...this [is the] fairest of all devices wherewith Satan hath ever perverted the right ways of the Lord!...Christianity is essentially a social religion, and to turn it into a solitary one is to destroy it (Wesley, 1984-87, I: pp. 532-33).

The flight from the body and the senses, and the passive removal of the will, indicate that Quietist spirituality relied upon trance states as a means to achieve perfection. The Committee on Psychiatry and Religion (1976, p. 775) maintain that in the trance state "the external world is excluded from consciousness more or less completely, or its impact is muted—attention is turned away from it." As a result of Quietism's world-renouncing character, Wesley could not accept the tenets of its doctrines. Moreover, although acceding that faith was passively received and that all righteousness was in Christ, Wesley refused to jettison the role of the will in the pursuit of holiness. In contrast to an introspective spirituality whose goal was to eradicate autonomy, willfulness and rationality, Wesley accentuated the integrity of the self. He made it clear that individuals were endowed with the ability to embrace or reject God's offer of saving grace. Because the Holy Spirit empowered volition, Christians were obligated to nurture and exercise their faith, among other means, by rendering service to others in the world. Hence Maddox (1994) speaks of a "responsible grace" that enhances initiative and personal agency.

Through collating the various designations and descriptions that appear in the writings of Wesley and his followers, I have argued that the term faith was understood *in its most inclusive sense* not only as pardon, but as a medium of ecstatic perception. As we have seen, the *normative* alternate states in early Methodism were reverie based. Wesley's description of the unitive perception of God's presence *in the world* was at once rational and object related. Several writers have pointed to a mystical component in Wesleyan spirituality (Dimond, 1926, pp. 86-87, 183-184; Outler, 1987, p. 187; Rack 1987, p. 40; Trickett, 1989, p. 358; Tuttle, 1989, op. cit). The evidence I have adduced suggests that he endorsed a non-dissociative "extroverted" form of mysticism (Stace, 1961, pp. 62-81). Wesley's mysticism differed from the trance-based experiences of the canonical Christian mystics, and more particularly, the Quietists, of whom Wesley was largely critical. If by "mystic" we mean Quietist, Wesley was not a mystic. However, he was indeed a mystic by the standards of the comparative study of mysticism. His objection to a particular kind of piety and a particular form of ecstasy has obscured the extent to which unitive experiences are central to early Methodist spirituality. Both men and women from a variety of cultural-religious backgrounds report them consistently. Neither were they exclusive to a particular class or vocational group. These findings are consistent with contemporary data on the demography of mysticism. Surveys indicate that one-third of the populations of Western cultures report "mystical and/or numinous experiences" (Hood, 1995 pp. 589, 594). Greeley, for example, found that four out of ten Americans have had, or believe they have had a mystical experience (cited in Ellwood, 1980, p. 1).

JUSTIFICATION, PEAK EXPERIENCES AND THE EGO-IDEAL

Maslow (1970, p. 59) held that the momentary perception of cosmic unity "can be so profound and shaking...that it can change the person's character and his Weltanschauung forever after." "Peak experiences," he writes, "sometimes have immediate effects or aftereffects...[which] are so profound and great as to remind us of the profound religious conversions which forever after changed the person." The effects upon the personality bear striking resemblance to what Wesley calls "the fruit of the spirit."

> [The fruit of the spirit may be known by] *love, joy, peace* always abiding; by invariable *long-suffering*, patience, resignation; by *Gentleness*, triumphing over all provocation; by *goodness*, mildness, sweetness, tenderness of spirit; by *fidelity*, simplicity, godly sincerity; by *meekness*, calmness, evenness of spirit; by *temperance*, not only in food and sleep, but in all things natural and spiritual (Wesley & Wesley, 1981, p. 355).

These dispositions, the aftereffects or "fruit" of God's pardon, flow from the apprehension of a unitive ideal. Following Maslow, we may say that the unitive inspirations that manifest during Methodist conversion encourage similar changes in temperament. The emergence of a symbolic ideal, encoded in the abstract perception of God's omnipresence, transforms the significance of what is taken in by the senses, and evokes emotions that invigorate the self.

For Wesley, profane consciousness proceeds according to the constraints of the body. In essence, he speaks of an "idolatry" that consists of straightforward, unelaborated sense perceptions. The simple meanings of these perceptions are limited by their materiality and the carnal appetites and desires that they provoke. "Love of the world," states Wesley, "is now as natural to every man as to love his own will" (1984-87, II: p. 179).

> What is more natural to us than to seek happiness in the creature instead of the creator? To seek that satisfaction in the works of his hands which can be found in God only? What more natural than the desire of the flesh? That is, of the pleasure of sense in every kind?...Sensual appetites, even those of the lowest kind, have, more or less, the dominion over him (II: pp. 179-80).

Spiritual senses promote a movement beyond the limitations of idolatry. Now the objects of sense perception take on transcendent significance—their *concrete physicality* becomes a *conceptual sign* of God's immanence. Entering into the new world and seeing the invisible and eternal things of God means beholding the creator in creation itself: "God is in all things...we are to see the Creator in the glass of every creature...we should use and look upon nothing as separate from God...who pervades and actuates the whole created frame, and is in a true sense the soul of the universe" (I: pp. 516-17). Methodist converts claimed that their justification left them feeling as if they had become an "entirely new person" (Abelove, 1990, p. 89). Some also felt "the release so strongly that the whole world of nature was transformed for them" (Rack, 1989, p. 425). As Starbuck (1911) observes, one of the commonest experiences after conversion is the "sense of newness." He writes: "The person is living in a new world. Old experiences are seen from a different point of view. The world bears a new face. It has likewise a new content and significance" (pp. 119-120). There is a "clarification of spiritual vision" such that one sees "beauty in every material object in the universe."

Upon receiving pardon, George Shadford (1866) saw Christ "by the eye of faith" (as opposed to his "bodily eyes") interceding for him. In that instant his soul was filled with "divine love." He wept "tears of joy and sorrow" (p. 150). The ecstasy subsequently transformed the content and meaning of his perceptions. Reminiscent of Maslow's (1970) claim that peak experiences furnish individuals with a "personally defined heaven" (p. 66), Shadford (1866) writes,

> As I walked home along the streets, I seemed to be in paradise. When I read my Bible, it seemed an entirely new book. When I meditated on God and Christ, angels or spirits; when I considered good or bad men, any or all the creatures which surrounded me on every side; everything appeared in a new relation to me. I was in Christ a new creature; old things were done away, and all things became new (p. 150).

We may view this phenomenon as a transformation of perceptual-cognitive patterns, as a heightened symbolic awareness. With this awareness the divergent data of sense perception are thematically aligned by a supraordinate value. Here the creation of what Winnicott (1971) calls "intermediate space" is achieved by an integrative synthesis of internal and external reality (compare Meissner, 1984, pp. 173-77). *God's pardon, or the ego-ideal's approval of the ego, is represented in consciousness by the abstract perception of unity in the external world* (Haartman, 1998). The world appears to bear a "new face." Unitive ideation endows the cosmos with the conceptual qualities of the loved and admired ideal.

Maslow distinguishes between the unitive content of peak experiences and the way that the content subsequently affects the personality. Wesley's distinction between the witness of the spirit of God and the witness of our own spirit, or the "fruits," presupposes the same logic (Wesley, 1984-87, I: pp. 289-90). The consequences for the personality include: self-esteem; empathy and the intensification of healthy conscience; motivation and initiative; and emotional equanimity and self-composure. Psychoanalytically understood, all are functions of the positive superego and the ego's integration of its ideals (compare Freud, 1933a [1932]; Loewald, 1962; Jacobson, 1964; Lederer, 1964; Furer, 1967; Saul, 1970; Kohut, 1977; Laplanche & Pontalis, 1988; Milrod, 1990; Eigen, 1993).

Self-esteem

The witness of God's spirit persuades individuals that their sins are "blotted out" (Wesley, 1984-87, I: p. 274). The assurance of love and pardon, a feeling that coincides with the ego-ideal's acceptance of the ego, brings with it an "inexpressible joy" that effects a dramatic boost in self-regard. Several writers argue that the correlation between the spirit of adoption and self-esteem is taken for granted in Wesley's work. Maddox (1994) explains that the "recovery of our own happiness" through divine love presupposes "proper esteem for self" (p. 146). "Self-regulated" love, according to Lindstrom (1946), is a necessary consequence of God's benevolence; the latter "legitimates" the former (pp. 195-197). In other words, *the subjective sense of divine pardon symbolizes self-acceptance.* Wesley's portrayal of the characteristic shift in the God image, the substitution of a "loving father" in lieu of an "angry judge" (1984-87, I: p. 261) is significant in this connection. In a study on attachment and religious practice, Kirkpatrick (1995) marshals evidence to show how loving images of deity correlate with self-esteem. He writes, "people who think of their attachment figures as available and responsive also regard themselves as worthy of love and care" (p. 454; compare: Benson & Spilka, 1977).

Moreover, self-esteem, as Maslow has shown, is a direct consequence of the unitive perceptions of peak experiences. Grof and Grof (1990) make the same point.

> Encounters with divine regions...are extremely healing...one often feels positive emotions such as ecstasy, rapture, joy, gratitude, love, and bliss, which can quickly relieve or dissolve negative states such as depression and anger. *Feeling oneself to be part of an all-encompassing cosmic network often gives a person who has problems with self-esteem a fresh, expanded self-image* (emphasis added; 1990, p. 68).

Merkur (1989b) holds that because unitive ecstasies provide "unparalleled access to the deepest and most unconscious core of the superego," they are "the most intensely pleasurable experiences possible for a human being" (p. 152). Their euphoric character is an expression of "positive self-regard in response to ego-ideals whose attainment form the cognitive contents" of the experience (1999, p. 113). One's self-esteem is "maximized when and because a unitive ideal is momentarily integrated in the self" (p. 113). This view coincides with the role of the superego as a self-esteem regulator (Sandler, 1960, p. 153) and the idea that well-being results from an identification with and obedience to internalized values.

Empathy and the Intensification of Healthy Conscience

One of the most common realizations that flow from peak experiences is a conviction that the core of life is love. Individuals frequently acknowledge a deepening of their interpersonal relationships (Pahnke et al, 1969, p. 146; Kurland et al, 1973, pp. 113-114). Similarly, Wesley states that the witness of our own spirit, which emerges in direct response to God's witness of pardon, engenders a reciprocal love for God, as well as a compassion that extends to all humankind. This compassion encompasses intimate relations, acquaintances, strangers and enemies (1984-87, I: pp. 163; 518-19).

> Then, and not till then—when the Spirit of God beareth that witness to our spirit, 'God hath loved thee and given his own son to be the propitiation for thy sins'...'we love God, because he first loved us,' and for his sake we love our brother also' (I: p. 275).

When those who are justified feel "the love of God is shed abroad in their hearts" (I: p. 123), they become eager to do good works (I: p. 138). They want to relieve the misery of others by assisting in their repentance (I: p. 166).

For this reason they are deemed "lovers of mankind" (I: p. 165). Again, the compassion of which Wesley speaks is firmly rooted in unitive thinking. God is "the Father of the spirits of the flesh" (I: p. 138). Christians love all of humankind because they are related as spiritual siblings: "Agreeably hereto, the affection of this lover of God embraced all mankind for his sake; not excepting those whom he had never seen in the flesh, or those of whom he knew nothing more than that they were 'the offspring of God'" (I: p. 163).

Maslow repeatedly emphasizes the "object-directed" nature of beta-cognition.

> The cognition of being (B-cognition) that occurs in peak experiences tends to perceive external objects, the world, and individual people as more detached from human concerns. Normally we perceive everything as relevant to human concerns and more particularly to our own private selfish concerns...perception in the peak experiences can be relatively ego-transcending, self-forgetful, egoless, unselfish...it becomes more object-centered than ego-centered (1970, pp. 61-62).

The object directed consciousness of peak experiences relates directly to an enlargement of the empathic imagination. In Methodism, the perception of a universalizing alliance through Christ establishes new identifications in the ego and intensifies one's empathic relatedness to others. In keeping with Ross's (1968, p. 271) assertion that mystical experiences can lead to an increased maturity in object relations, we find that unitive ideation heightens the ability to imaginatively adopt another's point of view, which, in turn, breeds compassion and altruism. In the autobiographies, Methodists regularly associate ecstatic interludes with strong feelings of affection, benevolence and charity. The following two extracts are taken from accounts by Sarah Crosby and Duncan Wright, respectively.

> At length, one day, while I was sitting at work, the Lord Jesus appeared to the eye of my mind, surrounded with glory, while his love overwhelmed me: I said, this is the power I have waited for...*My soul seemed all love, and I desired nothing so much as to lay down my life for others, that they might feel the same* (emphasis added; *Arminian Magazine*, 1806, p. 468)

> I think it was in April this year, that the Lord justified me by his grace. I used to spend all my time in bed, while awake, in weeping and prayer; and it was in one of these weeping nights, that in an instant the Lord brought me out of my darkness into his marvelous light. I did not know then what to call it, but its effects were many, *I found an uncommon concern for the souls of the soldiers; and the*

sight of a Methodist used to set my heart on fire with love (emphasis added; *Arminian Magazine*, 1781, p. 371).

In the main, Methodist justification conforms to what Conn (1986) refers to as "affective conversion" (p. 228). For him, this form of "moral" conversion is akin to falling in love. In both instances there "is a more or less radical transformation of a person's life" (p. 228). In the same way that love draws us beyond ourselves towards the needs and interests of the beloved, affective conversion leads to a "desire for generosity; a reorientation from the possessiveness rooted in obsessive concern for one's own needs to the self-giving of intimate love and generative care of others" (p. 228). From Freud onwards, psychoanalysts maintained that the experience of "being in love" involves a projection of the ego-ideal. Augmenting Freud's (1921) dictum that in romantic love, "the object has been put in the place of the ego ideal" (p. 113), Chasseguet-Smirgel (1976) writes, "In the state of love—from the outset, at the very moment of 'election'—the subject and its object represent the relationship between the ego (the subject) and ego ideal (the object)" (pp. 356-357). With one important exception, the same dynamic applies to unitive ecstasies. Because unitive ecstasies take recourse to universalizing abstractions, *the projection of the ego-ideal extends globally to include a plurality of other beings as a single category or object of devotion.*

Furer's (1967) observations on the development of empathy in the second year of life, an event that he identifies as a "superego precursor," add additional insight to the psychology of justification. He claims that between 14 and 18 months, the child identifies with the mother as a loving consoler. By identifying with the mother's ability to feel and respond to the child's pain, the latter engages in an empathic role reversal modeled on the parent's solicitude. A similar identificatory event occurs in Methodist conversion and is theologically expressed by the distinction between the first and second witness. Wesley stipulates that without the prior manifestation of God's pardon, believers would not be properly enabled to love and minister to one another. Personal pardon lays the basis for the altruistic sentiments of the second witness. Through identification with God's solicitude as a "consoler," the justified are empowered to love: "But every Christian loveth [others] also as himself; yea 'as Christ loved us'" (1984-87, I: p. 138). "Self-esteem" writes Merkur (1999), "is necessary not only to the capacity to be alone, but also to the capacity to relate healthfully to others" (p. 114).

Because the varieties of identification that characterize unitive thought enhance the empathic imagination, peak experiences either strengthen one's convictions in pre-existing moral values, or they spontaneously inspire new ones (Haartman, 1998a, p. 217). Wesley frequently remarked upon the intensification of conscience following justification. The "light of faith," which he sees as qualitatively distinct from the fear and self-recriminations of the repentance phase, not only entails a "greater tenderness of conscience, and a more exquisite sensibility of sin," it is also a function of the spiritual senses, "the steady sight of things eternal" (1984-87, II: pp. 42-43).

> Accordingly this is spoken of by St. Paul as one great end of our receiving the Spirit, 'that we may know the things which are freely given to us of God'; that he may strengthen the testimony of our conscience touching our 'simplicity and godly sincerity', and give us to discern in a fuller and stronger light that we now do the things which please him (I: p. 275).

Pardon presupposes a "conscience void of offense towards God and man" (I: p. 304). The joyful affirmation of a "good conscience" (I: p. 310), established through faith, subsequently "brings to light" a definitive set of value criteria or standards from which the judgments of conscience proceed. In other words, faith affords a clear sight of God's law.

> Faith alone is that evidence, that conviction, that demonstration of things invisible, whereby the eyes of our understanding being opened, and divine light poured in upon them, we 'see the wondrous things of' God's 'law', the excellency and purity of it; the height and depth and length and breadth thereof, and of every commandment contained therein...By this is that gracious promise fulfilled unto all the Israel of God, 'I will put my laws into their minds, and write (or engrave) them in their hearts;' hereby producing in their souls an entire agreement with his holy and perfect law (I: pp. 304-305).

Since the spiritual senses are "fitted to discern spiritual good and evil" (I: p. 311), one develops strong moral intuitions.

> And now the eye of his soul waxes not dim. He was never so sharpsighted before. He has so quick a perception of the smallest things as is quite amazing to the natural man. As a mote is visible in the sunbeam, so to him who is walking in the light, in the beams of the uncreated sun, every mote of sin is visible...a Christian has the most exquisite sensibility, such as he would not have conceived before. He never had such a tenderness of conscience as he has had since the love of God has reigned in his heart (I: pp. 311-312).

The intensification of conscience is due to the emergence of unitive values that form the basis of God's law. Wesley's description of this law of love, written "afresh in the hearts of all true believers" (II: p. 8), captures the ethics of mutual reciprocity.

> [The law is just]. It renders to all their due. It prescribes exactly what is right, precisely what ought to be done, said, or thought, both with regard to the Author of our being, with regard to ourselves, and with regard to every creature which he has made. It is adapted in all respects to the nature of things, of the whole universe and every individual. It is suited to all the circumstances of each, and to all their mutual relations, whether such as have existed from the beginning, or such as commenced in any following period. It is exactly agreeable to the fitness of things, whether essential or accidental...there is nothing *arbitrary* in the law of God (II: p. 12).

In so far as all things meaningfully interrelate and participate in a larger whole, the law reveals the underlying order and harmony of creation (Lindstrom, 1946, p. 182). Wesley's rendering of the law corresponds to a particular mode of unitive ideation that Merkur (1998) identifies as "propriety": "The simplest form of the propriety mode involves an intense experience that the present time, place and events are proper, right, or appropriate to themselves" (p. 121). "The propriety mode presents temporally present phenomena as right, proper, harmonious, utilitarian, functional, and perfect, in and of themselves...the mode presents the idea that their function in relation to each other causes things to be as they should be" (p. 151).

Mutual reciprocity is an imperative revealed by the law. From it stems the golden rule: "Though shall love thy neighbor as thyself" (Lindstrom, 1946, p. 182). According to Merkur (2001b), unitive ideation bolsters conscience because moral judgments themselves rely on the unconscious assumption "that in hurting another person, one hurts oneself" (p. 127): "Moral thinking evaluates and treats people as though they were oneself, even in situations when the self neither is dependent on others nor has any reasonable expectation of becoming so" (p. 128). Sandler (1960) and Breen (1986) trace the origins of empathy and morality back to an early phase of primary identification with the mother. Although recent findings in infant observation flatly contradict the psychoanalytic myth of "primary narcissism" (Stern, 1985)—a neonatal stage of self-object nondifferentiation—a consensus exists among developmental theorists that in tandem with the conscious ability to distinguish between self and object, the baby also entertains unconscious fantasies of merging and becoming one with the mother (Bergmann, 1971; Silverman et al, 1982; Harrison, 1986; Pine, 1990). Merkur (2001b) suggests these fantasies are developmental precursors of, and therefore, the foundation for the moral and empathic imagination. He writes, "The capacity for the empathic beginnings of morality arises, I suggest, through the resolution of unconscious merger fantasies, precisely as generalized moral self-regulations arise through the resolution of the unconscious Oedipus complex (p. 131)." In a similar vein, Jacobson (1964) speaks of the unitive basis of ego-ideals. According to her, in the "deep, unconscious core" of the ego-ideal, "we may detect fusions of the early infantile images of both the love object and the self" (p. 95).

These views underscore the object related origin of ideals. Even after they are subject to a process of abstraction, ego-ideals maintain their affective tie to the concrete parental representations upon which they are modeled. They are de-anthropomorphized but never depersonified (Merkur, 1999b, p. 127). Indeed, as Pruyser (1974) shows, the ego is bound to its ideals as love objects: they are "cherished," "loved," "defended" and "clung to"; ideals inspire "loyalty" and "commitment" (p. 254). For Wesley too, the law is clearly object bound since it expresses the essential being of God.

> [The law] is the face of God unveiled; God manifested to his creatures as they are able to bear it...It is the heart of God disclosed to man...the express image of his person...a copy of eternal mind, a transcript of the divine nature...And this law which the goodness of God gave at first, and has preserved through all ages, is, like the fountain from whence it springs, full of goodness and benignity. It is mild and kind; it is (as the Psalmist expresses it) 'sweeter than honey and the honey comb'. It is winning and amiable...[in it] are hid all the treasures of the divine wisdom and knowledge and love (1984-87, II: pp.10-14).

In the optimal outcome of the desolation crisis, the lifting of repression allows the ego to regain access to intrapsychic representations of the good parent. The conscious acknowledgment of rage achieved through symbolic means temporarily allays the conflict of ambivalence. *Early memories and fantasies of loving intimacy can now be processed in consciousness and sublimated into an abstract ideal.* For this reason, the unitive form of the law preserves the trace of the "good object" from which it is derived. The law represents a figurative revelation of God's personhood. In it one beholds his face, his heart and his mind, all of which are sweet, winning and amiable. In her study of contemporary religious conversions, Ullman (1989) found that converts' attraction to new ideological truths was inseparable from the discovery of a new relationship with either "a real or imagined figure" (p. xvi).

Motivation and Initiative

The ego-ideal's developmental tie to the love object arouses the ego's devotion and compels it to act in accordance with what it regards as exemplary. When conflict does not intervene, the ego's willingness to conform to the behavioral dictates of its values is ensured by affects that produce initiative, commitment and loyalty. In health, obedience to one's ideals is spontaneous, inherently gratifying and free of the compulsive quality that characterizes the punitive mentality of a fixated superego. As Maslow (1970, p. 67) states, "[In peak experiences] the person feels himself more than at other times to be responsible, active, the creative center of his own activities and of his own perceptions, more self-determined...with more free will than at other times."

Wesley assumed that the will aligned itself with the affections (Lovin, 1985; Clapper, 1989; Steele, 1994). Self-consciousness and volition are not only a function of reason, "but likewise of love, hatred, joy, sorrow, desire, fear, hope, etc., and a whole train of other inward emotions which are commonly called 'passions' or 'affections'." "They are styled, by a general appellation, 'the will', and are mixed and diversified a thousand ways" (Wesley, 1984-87, IV: p. 22). Since Wesley regarded the characterological effects of conversion as a change in one's emotional capacities (Clapper, 1989, pp. 123, 130), he held that faith arms the will with a new set of motivating dispositions (Maddox, 1994, p. 69). Prior to justification, service to God is psychologically structured in terms of coercion. More specifically, because unjustified individuals remain subject to the "wrath and curse of God," and because obedience is motivated by guilt and "slavish fear," they cannot properly identify with the spirit and dictates of the law. Conflict precludes the possibility of fully embracing one's values (Wesley, 1984-87, II: p. 29). Through pardon, love becomes the affective basis for willful action.

> As he is not obliged to keep even the moral law as the condition of his acceptance, so he is delivered from the wrath and the curse of God, from all sense of guilt and condemnation, and from all that horror and fear of death and hell whereby he was 'all his life' before 'subject to bondage'. And he now performs (which while under the law he could not do) a willing and universal obedience. He obeys not from the motive of slavish fear, but on a nobler principle, namely, the grace of God ruling in his heart, and causing all his works to be wrought in love (II: pp. 29-30).

The faith that works through love produces all obedience and holiness (II: p. 27). Notions of the "power of Christ" (I: p. 581) and "Christian Freedom" (Lindstrom, 1946, p. 180; Deiter et al., 1987, p. 35) refer to the dynamism of the ego-ideal, and the way in which the ego gladly "yields," as opposed to "submits" to its imperatives. When ecstatically presented to consciousness, ideals provide the ego with a sense of direction (Laplanche & Pontalis, 1988, p. 144). Since they vitalize the will by summoning the ego's enthusiasm and resourcefulness, ideals act as a constant motivational source.

Methodist autobiographers repeatedly describe how their initial excitement during conversion rapidly crystallized into an aspiration to become circuit preachers. For George Brown, the witness of assurance came in the form of an "inward voice (sweeter than the harmony of angels)" (*Arminian Magazine*, 1784, p. 521). The voice whispered to him, "Be of good cheer, thy sins are forgiven. Go in peace and sin no more." "Now indeed," he writes, "heaven was opened in my new born soul." Weeping for joy, Brown immediately wondered how to apply himself to his ideal: "Lord, what wouldst thou have me to do? What return shall I make for the heaven I enjoy?...I slept none all night; but my soul rested in the peace of God, and I continued with him, as one would do with a beloved and intimate friend." After communing intimately with an imagined personified presence, an abstract vocational ideal gradually takes shape and enters into his awareness: "In a short time the Lord let me see that I must preach the Gospel. When this was deeply impressed, I solemnly promised to obey the Call, and intended to begin in a very few days."

Following his justification, Thomas Rankin entertained thoughts of becoming a preacher. As a result of ongoing conflict, however, bouts of depression interfered with his ability to fully consolidate his ideal. His resolve was clinched during an ecstatic episode.

> I awoke very early, and found my heart drawn out after God. I quickly arose and kneeled down to prayers: all the clouds fled away, and divine light and love shone with such brightness upon my soul, as I had not found in that degree since my conversion to God. I cried out with amazement, "O Lord, what dost thou intend concerning thy servant?" I walked about the room with streaming eyes, and an heart burning with love; and then kneeled down to pray again. While I was upon my knees, I beheld the fallen race of mankind in such misery and ruin, that I almost fainted away. Soon after these words were applied with mighty power, "Whom shall I send? whom shall I send?" I cried out, "Lord, here am I; send me if it will bring any glory to thy name. Then these words were applied, Depart ye, depart ye, go ye out from thence, touch no unclean thing, go ye out of the midst of here; be ye clean that bear the vessels of the Lord! For ye shall not go with haste, nor go by flight; for the Lord shall go before you; and the God of Israel will be your reward. And soon after these words. They that be wise, shall shine as the brightness of the firmament, and they that turn many to righteousness, as the stars for ever and ever!
>
> At the application of these words, I was so overwhelmed with the divine presence, that my soul seemed to be lost in the inexpressible enjoyment of God (*Arminian Magazine*, 1779, pp. 191-92).

Rankin's ecstasy commences with a unitive vision of the "fallen race of man." The emotional force of the image, which causes him to swoon, overrides the resistances that previously inhibited his intention to preach. The vision then shifts into an interior dialogue whose verbal content continues to reassure him of the validity of his aspiration. When his doubts subside, Rankin receives the full approval of his ideal, and the ecstasy climaxes in the rapturous enjoyment of "divine presence." He attains a "clear conviction" that he is chosen by God to preach the gospel. His newly found determination is inextricably tied to the affective power of the unitive vision. He writes, "I felt such love *for the souls* of my fellow creatures, that I could have burnt at the stake, to rescue them from eternal misery. In short I felt such a change through all my powers, that when I was brought from nature to grace, it was not more conspicuous" (p. 192).

Emotional Equanimity and Self-Composure

Maslow (1970) explains that in peak experiences "there tends to be a loss, although transient, of fear, anxiety, inhibition, of defense and control, of perplexity, confusion, conflict, of delay and restraint" (p. 66). Because this mood correlates with an increase in self-determination and "free-will" (p. 67), we may alternatively speak of heightened impulse control and greater degrees of emotional equilibrium, or, in short, an even temperament. Wesley holds that one of the fruits of the spirit is "meekness," which he defines as self-composure.

> [Christian Meekness] keeps clear of every extreme, whether in excess or defect. It does not destroy but balances the affections...It poises the mind aright. It holds an even scale with respect to anger and sorrow and fear; preserving the mean in every circumstance of life...When this due composure of mind has reference to God, it is usually termed resignation—a calm acquiescence in whatsoever is his will concerning us...When we consider it more strictly in regard to ourselves we style it patience or contentedness. When it is exerted towards other men then it is mildness to the good and gentleness to the evil (Wesley, 1984-87, I: pp. 489-90).

Meekness denotes the ability to regulate and temper one's emotions. Individuals who tame the unruly and overwhelming intensity of their affects remain, as it were, in calm possession of themselves. For Wesley, this trait is brought into being by devotion: "meekness holds the reins...their zeal is always guided by knowledge, and tempered in every thought and word and work with the love of man as well as the love of God" (I: p. 490). The reconciliation of passion and volition accomplishes the equivalent of sublimation.

> But they have the mastery of all; they hold [the passions] in subjection, and employ them only in subservience to those ends [that is, the will of God]. And thus even the harsher and more unpleasing passions are applicable to the noblest purposes. Even hate and anger and fear, when engaged against sin, and regulated by faith and love, are as walls and bulwarks to the soul (I: p. 490).

Emotional equanimity reduces anxiety and fear (compare: Maslow, 1970, p. 66). Pardon dispels the chronic preoccupation with death and damnation so that, ideally, those whose hearts are filled with "love to every soul" feel prepared to lay down their lives for others (Wesley, 1984-87, I: p. 509). Elsewhere Wesley writes,

> [Justification by faith] delivers us from all perplexing doubts, from all tormenting fears, and in particular from that 'fear of death, whereby we were all our lifetime subject to bondage (II: p. 481).

In *A Plain Account of Christian Perfection* (Wesley & Wesley, 1981, pp. 342-347), Wesley provides an account of the death of an ardent follower, Jane Cooper. The extract shows that Cooper's continual involvement with Jesus through watchfulness and prayer prompted a series of autonomous moral inspirations that she interpreted as evidence of her savior's immanent presence.

> It was mine, to be reserved, to be very quiet, to suffer much, and to say little...But the thing is to live in the will of God. For some months past, when I have been particularly devoted to this, I have felt such a guidance of his Spirit, and *the unction which I have received from the Holy One has so taught me of all things, that I needed not any man should teach me, save as this anointing teaches*...'Lord, I bless you that you are ever with me, and all you have is mine...' (p. 345).

Cooper's communion with Jesus assuages her fears and gives her strength to suffer "the agonies of death" (p. 345) with joyous resignation. Through prayer and introspection, she actualizes a reciprocal, dynamic rapport or dialogue with her ideal. Her efforts to conform to the will of God are rewarded by personalized revelations of conscience, that is, by the guidance of the Spirit. The satisfaction of receiving such signs of approval helps her to internally regulate her own anxieties: "I needed not any man should teach me, save as this anointing teaches." Here the emotional equanimity achieved through the personalization of a moral ideal fosters courage, endurance and the ability to withstand deprivation. Each of these items represents a provision of the positive superego (Schafer, 1960, 175-178; see also Kohut, 1977, p. 46, on the tension-relieving and self-soothing functions of internalized ideals). Several Methodist deathbed accounts refer to the way in which ecstatic manifestations of divine presence soothe the physical and mental anguish of the dying (for example Carvosso, 1835, pp. 50-51, 134; Rogers, 1832, pp. 59, 216). Hester Anne Rogers speaks of an "extraordinary exertion of [God's] power and love, which, indeed, we often see manifested in the dying hours of those who love God" (p. 21). Humanistic psychologists report similar findings. In a series of clinical experiments conducted in the 1960s with terminal cancer patients, researchers found that peak experiences induced through psychedelic use led to significantly positive changes in individuals' attitudes towards death. Feeling themselves identified with a larger spectrum of being, patients comprehended their mortality in different terms:

> Some of the patients who experienced the shattering phenomenon of death and rebirth followed by an experience of cosmic unity seemed to show a radical and lasting change in their fundamental concepts of man's relation to the universe. Death, instead of being seen as the ultimate end of everything and a step into nothingness, appeared suddenly as a transition into a different type of existence; the idea of a possible continuity of consciousness beyond physical death seemed to be much more plausible than the opposite (Kurland et al., 1973, p. 113).

VICISSITUDES OF JUSTIFICATION AND THE NEW BIRTH

Because Wesley's account of justification and the new birth is theologically framed, it reflects an optimal ideal of transformation that does not and cannot address the diversity of experiences that are unique to single individuals. Personality differences introduce a series of idiosyncratic variables. Not surprisingly, converts' accounts are manifold and distinctively nuanced. Most writers prioritize the sense of pardon. For some, however, pardon is conveyed by visionary experiences that are subject to variation in terms of both content and mode (for example, visual versus auditory). Moreover, in many instances, only a partial or uncertain manifestation of the Spirit occurs. A more complete array of doctrinally prescribed experiences may only emerge gradually over a period of time. I have assembled a set of extracts that both attest to this diversity *and* reveal the essential features and effects of the justification ecstasy as described above.

Following a prolonged period of depression marked by fasting and sleep deprivation, John Mason finally felt God's benevolence.

> While I was exercised in this gloomy manner, I, one evening, took up the New Testament to read, and I hope never to forget the time and place. As I read, I felt, I cannot tell how, an unusual going out after God and Christ. At once my eye, and all the powers of my soul were fixed on those words, Heb. ii. 9, *But we see Jesus, who was made a little lower than the angels, for the suffering of death, crowned with glory, and honor, that by the grace of God should take death for every man.* The deep silence that rested on me gave way, and I broke out as in an extasy of joy, not regarding who might hear,
> "For me he lived, and for me he died."
> In a moment, all my burthen of pain and sorrow fled away, and all my soul was filled with peace and joy. I was all love to God and man (*Arminian Magazine*, 1780, pp. 651-652).

A verse of scripture triggered Mason's justification. He emphasizes the feeling of extreme joy and relief in knowing that Christ died for his sins.

Father Reeves provides no details of the actual content of his justification, claiming only that "the Lord was pleased to set [his] soul at liberty." What Reeves does convey are the immediate after-effects of the conversion.

> I then began to see the worth of precious souls, and that I had something more to do than merely save my own soul. I began to rebuke sin wherever I saw it, and when I heard of any person sick, I could not rest until I had been to see them and told them of heaven and hell, and that they must repent, and what God had done for my soul. I was so ignorant that I thought they would believe all and receive all I said, and be saved. If they were in distress, I gave them all I had in my pocket (Corderoy, 1873, p. 16).

Since Reeves's conversion establishes empathic identifications, he becomes less preoccupied with himself. As is consistent with a typical post-conversion pattern that I examine in greater detail in the following chapter, Reeves's altruism appears somewhat inflated. His feelings of concern momentarily obscure his ability to appreciate the difference between his own exalted state of mind and that of others. Reeves assumes that what is self-evident to him is perceived similarly by everyone else. There is also a manic quality in the urgency with which he rebukes sin, admonishes the ill ("when I heard of any person sick, I could not rest till I had been to see them"), and gives away his money. However, what is most apparent in this extract is Reeves's pronounced compassion.

The moments leading up to Richard Whatcoat's justification point to a resistance that led to a fantasy of corporal punishment.

> On Sept. 3, 1758, being overwhelmed with guilt and fear, as I was reading, it was as if one whispered to me, "Thou hast better read no more; for the more thou readest, the more thou wilt know, *And he that knoweth not the Lord's will and doth it not, shall be beaten with many stripes*" (*Arminian Magazine*, 1881, p. 191).

Whatcoat resigned himself to whatever consequences lay ahead, and continued reading his Bible.

> When I came to those words, *The Spirit itself beareth witness with our own Spirits, that we are the children of God*, as I fixt my eyes upon them, in a moment, my darkness was removed, and the Spirit did bear witness with my Spirit, that I was a child of God. In the same instant I was filled with unspeakable peace and joy in believing: and all fear of death, judgment and hell, suddenly vanished away. Before this, I was kept awake by anguish and fear, so that I could not get an hour's sleep in a night. Now I wanted no sleep, being abundantly refreshed by contemplating the rich display of God's mercy, in adopting so unworthy a creature as me to be an heir of the kingdom of heaven! (pp. 191-192).

Scripture activated Whatcoat's conversion, like that of John Mason. In receiving the spirit of adoption and becoming a child of God, he emphasizes his blissfulness, as well as the demise of his persecutory fear of death and damnation. Along with many other converts, he alludes to a common phenomenon: an exuberance that temporarily overrides the desire for sleep. This again lines up with certain manic trends associated with the emotional intensity of the new birth.

Charles Hopper, who had become thoroughly "undone" by his own sense of corruption, "quietly retired to a little parlor" to "cover" his shame, and to plead with the Lord for his salvation (*Arminian Magazine*, 1881, p. 32).

> He then heard my cry, and sent me relief. A glorious light shone into my heart, and discovered to me the blessed plan of man's redemption, through the blood of a crucified Savior...He sent his Son to save sinners, the chief of sinners...The love of God is shed abroad in my heart, by the Holy Ghost given unto me. The Spirit of bondage is gone. The Spirit of Adoption is come. I can now cry, Abba father...No enmity—No wrath—No curse—No condemnation—The ruined sinner is saved. I then found a glorious and undeniable change. God, Christ, Angels, Men, Heaven, Earth, and

> the whole creation appeared to me in a new light, and stood related to me in a manner I never knew before. I found love to God, to his yoke, to his cross, to his saints, and to friends and enemies...I then went my way rejoicing; a wonder to my Father's family; to all that knew me; and to myself. All my idols fell to the ground, before the ark of God. I found a perfect hatred to sin, and a compleat victory over it.
> The whole tenor of my life and conversation was new. *Free grace, infinite mercy, boundless love*, made the change. My heart, my tongue, my hands, were now, in my little way, employed for my loving God (pp. 32-34).

Hopper's pardon not only dispels his guilt, but also instills a different perception of the cosmos: "the whole creation appeared to me in a new light." As mentioned above, this effect is a function of unitive thinking. After he states that creation stood related to him in a manner he had never known before, he immediately refers to a universalizing love that encompasses God and all beings. Furthermore, Hopper emphasizes that the transformation was both dramatic and conspicuous. He claims that he was a "wonder" to his father's family and to all who knew him. The affective conversion enabled him to adopt a set of values whose emotional appeal led to significant behavioral and characterological changes. As a direct consequence of "infinite mercy" and "boundless love," the "whole tenor" of his life and conversation was altered: "My heart, my tongue, my hands, were now, in my little way, employed for my loving God."

Many accounts of the new birth include visual and auditory pseudo-hallucinations that express divine pardon in pictorial or verbal registers. As is the case with the spontaneous and passive remission of guilt, an event that proceeds independently of the will, the autonomous character of the pseudo-hallucinations accentuates the sense of presence. Several examples of the vision of Christ crucified are provided above. Since the imagery straightforwardly represents the means by which the Savior atoned for the sins of human kind, the vision is almost invariably presented during justification "to the eye of the mind" or the "eye of faith." John Nelson (1842), for example, resolved to abstain from all food and drink until he "found the kingdom of God" (p. 18).

> But now I was as dumb as a beast, and could not put up one petition, if it would have saved my soul. I kneeled before the Lord some time; and saw myself a criminal before the judge: then I said, "Lord, thy will be done: damn or save!" That moment Jesus Christ was as evidently set before the eye of my mind, as crucified for my sins, as if I had seen him with my bodily eyes; and in that instant

my heart was set at liberty from guilt and tormenting fear, and filled with a calm and serene peace. I could then say without any dread or fear, "thou art my Lord and my God." Now did I begin to sing that part of the 12th chapter of Isaiah, "O Lord, I will praise thee: though thou wast angry with me, thine anger is turned away, and thou comfortest me. Behold, God is my salvation; I shall trust and not be afraid: for me the Lord Jehova is my strength and my song; he is also become my salvation." My heart was filled with love to God and every soul of man: next to my wife and children, my mother, brethren, and sisters, my greatest enemies had an interest in my prayers; and I cried, "O Lord, give me to see my desire on them: let them experience thy redeeming love!" (pp. 18-19).

Nelson's vision, precipitated in part by his mental exhaustion ("now I was dumb as a beast"), allays his troubled conscience. Convinced that God's anger had vanished, Nelson surrenders himself to his ideal: "I shall trust and not be afraid." His love for God is abstracted and extended towards "every soul of man." He wishes that all could feel his own "desire" and experience God's "redeeming love." His gratitude releases a flood of tears:

I was so affected that I could not read for weeping. That evening, under Mr. Wesley's sermon, I could do nothing but weep, and love, and praise God, for sending his servant into the fields to show me the way of salvation" (p. 19).

Furthermore, Nelson's elation creates a temporary sense of inflated self-sufficiency. Being so filled with the Spirit, he denies the need for food.

All that day I neither ate nor drank any thing; for before I found peace, the hand of God was so heavy upon me, that I refused to eat; and after I had found peace, I was so filled with the manna of redeeming love, that I had no need of the bread that perisheth for that season (pp. 19-20).

James Rogers, whose vision of Christ's sufferings on Calvary has already been cited above, experienced "an inexpressible degree of approbation."

In that moment my burden was gone; my heart was changed from a state of bondage into glorious liberty: and I was constrained to tell all those who feared the Lord, what he had done for my soul...I now went about among my old acquaintances, with a confidence that they would all repent and be converted if they knew how ready Christ was to convert them. Some I found willing to hear what I had to say; others stared at me as one quite out of his senses (*Arminian Magazine*, 1789, p. 462).

Like Father Reeves, Rogers's unitive identifications and his need to convert others cause him to overestimate the ease with which this task would be accomplished.

Thomas Hanson's justification commences with a dissociative phenomenon that contemporary evangelical circles refer to as "slain in the spirit" or "resting in the spirit" (MacNutt, 1984). Although it admits of variations, the phenomenon is generally characterized by a hypnotic element—a loss of motor control and a "detached awareness" (p. 34). MacNutt states, "By and large people do not become unconscious" (p. 34) but experience a peaceful sense of God's presence. "With the body out of the way, so to speak, the person can concentrate more fully on what is happening within...Distractions grow less and we are better able to listen" (p. 47). Similarly, Hanson writes,

> Under my brother Joseph's prayer, I yielded, sunk, and, as it were, died away. My heart with a kind, sweet struggle melted into the hands of God. I was for some hours lost in wonder, by the astonishing peace, love, and joy which flowed into my heart like a mighty torrent. When I came to recollect myself, I asked what hast thou done? It was sweetly, but deeply impressed, "I have made thee mine." No tongue can tell what peace, love, joy and assurance I then felt. My willing heart and tongue replied, hast thou thus loved me? Here I am, willing to spend and be spent for thee. God now gave me to see all creation, redemption, grace and glory in a new light: and everything led me to love and praise him (*Arminian Magazine*, 1780, p. 481).

The hypnotic onset of Hanson's conversion is punctuated by the disappearance of both bodily control and conscious perception of the external world. However, he remains passively aware of highly pleasurable emotions that signify God's presence; he "melted into the hands of God." When the hypnotic interlude subsides, and Hanson "recollects himself," the sense of presence continues to manifest in the form of an interior dialogue. After asking God for the meaning of the ecstasy to be revealed to him, Hanson experiences an autonomous verbal inspiration that he construes as a direct response: "I have made thee mine." The fact that the ecstatic inspiration flows from an active and lucid inquiry indicates that the alternate state switches from hypnosis to reverie. Persuaded of his "assurance," Hanson continues the dialogue and vows to "spend" himself for God. In turn, he is granted a vision. Here again the theme of newness correlates with unitive ideation: "God now gave me to see all creation, redemption, grace and glory in a new light: and everything led me to love and praise him." Hanson's dialogue with God leads to the conscious emergence of a unitive moral ideal. The spontaneous onset of a trance state suggests that when the ideal first entered into his awareness it was resisted. However, as the trance dissolves and Hanson recovers his normal sensibilities, the ecstatic exchange permits him to reflect upon and assimilate the material gradually. The full impact of the insight is represented symbolically by a unitive view of creation in which all things are emblematic of God.

The ecstatic content of Thomas Joyce's justification combined both visual and auditory modes. He writes,

> I felt such a load as I was scarce able to bear. I looked down, and I thought I must drop into Hell forthwith: when in a moment I saw a great light, and heard a voice saying, "Rejoice in the Lord always, and again I say rejoice." This came twice, and I answered in my heart, "Yea, and I will rejoice." Since that time, I never lost the sense of God's love, nor ever yielded to any known sin (*Arminian Magazine*, 1781, p. 420).

Ruth Hall's conversion was effected by an audible inspiration alone.

> Being in great agony, I was crying to God to have mercy upon me, when I heard a voice (inwardly or outwardly I cannot tell,) "Jesus Christ maketh thee whole." I could not believe it. I cried out, "Me, Lord! It cannot be me!" But it was repeated again and again, it may be twenty times, till I could not but believe it. I was quite overwhelmed with peace and love, and was unspeakably happy. From that moment I could never doubt at all, nor did I never the loose the love I then received (*Arminian Magazine*, 1781, p. 478).

Non-auditory verbal inspirations are commonly said to be "impressed" or "applied." In other instances, like that of Ruth Hall's, verbal inspirations instead manifest as a spoken voice that magnifies the sense of presence and lends further credence to the revelation.

Some individuals describe an incomplete manifestation of the spirit. Certain core characteristics of the new birth fail to materialize. This may be due to resistance, or it may simply reflect differences in temperamental dispositions across personalities. For example, when Alexander Mathers' heart was set at liberty, and his load taken away, he praised God from the ground of his heart: "All my sorrow, and fear, and anguish of spirit [was] changed into solid peace" (*Arminian Magazine*, 1780, p. 99). Yet he remarks that he had "no great transport of joy," intimating that his expectations were not entirely fulfilled. For J. B. of St. Hellier's, the normative theological sequence of testimonies is actually reversed—the fruits of the spirit precede the witness of pardon.

> I saw by faith the Lord Jesus on the cross, and the blood streaming from his side. Immediately my load dropped off and I believed my sins were blotted out, *though I had not yet a testimony from his Spirit, that I was a child of God.* Yet I enjoyed a calm, serene peace, and had no fear either of death or hell (emphasis added; *Arminian Magazine,* 1788, p. 72).

Here we may safely infer that the testimony was missing as a result of a conflict that was also expressed in terms of physical exhaustion: "But the work of God in my soul, so weakened my body that I was obliged to take to my bed for some days" (p. 72).

Incomplete manifestations must be viewed in a larger psychological context. Most often, the transformative characteristics that Wesley attributed specifically to the new birth emerge intermittently over time. Wesley's adherence to reformation theology led him and his followers to identify ecstasies that included the distinct sense of pardon as the decisive indicators of instantaneous justification. However, if we examine the experiences of Richard Moss, we find that the personality changes associated with justification are established successively in tandem with several ecstatic episodes. The first ecstasy he reports in his narrative occurs during a service given by Wesley, whose very presence immediately elicits an idealizing transference in Moss. As the service proceeds, Moss's infatuation steadily builds until he is literally enraptured.

> When Mr. Wesley came out of the kitchen door, I rose up to look at him. I felt something I had never felt before. I thought, "I have read or heard of saints: Surely this is one." He went up into the pulpit, but I could not keep my eyes off him. He prayed, and I thought, "Well, this is such a prayer as I never heard in my life." Then he gave out a verse of hymn. Immediately I felt much love in my heart, and such joy, that I could not refrain from tears...Now I was happy: I was as in heaven: The hymn, the singing, all was heavenly round about me. And I knew, that till this hour, I had never known what happiness meant...I found all my prejudice vanish away, and I had such a love, both to the preachers and to all the people, as I cannot express (*Arminian Magazine,* 1798, p. 7).

After this event, Moss "could only talk of the things of God" and continually reproved the sins of his companions (p. 7-8). At the same time, he believed that he remained "under conviction" and continued "mourning after

God." Several months passed before he experienced a second ecstasy in which he received pardon.

> In the midst of my prayer, my eyes being shut, I saw Christ by faith, as if he was standing by me, and I saw plainly the prints of the nails in his hands. All my burden dropped off. My fears and doubts and sense of guilt vanished away. I knew Christ was mine. I knew that God for his sake, had blotted out all my sins. I was filled with such a love to God, and such a joy, as cannot be uttered. All the love and joy I had felt before, was nothing in comparison of this. And I now no longer rejoiced I new not why; but I had a clear sight of the Love of God in Christ Jesus (p. 53).

For three days Moss "walked as one out of the body, in the broad light of God's countenance" (p. 53). In keeping with a developmental pattern Wesley himself identified as a normal vicissitude in spiritual growth, Moss abruptly lost the sense of divine presence: "But when I waked the fourth morning, all was dark. My comfort and my God was gone."

> I had no fear of death or hell; and I had continual power over outward sin (as indeed I had from the very hour when I first tasted that God was Love, at the Foundery.) But I could not see Christ; and therefore I was in sorrow and heaviness (p. 53).

Moss was "pressed down to earth" by the "absence of divine comfort." For an unspecified period of time, he had a sense of his "inward sins and temptations" before he again attended one of Wesley's services.

> In the middle of the sermon I felt my soul united to the Lord. I had closer communion with him than ever. I found his Spirit witnessing with my spirit, not only that I was a child of God, but that he would depart from me no more, that he would abide with me forever. All sorrow and doubt and fear fled away. I was filled with light and peace. I had such a solid, settled joy in the Holy Ghost, as I was a stranger to, till that very hour. I felt a fuller and stronger love to God than ever, as well as to all mankind. And from that time I never lost for a moment the Light of God's countenance (p. 54).

We observe in this sequence of ecstasies the *protracted* emergence and consolidation of a unitive ideal. Moss's acquisition of the witness and its fruits occurs progressively in a series of discrete revelations. In the first episode, an idealization focused upon the person of Wesley catalyzes a further process of sublimation. By the end of the sermon, Moss extends affection towards God, the preachers, and all the people present at the service. This enlarged sense of affiliation extinguishes his fear of death, and offers an identificatory source through which he resists temptation and acts in vigorous accord with a new set of ideals. After conscientiously applying himself in this manner, he eventually experiences a second ecstasy, a pardoning vision of the Savior that represents his self-acceptance vis-à-vis his ego-ideal. For three days, Moss is acutely aware of God's immediate presence in his life. However, the rapid onset of a depression attests to a resistance that requires further working through. Despite this temporary setback, Moss did not fully regress back into blind despair. He did not experience a resurgence of anxiety about death and damnation, and he was able to prevent himself from backsliding into sin. In other words, certain self-regulatory features of the positive superego became durable despite his awareness that the previous intensity of his emotions waned: "I could not keep my heart fixed in prayer. I could not love God. I could not love my neighbor. I felt peevishness and discontent" (p. 54). Moss's depressive trial culminates in yet another ecstatic conferral of self-acceptance. The insight that he has attained sufficient equanimity to console himself, that is, to tolerate his doubts without succumbing to old habits opposed to faith, is expressed symbolically in a communion with the Lord—one that is "closer" or more intimate than ever. His sense of presence is now continuous: "And from that time I never lost for a moment the Light of God's countenance." He reciprocates with affect for both God and humanity: "I felt a fuller and stronger love to God than ever, as well as to all mankind."

In summary, the foregoing extracts reveal that the content and transformative effects of the justification ecstasy differed from individual to individual. In some cases it consisted primarily of an outpouring of extremely positive emotions associated with the autonomous and intuitive conviction of pardon. For others, visionary experiences reinforced the sense of acceptance. Furthermore, it was not uncommon that aspects the new birth were acquired episodically over a series of ecstatic interludes. Even so, we find that all the core components listed in Wesley's description of justification—those that coincide with the beta-cognition of peak experiences—appear in the autobiographical narratives. These include forgiveness, joy, self-esteem; empathy, compassion, the intensification of conscience; abstractions of unitive love and an altered perception of the cosmos; the sense of presence; and increased initiative and commitment to a new set of values and ideals.

SUMMARY

All the major components of faith doctrinally stipulated by Wesley, and reflected in the autobiographical narratives of his followers, coincide with Merkur's definition of ecstasy as an autonomous or involuntary conviction of the reality of the numinous. Justification by faith was depicted as both passive and instantaneous. It provided "perceptible inspiration," an "experimental knowledge of God" that was characterized not only by an affective sense of pardon, but also by a cognitive dimension that typically involved discursive inspirations, imaginary pseudo-hallucinations and the intellectual vision of presence. Furthermore, although descriptions of trance do sometimes appear in the autobiographical literature, the normative alternate states associated with Methodist ecstasies were reveries. In reverie, individuals remain aware of the intrapsychic nature of the ecstasies. Ego functions remain intact and reality testing persists. Ecstatic reverie went hand in hand with Wesley's synthesis of reason, Lockean empiricism and supernatural enthusiasm, as well as his commitment to a worldly or "object related" spirituality.

The Wesleyan conception of faith is permeated through and through with various modes of unitive thinking. The most notable is the sense of divine omnipresence. The abstract perception of the "eternal world" or "invisible things of God" instills a series of dramatic psychological effects that Wesley deemed "the fruit of the spirit." In his discussion of peak experiences, Maslow similarly refers to a unitive abstraction bound to a common set of ego-enhancing traits. I argue that in psychoanalytic terms these features indicate the emergence of ego-ideals. The transformative potential of these ecstasies is directly attributable to the alternate state because it provides immediate access to previously unconscious superego materials. Any number of internalizations capable of strengthening the ego through identification may remain dormant due to fixations and defenses that block their proper manifestation. Hartmann and Loewenstein (1962) allude to a particular variation of this phenomenon:

> In some cases the abolishment of the idealization of the parents will also interfere with, instead of strengthening, the child's self-esteem and ego ideal development. In later life the loss of ideals, related either to objects or to factors of a more impersonal nature may lead to what one usually terms cynicism—behind which, however, another set of ideals may be hidden (frequently, for example, truth values) (pp. 62-63).

Alternate states allow for a dramatic externalization of these frozen materials. In observing the significant improvement of terminal cancer patients who had peak experiences while undergoing psychedelic psychotherapy, Pahnke (1969) writes:

> I suggest that this experience has the potential for opening up positive experience *that may have been previously closed or clogged.* Our experiments have indicated that deep within every human be-

ing there are vast usually untapped resources of love, joy and peace (emphasis added; p. 15).

In the Methodist context, the initial work of mourning permits unconscious self and object images to emerge into consciousness during conversion. Rizzuto (1979, p. 51) writes, "For other individuals the elaboration of the God representation is enmeshed in the repression of the parental representations....In short, I understand conversion to be the ego-syntonic release from repression...of an earlier (or even present) parental representation linked to a God representation." The favorable representations of the parent—which belong to the positive pole of the split imago—become accessible to the "synthetic" or innate organizing functions of the ego (Blanck & Blanck, 1979, pp. 15-30). Representations of loving intimacy, not the least of which are the unconscious merger fantasies of early infancy, become subject to a process of abstraction. They transform into unitive ego-ideals that form the basis of conscience.

My formulation of this process, which places emphasis on the dynamic elaboration of ideals, may be compared to what Frick (1983; 1987; 1990) calls the "symbolic growth experience (SGE)." Frick (1983), who approaches similar phenomena from the perspective of humanistic psychology, defines SGEs as sudden developmental acquisitions, significant life moments in which "we create personal meaning by symbolizing our immediate experience in the interest of heightened consciousness and personal growth" (p. 108).

> Any experience containing symbolic potential for the individual clearly stands for something "beyond itself." As we move deeper into the symbolic nature of the experience, its "objective" structure and content are transcended. The SGE, therefore, discloses hidden potentials within experience. The SGE enables us to perceive and extend experience metaphorically to establish ontological significance in our lives. Thus our experience is transformed to reveal unseen potentialities. It is through this transformation that the facts and events of experience become charged with emotional power and personal meaning...This symbolic dimension of experience becomes a major source of learning and a powerful catalyst for dynamic personality change and growth...The perception of boundaries between person and environment is also erased during the SGE. The external and "objective" facts of experience fuse with deeply personal needs, meanings and values (pp. 111-13).

Eigen (1993, p. 70) explicitly ties the foregoing phenomenon to the "growth of a supportive and stimulating ego ideal."

> The mind spontaneously creates ideal images which enter into varied points of tension and harmony with representations of material reality. The ability to sustain the tension between representations of ideal and material realities is an essential condition of creative growth and work. A vital ego-ideal provides an ideal pole of experience which attracts representations of material reality which are relevant for its purposes. Thus the ego-ideal may come to act as a nodal point for the convergence and transformation of symbolic expressions of ideal and material experience (p. 78).

Both Frick and Eigen describe the alteration of perceptual-cognitive patterns that epitomize the spiritual senses in Methodism. Unitive ideals produce a heightened symbolic awareness. Concrete perceptions become conceptualized as evidence of divine immanence. As a result, they grow richer cognitively.

Six

Inflation and Depression

In an essay on typical disturbances that accompany spiritual illuminations, Assagioli (1990) identifies two kinds of complications that unfold sequentially and relate dynamically to one another. First, revelations of "higher" values "such as the ethical, the esthetic, the heroic, the humanitarian, and the altruistic" (p. 38) sometimes "feed" and "inflate" the ego" (p. 44). The inflation ranges from an exuberant overestimation of the self and its powers, to "uncontrolled, unbalanced and disordered behavior," and an "unrealistic, zealous and fanatical ambitiousness." One "may be easily impelled by the excitement of the inner awakening to play the role of the prophet or savior; [one] may found a new sect and start a campaign of spectacular proselytism" (pp. 45-46). According to Assagioli, these grandiose reactions betray a confusion between potential and actuality. The ecstatic contemplation of ideals can be emotionally profound and overwhelming. Individuals may readily assume that they have been permanently altered, that no discrepancy remains between their actual selves and an imagined state of perfection. But the euphoria eventually subsides when the self faces up to its ineluctable shortcomings. A second complication then arises, a danger that disillusionment will foment an equally powerful depression. Bitterly disappointed that the "rocks and rubbish, which had been covered and concealed at high tide, emerge again" (p. 47), individuals doubt or deny the "value and reality" (p. 47) of their experience. Sometimes the reaction takes on pathological overtones, producing a state similar to "psychotic depression or 'melancholia'" (p. 47). Symptoms include despair, suicidal impulses, self-deprecation, self-accusation and a loss of will power and self-control.

Rambo (1993), in his study of conversion, also identifies a "postconversion depression" (p. 136), a common inability to sustain the euphoria and the sense of empowerment. With the "tapering off from the emotional peak of decisive commitment," "old temptations and doubts" creep in again. The degree of disappointment dictates the severity of the depression. Both Assagioli and Rambo stress that the transformation of ingrained personality traits is not instantaneous, but rather, a long-term process requiring patience and commitment.

The conscious emergence of ideals and their integration into the personality are independent variables. Feeling partially responsible for the misuse of LSD in the 1960s, Maslow lamented the "big bang" theory of self-actualization (Krippner, 1972, p. 120). By this, he meant the chronic and repetitive induction of psychedelic ecstasies without any actual integration of their content and significance into the fabric of one's life. Maslow insisted that the long term consolidation of unitive values is slowly and painstakingly effected through self-reflection and the on-going application of ideals to the exigencies of ordinary events.

POST-CONVERSION INFLATION

Wesley regarded the post-conversion pattern of inflation and depression as a standard vicissitude in spiritual growth. For him, the overestimation of the self implied a confusion between justification and the new birth on the one hand, and entire sanctification, on the other (1984-87, I: pp. 336). The former terms, more modest in their scope, granted power to overcome temptation, whereas the latter eradicated the very root of sin. In the days and weeks that followed justification, the natural tendency of individuals to feel rapturously swept away meant that many lost sight of these distinctions. Their unchecked exhilaration led them to collapse the categories: "When the love of God is first shed abroad in our hearts...it is natural to suppose that we are no longer sinners, that all our sins are not only covered but destroyed...[some persuaded] themselves that when they were justified they were entirely sanctified" (I: p. 336).

> I know there are also children of God who, being now 'justified freely', having found 'redemption in the blood of Christ', for the present feel no temptation. God hath said to their enemies, 'Touch not mine anointed, and do my children no harm.' And for this season, it may be for weeks or months, he causeth them to 'ride on high places'; he beareth them on eagles' wings, above all the fiery darts of the wicked one. But this state will not last always (II: p. 104)

> When the candle of the Lord first shines on our head, temptation frequently flees away, and totally disappears. All is calm within: perhaps without, too, while God makes our enemies to be at peace with us. It is then very natural to suppose that we shall not see war any more. And there are instances wherein this calm has continued, not only for weeks, but for months or years. But commonly it is otherwise: in a short time 'the winds blow, the rains descend, and the floods arise' anew...The evil which yet remains in the heart will then also move afresh; anger and many other 'roots of bitterness' will endeavor to spring up. At the same time Satan will not be wanting to cast in his fiery darts...Now when so various assaults are made at once, and perhaps with the utmost violence, it is not strange if it should occasion not only heaviness, but even darkness in a weak believer. More especially if he was not watching, if these

assaults are made in an hour when he looked not for them; if he expected nothing less, but had fondly told himself (II: pp. 212-213).

For Wesley, conversion inflation refers to the belief that one has already resolved the struggle between ideal aspirations and the narcissistic and instinctual currents that oppose them. Inflated believers assume prematurely that the opposition of "the flesh lusting against the spirit" (II: p. 159) has been permanently laid to rest. Invoking the traditional concept of spiritual warfare between human nature and divine grace, Wesley summarizes: "It is very natural to suppose that we shall not see war anymore."

Methodist autobiographies certainly confirm Wesley's view of inflation. Yet they also paint an even more complex picture by depicting states complicated by manic features. For example, several extracts cited in the previous chapter show how some individuals, shortly after their justification, experienced insomnia and restlessness. In an early study on sudden religious conversions, Prince (1906) noted the same pattern. He describes the case of Miss B., a woman who had undergone a sudden conversion to Catholicism. Thanks to a "sudden change in her personality" (p. 44), a host of chronic physical symptoms vanished abruptly. Prince writes:

> On examination I found her to be in a high state of mental exhilaration, because, as she averred, she was cured at last. All her symptoms had vanished, and she experienced a feeling of well-being and physical health. She believed herself well, and plainly interpreted every event through her dominant idea of physical, if not spiritual "conversion" to health...The recovery of her health would allow her to follow a religious life in accordance with her ideals. Her condition was one of ecstasy. *Although she had not slept more than an hour a night for several nights, nevertheless she was not a bit tired, although under ordinary circumstances she would have been a physical wreck.*
>
> Psychologically, this new mental condition plainly afforded an opportunity to observe an example of that state of exaltation into which notoriously so many religious enthusiasts have fallen when the feeling of a new spiritual life was awakened in them (emphasis added; p. 45).

Miss B.'s miraculous cure, as well as her prolonged sleeplessness, suggests strongly that a manic component had infiltrated the conversion.

We see similar phenomena in Methodism. Benjamin Rhodes writes that when he was justified, he beheld the truths of Christianity "in the clearest light," and entertained a "deep sense of a present God" whom he approached "with reverential awe, confidence, gratitude, and love" (*Arminian Magazine*, 1779, p. 362).

> In this happy season, my joy frequently prevented my sleep, while my soul was taken up with him, who is *altogether lovely*: and in the extasies of joy, in the stillness of the night, I often sung my great Deliverer's praise. All things earthly appeared so empty, that I thought nothing here below worth a thought only as it tended to promote my eternal interest: I only desired grace and glory. I then began to conclude, that my adversaries were quite overthrown; and that I had only to march forward, and take possession of the "Land of Promise": I therefore pressed forward rejoicing for some months. At length, through unwatchfulness, and giving way to levity, my comforts gradually diminished till, imperceptibly, I was then drawn into a wilderness state; and though I was diligent in the outward means, yet I had lost the pleasing sensations which I formerly had found therein (p. 362).

Rhodes explains that "exstasies of joy" that came "in the stillness of the night" were so stirring that they prevented him from sleeping. Instead of resting, he felt compelled to sing his "great Deliverer's praise." Note that these "exstasies" presuppose a stark dichotomy between the eternal heavens and the lower "earthly" sphere that Rhodes disparagingly portrays as "empty" and not "worth a thought." Rhodes also assumes that his previous conflicts and doubts were finally allayed and that he had attained the equivalent of entire sanctification. "I then began to conclude, that my adversaries were quite overthrown." This constellation of features—hyperarousal, idealization coupled with splitting and devaluation, and inflation—all point to a manic defense (Segal, 1974, pp. 82-91; Klein, 1988, pp. 278, 349; Hinshelwood, 1991, pp. 344-346). Rhodes's rejection of the created world is an extension of his denial of inner "adversaries," split off feelings and impulses that have yet to be worked through. His *exclusive* identification with the higher realm of "grace and glory" reinforces a belief in his own perfection. Because he is inflated, Rhodes feels less obliged to examine his thoughts prayerfully. This neglect coincides with the defensive function of the inflation: *to ward off an awareness of residual conflict that, if brought into consciousness through meditative introspection, would prompt a renewed depression.* Ironically, Rhodes's failure to exercise his faith via watchfulness eventually leads to a dissipation of his "comforts" and "pleasing sensations."

Sometimes, a loss of appetite accompanied sleeplessness. After receiving pardon, Thomas Rankin was so overwhelmed with the love of God that he thought he "should then have died": "I was so swallowed up in the love of God all that day, and for many days and nights following, that the desire of food and sleep departed from me" (*Arminian Magazine*, 1779, p. 189). Methodists frequently rationalized their losses of hunger as a substitution of spiritual for physical nourishment. Hester Ann Rogers (1832) writes that her justification doubled her bodily strength, even though she could "neither eat nor sleep for many days and nights": "The love of God was now my meat and drink" (p. 32). Similarly, after John Nelson found peace, he was "so filled with the manna of redeeming love" that he had "no need of the bread that perisheth for that season" (pp. 19-20). The denial of basic bodily needs found its rationale in the theme of self-sufficiency, that God's manna is enough. Yet this sublime refusal also points to a manic defense. Methodists circumvented frustration by splitting off and disavowing the degraded realm of the flesh, the locus of unholy passions and appetites.

Two related phenomena that also point to a manic defense are the exaggerated urgency of the convert's need to rebuke sin and evangelize, and the naive overestimation of other people's willingness to be persuaded (for example, Corderoy, 1873, p. 16; *Arminian Magazine*, 1789, p. 462). For Morentz (1987, p. 258), these "noisy" reactions relate directly to the misguided conviction that one's conflicts have been forever resolved. "Noisy" converts are inordinately active, expansive, and generous. They want everybody to share in their experience.

I am not alone in viewing certain after-effects of unitive ecstasies as manic. Rammage (1967) too made use of the concept in connection with Methodist justification. He suggests that the depressed convert's swing into elation resembles the state of "hypomania" (p. 163). The analogy proves valid given that depression both precedes and succeeds the inflation.

Several psychoanalytic writers draw connections between aspects of mania and religious ecstasy. For Lewin (1951) and Linn and Schwartz (1958), mystical experiences are intrinsically pathological. Instigated by severe emotional conflict, they are the product of a regression to the early oral period of development. Because they obliterate the space between the ego and the superego, unitive ecstasies represent fusions with an idealized maternal breast. For these writers, it follows that mystical experiences are elaborate forms of manic denial. Hartocollis (1974; 1975), who advances a similar argument, holds that mystical experiences defend against dangerous feelings of rage. Because mystics try to flee from their own hostility, the mystical quest represents a massive reaction formation, a passive-regressive fusion of the self and the nurturing breast. By employing Kris's notion of regression in the service of the ego, Prince and Savage (1965) provide a more plausible link between some features of the psychoses and mystical states *without completely equating the latter category with the former and all of its morbid implications*. They hold that, for some, ecstatic bliss *may* function as a manic denial of pain. In the same way, Modell (1968) claims that merger with the good object in religious mysticism *could* be a form of manic denial. For Aberbach (1987), the mystical "dream of perfect harmony" (p. 512) contrasts with the dark night of the soul in the same way mania contrasts with depression. The dark night—the sense of being deserted by God—allows mystics to grieve over previous losses that were insufficiently mourned. Auberbach, who endorses the Kleinian view of idealization, states that periods of mystical illumination may reflect a defense against "hatred of the lost person for disappearing, and irrational fears that the lost person will retaliate" (p. 512). Fauteux (1994) offers a perspective comparable to Auberbach's. He too presupposes the manic defense. Using Mahler's model of ego development, Fauteux explains mystical unity as a regression to the symbiotic phase of undifferentiated unity with the mother. The regression "recreates a psychological paradise characterized by the exclusive presence of good libidinal feelings and images" (p. 75). To safeguard the regression, mystics split off the aggression that threatens to destroy the good imago.

The wholesale pathologization of unitive ecstasies is theoretically myopic and diagnostically limited. Lewin's claim that mystical states are *by definition* specimens of the manic defense is simplistic and ignores the empirical complexity of the data. The blanket application of this label presupposes that apart from the defense, no redeeming or unequivocally adaptive qualities obtain. Yet we have seen how justification ecstasies provide a medium through which ego-ideals present themselves to consciousness and promote a series of positive traits that clearly vitalize the ego. The reduction of these integrative phenomena to by products of a defense ignores the cardinal principal of multiple function (Waelder, 1930). As with all aspects of psychic life, the nature and uses of ideals are variable and overdetermined. Although paradoxical, certain functions of idealization may be used *simultaneously*, as both a source of strength to the ego—augmenting a poor sense of identity, providing hope, purpose, courage and initiative—as well as a defense against unacceptable hostility or sexual feelings.

Some schools of psychoanalytic thought remain polarized by isolating particular facets of the idealization process. For example, Kleinians tend to focus on splitting and the denial of aggression, while self-psychologists emphasize the therapeutic growth potential of idealizing transferences. However, we find that even Klein (1988) understood the integrative role of otherwise defense driven idealizations. Her comments pertain to the universality of the manic defense in the early development of the ego. Idealization, omnipotence and denial "enable the early ego to assert itself to a certain degree...and thus to make further advances in development" (p. 349). Klein holds that in normal development splitting and idealization do not only ward off destructive rage. The identification with the good object additionally strengthens the ego, so that it acquires greater confidence in its own goodness and begins to assimilate the more painful aspects of psychic experience (p. 350). Steiner (1993) points out that although manic idealizations entail a temporary distortion of reality, they may ultimately lead to a reduction of splitting: "the periods of integration, which at this stage take place in relation to good objects, can be seen as precursors of the depressive position" (p. 29). So, we can more realistically assume that healthy and morbid structures are not mutually exclusive. They interrelate dynamically and fluidly (compare: Brenner, 1982). Eigen (1993) echoes this idea when he states, "Much excellent psychoanalytic literature...has followed Freud in deciphering the pathological element in attachment to ideal states, relatively neglecting their healing aspect" (p. 62).

I have elsewhere suggested that in some instances unresolved unconscious conflicts directly attach themselves to otherwise healthy and non-conflicted ideals (that is, beta-cognition) and convert them into complex neurotic compromise formations. I term these compromises "unitive distortions" (Haartman, 2001). Pathologically conflicted forms of unitive thinking may enhance certain facets of psychological functioning while they concurrently reinforce other dissociative trends. The concept of unitive distortions illuminates the data we are presently considering. We may regard the manic patterns found in Methodist and other forms of conversion as defensive exaggerations, pathological transformations of integrative ego-ideal functions. Specifically, self-esteem distorts into conceit or grandiosity, initiative into compulsion, hope into rigid certainty, and trust and safety into omnipotence. We can assesss the pathological magnitude of any unitive experience by at least two indices: the degree of exaggeration of any particular distortion, and the spread of distortion across a number of discrete items such as self-esteem, empathy, trust, initiative, abstraction and so forth.

Commenting on psychedelically induced peak experiences, Grof (1976) *emphasizes how latent and unintegrated materials augment the specifically therapeutic dimensions of the ecstasy*. In the following extract, the abbreviation "BPM IV" refers to states of unitive consciousness that follow the resolution of depressive crises and/or anxiety attacks.

> In an individual who has completed the death-rebirth sequence and stabilized under the influence of BPM IV, the feelings of joy and relief are accompanied by deep emotional and physical relaxation, serenity and tranquility. Occasionally, it can be observed that the feelings of liberation and personal triumph are accentuated and exaggerated to the point of becoming a caricature. The behavior of a person in this state has a driven and manic quality; he cannot sit or lie quietly, runs around advertising loudly the overwhelming beauty and significance of his experience, wants to arrange a big party to celebrate this event, and makes grandiose plans for changing the world. This situation indicates that the experience of rebirth has not been fully completed. Such an individual is already experien-

tially tuned into BPM IV but is still under the influence of unresolved elements...particularly anxiety and aggression (p. 140).

Grof here describes what I have termed a unitive distortion, a response to peak experiences that involves the manic defense and coincides with the Methodist data presented above.

POST-CONVERSION DEPRESSION

Intrapsychic conflict produces post-conversion inflation and mania. Not surprisingly, unintegrated materials that contradict unitive ideals eventually force their way into awareness and initiate a fresh depression. But the resurgence of melancholy in Methodist spiritual development is not cyclical as with manic-depressive psychoses. It is not simply a reversion to the previous state of desolation. Ideally, believers now possess new leverage in the struggle against despair. In Methodist terms, they have recourse to the witness of pardon. Phrased psychoanalytically, the emotional and cognitive residues of the conversion ecstasy, the memory of the event and its undeniable aftereffects, serve as transitional objects that further empower the therapeutic alliance, and ensure that the outcome will be psychologically productive.

For Horton (1973, 1974), mystical states of consciousness conform to Winnicott's notion of transitional phenomena. Horton reviews several case histories of severely depressed, suicidal patients. In each instance, self-destructive behavior commenced after the loss of a symbiotic attachment. Following either psychedelically induced or spontaneously occurring mystical experiences, these individuals gave up their suicidal activities. Horton makes no mention of the role of ego-ideals. Instead, he adheres to the now obsolete psychoanalytic view that varieties of mystical unity are adaptive regressions to primary narcissism: "Residues of primary narcissism may represent the human being's last refuge in life's storms...one alternative to suicide may be the mystical state" (Horton, 1973, p. 296). Horton claims that as transitional phenomena, *mystical experiences are reliably soothing and provide a holding space for maturational growth.*

Wesley regarded this current round of sorrow as a fiery trial that brings forth "peaceable fruit" and further refines Christian character (Wesley, 1984-87, I: p. 485). Psychologically, this refinement involves the creation of ego structures that both enhance impulse control—a further mastery of aggression, anxiety and grief—and correspond to matching superego directives. The growth of these structures promotes a more constant degree of acceptance by the ego-ideal. This leads to object constancy, or, as Wesley puts it, an abiding or uninterrupted sense of pardon (Wesley & Wesley, 1981, pp. 312-313).

In his elucidation of the *Sermon on the Mount*, Wesley discusses at length the dual periods of inflation and mourning that follow the new birth. In essence, when believers receive the witness of pardon, their conviction of inbred sin grows "deeper and deeper everyday" (Wesley, 1984-87, I: p. 482). Because "the sin which still remains in one's heart is no longer imputed to one's condemnation," forgiveness acts as a vehicle through which repentance, or self-knowledge, grows even more profound.

> The more we grow in grace the more do we see of the desperate wickedness of our heart. The more we advance in the knowledge and love of God, through our Lord Jesus Christ... the more do we discern of our alienation from God, of the enmity that is in our carnal mind, and the necessity of our being entirely renewed in righteousness and true holiness...
>
> A new believer, however, has "scarce any conception of this"...
>
> Sin is so utterly bruised beneath his feet that he can scarcely believe it remaineth in him. Even temptation is silenced and speaks not again; it cannot approach, but stands afar off. He is borne aloft on the chariots of joy and love; he soars 'as upon the wings of an eagle'. *But our Lord well knew that this triumphant state does not often continue long. He therefore presently subjoins, 'Blessed are those who mourn; for they shall be comforted'* (Emphasis added; I: pp. 482-83).

A dark night now ensues. Believers who so recently felt enamored by the immediate presence of God lose "the joy of his countenance" (I: p. 485) and mourn his absence.

> But [God] now 'hides his face, and they are troubled'; they cannot see him through the dark cloud. But they see temptation and sin—which they fondly supposed were gone never to return—arising again, following after them amain, and holding them on every side. It is not strange if their soul is now disquieted within them, if trouble and heaviness take hold upon them. Nor will their great enemy fail to improve the occasion; to ask, 'Where is now thy God? Where is now the blessedness whereof thou spakest? The beginning of the kingdom of heaven? Yea, hath God said, "Thy sins are forgiven thee?" Surely God hath not said it. It was only a dream, a mere delusion, a creature of thy own imagination. If thy sins are forgiven why are thou thus? Can a pardoned sinner be thus unholy?' And if then, instead of immediately crying to God, they reason with him that is wiser than they, they will be in heaviness indeed, in sorrow of heart, in anguish not to be expressed (I: p. 484).

The decline of the sense of presence occurs in unison with an awareness of sin and temptation. In the foregoing passage, Wesley focuses on the temptation to doubt, a state of mind personified in demonic terms and elsewhere portrayed as Satan's "fiery darts" (II: p. 212). The waning of the initial exaltation, and the resurgence of "sin," of improper affects, impulses and ideas, lead believers to question their spiritual status and wonder whether they were actually justified. "Is it possible," they ask, "that one who is pardoned can be so bereft of God and so assailed by temptation?" Wesley advises believers to refrain from "reasoning with the Devil." In other words, he understood that obsessive questioning only exacerbates anguish. Instead of invoking the bad parental introject (for example, "you *are not* pardoned"), Wesley again recommends a turn towards the therapeutic alliance: do not reason but "cry" to God. The effort to endure the frustrations and anxieties that accompany the awareness of sin, as well as the acute feelings of loss, lead to spiritual gain: They "bringeth forth peaceable fruit unto them that are exercised thereby" (I: p. 485).

> 'Blessed' therefore 'are they that' thus 'mourn' if they 'tarry the Lord's leisure', and suffer not themselves to be turned out of the way by the miserable comforts of the world; if they resolutely reject all the comforts of sin, of folly, and vanity; all the idle diversions and amusements of the world, all the pleasures which 'perish in the using', and which only tend to benumb and stupefy the soul, that it may neither be sensible of itself nor God. Blessed are they who 'follow on to know the Lord', and steadily refuse all other comfort. They shall be comforted by the consolations of his Spirit, by a fresh manifestation of his love: by such a witness of his accepting them in the Beloved as shall never more be taken away from them. This 'full assurance of faith' swallows up all doubt, as well as all tormenting fear, God now giving them a sure hope of an enduring substance and 'strong consolation through grace' (I: p. 485).

In refusing to mollify the depression by turning to the "comforts of the world...of sin," that is, by refraining to "rebel" or act out the underlying aggression that lies at the root of the melancholy and doubt, one is blessed by the return of the comforter, the witness of pardon. Wesley holds that at this juncture, good conscience turns into an abiding disposition. It "shall never more be taken away from them." In this *ideal* developmental sequence, as one prevails through the depression, one achieves the equivalent of object constancy with respect to the positive superego (compare McDevitt & Mahler, 1989). Forgiveness, or self-acceptance, becomes steadfast in spite of persisting conflict and ambivalence. For this reason, one can begin to engage in sustained introspective meditation without the immediate threat of incurring a debilitating depression or an anxiety attack.

Wesley's sermon confirms the idea that the post-conversion depression leads to a further consolidation of the positive superego. For example, after the depression passes, another kind of mourning comes to the fore. *Concern* for the self in relation to God's judgment is replaced by *concern* for the welfare of others. Self-centered mourning is replaced by a mourning for "mankind," for sinners "that weep not for themselves," and "for the weakness and unfaithfulness of those that are in some measure saved from their sins" (I: p. 486)

Secondly, the recovery of the witness promotes "meekness," a term that refers to self-composure and equanimity, the ability to regulate and temper one's emotions. Christian meekness "keeps clear of every extreme...it balance[s] the affections" (I: p. 489). It represents a "due composure of mind...a calm acquiescence in whatsoever is [God's] will concerning us." Meekness is styled as "patience or contentedness" (I: p. 490).

In the same way that the values of the ego-ideal provide a direction for sexual and aggressive drives (Lederer, 1964, p. 28), and play a significant role in the process of sublimation, the meek do not "extinguish" their passions but employ them towards "wise" and "noble" ends (Wesley 1984-87, I: p. 490). Reminiscent of the metaphoric idea in ego psychology that sublimation occurs through the "neutralization" of a "confluence of sexual and aggressive drives" (Giovacchini, 1987, p. 278), Wesley holds that when hate, anger and fear are "regulated by faith and love," they can be usefully engaged against sin.

The emergence of adaptive structures in the ego links up with an improved ability to withstand the temptations that ensue during the second dark night. Wesley discusses this process in his sermon *On Patience*.

> Yet we shall surely 'fall into divers temptations'—temptations innumerable as the stars of heaven, and those varied and complicated a thousand ways. But instead of counting this as a loss, as unbelievers do, 'count it all joy; knowing that the trial of your faith', even when it is 'tried as by fire', 'worketh patience'. But 'let patience have its perfect work, and ye shall be perfect and entire, wanting nothing'...[Patience] is a gracious temper wrought in the heart of a believer by the power of the Holy Ghost. It is a disposition to suffer whatever pleases God, in the manner and for the time that pleases him (1984-87, III: p. 171).

The "middle way," as Wesley calls it, generates patience, or impulse control. Patience keeps the believer from falling into one of two extremes.

Patience avoids "making little" of one's sufferings and "passing over them lightly." It also prevents being "affected too much," "unnerved" and "dissolved" (III: pp. 171-172). One must endure temptation lucidly and calmly for it to bear fruit. The middle way describes a position between the manic denial of psychic pain and depressive breakdown. Interestingly, in the previous sermon of the same series (III: p. 158), Wesley cites I Corinthians 10:13: "[God] will not suffer you to be tempted above that ye are able; but will with the temptation also make a way to escape, that ye may be able to bear it." In essence, this view coincides with a fundamental assumption in classical psychoanalysis, shared by both ego and self psychologies: tolerable doses of frustration catalyze the growth of psychic structures. The "work of patience" promotes meekness and "peace—a sweet tranquility of mind" (III: p. 172). "This peace," Wesley writes, "often rises into joy...triumph and exaltation," as well as courage, zeal and activity (III: p. 173-174).

Wesley refers to the "perfect work" of patience (I: p. 173), the growing ability to bear pain and frustration, to both soothe and enliven the self. The work of patience implies an intensification of the positive superego in response to what we may call the "rehabilitation" of the ego. This involves an increase in the constancy of self-esteem, due to the ego-ideal's approval of the ego. Believers experience the self-esteem as a reaction to an increased sense of God's loving and approving presence. We can conceptualize the intensified presence as an increase in superego object constancy.

In "the work of patience," a provisional measure of faith, the emotional memory of justification, helps one to resist temptation. Although the process may at first be difficult and frustrating, success brings the pleasurable affects of self-esteem, which, in turn, makes the next round of temptation incrementally less painful and easier to withstand. Over time, ego structures related to impulse control proliferate and grow more and more stable. Because these structures coincide with ego ideal imperatives, their increasing permanence ensures an abiding sense of pardon—a lasting good conscience.

These dynamics also parallel the development of "superego autonomy" at the close of the Oedipal phase. In the successful working through of the Oedipal dilemma, the child must also relinquish grandiosity and learn to tolerate frustration, aggression and loss. For Jacobson (1964), one of the most important outcomes of this process is "a more enduring and stable libidinal cathexis" of the self-representation (p. 132). A high level of self-esteem, regulated internally by the harmonious relations between the ego and the ego-ideal, leads to a stable, basic mood, a "limited margin" of emotional vacillations that "withstand...psychic or even physical injuries to the self" (p. 132). For Jacobson, this is a "safety device of the highest order." It protects the child from dangerous inner and outer stimuli, as well as from narcissistic harm (p. 133). Analogously, in Wesley's developmental model, emotional equilibrium, that is, meekness, replaces the vacillations between inflation and melancholy. Jacobson's "stabilization of a basic mood" corresponds to the continual witness of the Holy Sprit, the abiding sense of good conscience. This is the "safety device" that permits systematic introspection.

Wesley intuits the spiritual equivalent of object constancy and its role in the vicissitudes of depression, when he differentiates between two kinds of melancholy. "Darkness," the more dire form of the two, Wesley defines principally as a complete loss of faith. In this state believers "come into a 'waste land and howling desert', where they are variously tempted and tormented" (1984-87, II: p. 205). Wesley points out that some have deemed this "a wilderness state....in allusion to the case of the Israelites" (II: p. 205). Darkness represents a total obliteration of the unitive ideal.

> They that are 'in the wilderness' have not now that divine 'evidence', that satisfactory 'conviction of things not seen', which they once enjoyed. They have not now that inward demonstration of the Spirit which before enabled each of them to say, 'The life I live, I live by faith in the Son of God, who loved *me* and gave himself for *me*'. The light of heaven does not now 'shine in their hearts', neither do they 'see him that is invisible'; but darkness is again on the face of their souls, and blindness on the eyes of their understanding. The Spirit no longer 'witnesses with their spirits that they are the children of God'...Hence, secondly, proceeds the loss of love...Accordingly they that are deprived of their faith are deprived of the love of God also...And as their love of God is 'waxed cold', so is also their love of their neighbor. They have not now that zeal for the souls of men, that longing after their welfare, that fervent, restless, active desire of their being reconciled to God...But after a suspense perhaps of many days, anger begins to regain its power. Yea, peevishness and impatience thrust sore at them, that they may fall...In consequence of the loss of faith and love follows, thirdly, loss of joy in the Holy Ghost. For if the loving consciousness of pardon be no more, the joy resulting therefrom cannot remain...With loss of faith and love and joy there is also joined, fourthly, the loss of that peace which once passed all understanding. That sweet tranquillity of mind, that composure of spirit is gone. Painful doubt returns...And these doubts are again joined with servile fear, with that 'fear' which 'hath torment'. We fear the wrath of God, even as before we believed...For loss of peace is accompanied with loss of power...the power over sin (II: pp. 206-208).

Because darkness results from various kinds of unrepented sin, it is alleviated by introspection, by a conscious recognition of one's wrongdoing so that it can be corrected and atoned for (II: pp. 208-214). With respect to the "torment" (II: p. 205) that accompanies this loss of faith, Wesley rejects the mystical understanding of the purgative nature of darkness, a view advanced, for example, by his former spiritual mentor, William Law (II: p. 205, see footnote 121). Wesley writes:

> 'But is not darkness much more profitable for the soul than light?...Is not a believer more swiftly and thoroughly purified by sorrow than by joy? By anguish and pain and distress and spiritual martyrdoms than by continual peace?' So the *mystics* teach...The Scripture nowhere says that the absence of God best perfects his work in the heart! Rather his presence, and a clear communion with the Father and the Son...Joy in the Holy Ghost will far more effectually purify the soul than the want of that joy (II: pp. 219-220).

One is saved not by "despair" and "unbelief," but by "faith" and "hope" (II: p. 220). Wesley underscores the idea that psychic integration proceeds by maintaining the alliance with the loved and admired values of the ideal rather than submitting to the castigation of the abandoning and punishing bad object. What is more, his whole discourse on darkness valorizes personal responsibility, a critical ingredient that he regarded as conspicuously absent in the mystical rationale. Because the "most usual cause of inward darkness is *sin* of some kind or another," Wesley concludes that God "never *deserts* us...it is we only who *desert* him" (II: p.208).

In contrast to darkness, "heaviness" (II: p. 222), the other species of melancholy, is characterized by a greater degree of object constancy. The crucial distinction resides in the fact that heaviness does not eventuate in a loss of faith. Metaphorically, instead of impenetrable darkness, Wesley speaks of the partial opacity of dark clouds, a temporary dimming of faith (Wesley & Wesley, 1981, p. 312; Wesley, 1984-87, I: p. 484). Again, in terms of his *ideal* developmental model, melancholic *heaviness* succeeds the period of inflation. Thanks to the preservation of faith, believers use heaviness to their advantage. Wesley's description of heaviness rests on the scriptural authority of St. Paul.

> I am in the first place to show what manner of persons those were to whom the Apostle says, 'Ye are in heaviness.' And, first, it is beyond all dispute that they were believers at the time the Apostle thus addressed them. For so he expressly says, verse five: Ye 'who are kept through the power of God by *faith* unto salvation'. Again, verse seven, he mentions 'the trial of their *faith*, much more precious than that of gold which perisheth'...Neither did their heaviness destroy their peace, the peace that passeth all understanding, which is inseparable from true, living faith...[They] were also

> full of a living hope...So that notwithstanding their heaviness they still retained an hope full of immortality...Their heaviness therefore was not only consistent with living hope, but also with 'joy unspeakable'. At the same time they were thus heavy they nevertheless rejoiced with 'joy full of glory'...they likewise still enjoyed the love of God which had been shed abroad in their hearts...They retained the same power over sin. They were still 'kept' from this 'by the power of God' (II: pp. 223-224).

Outward sin ushers in darkness. Darkness represents a bad conscience in response to deeds actually committed. Heaviness, on the other hand, comes from temptations that at most create distressing effects by precipitating a depression. Regardless of whatever desire or intention the temptation may be, the believer possesses enough strength to refrain from committing it. This restraint, the willfulness deemed "power over sin," is rooted in the preservation of faith.

Again, the work of faith is an incremental process. For Wesley, the unitive ecstasy—or, to be precise, *ecstasies*—that mark an individual's justifying conversion provide a provisional degree of object constancy that is later "exercised" and increased during the "fiery trial." The memories and aftereffects of the conversion experience serve as transitional objects that contribute to a productive outcome.

In order to illustrate this process, I return to a set of data already adduced in the previous chapter. Richard Moss was justified during a service at Short's Gardens. Closing his eyes in the midst of prayer, he beheld Christ hanging on the cross. At this instant, Moss's "burden dropt off." His "fears and doubts and sense of guilt vanished away" (*Arminian Magazine*, 1798, p. 53). He was then "filled with such a love to God, and such joy as cannot be uttered." Moss became inflated for a brief period of time. His inflation was marked by the immediate sense of presence and the conviction that he was now sanctified. "For three days I walked as one out of the body, in the broad light of God's countenance. And then I said in my heart, 'I shall never be moved: Neither shall I see war any more'" (p. 53). His elation, however, terminated abruptly.

> But when I waked in the fourth morning, all was dark. My comfort and my God were gone. I had no fear of death or hell; and I had continual power over all outward sin as indeed I had when I first tasted that God was Love at the Foundery. But I could not see God; I could not see Christ; and therefore I was in sorrow and heaviness (p. 53).

At the start of the passage, Moss states that "all was dark." However, the way in which he describes his state of mind during this early phase of the depression clearly coincides with heaviness, a term he uses to conclude the extract. Moss complains of a "loss of comfort" that accompanies the sudden disappearance of the sense of presence. More importantly, we see that he retains a provisional degree of faith. He continues to be free of the fear of "death and hell" and maintains "power over all outward sin." Indeed, Moss indicates that this power, or, impulse control, arose during an ecstasy that occurred at the Foundery and preceded his more recent justifying vision. In that episode, the first in a series of ecstatic interludes, Moss was initially enraptured by Wesley's captivating presence (p. 7). He subsequently experienced an intense happiness and an affection that grew to encompass the entire entourage of preachers, as well all those in attendance at the service. Moss reacts to his current feelings of "sorrow and heaviness" by trying "every means of recovering the Light" (p. 53).

> I poured out my soul in prayer. I read and heard God's Word at every opportunity. But still I could not find God. Then I doubted, whether my sins were forgiven or no, altho' I did not dare to deny it. Then I thought, it might help me to join with the children of God. So, on Mr. Wright's recommendation, I was admitted into the Society (p. 53).

Even as he exercises his faith through prayer and scripture, and enlists as a member of the Methodist society, Moss's heaviness takes a slight turn for the worse when he doubts whether God truly forgave him his sins. As a result, he fasts in a masochistically exaggerated manner.

> I resolved to leave nothing undone that was in my power. I used all the ordinances of God. I never ate a full meal, so that I was hungry from the beginning of the week to the end. From Thursday noon till Saturday noon, I tasted no food at all. Insomuch, that I was quite worn away, and grown so weak, that I could scarcely walk (p. 53).

The strain that Moss experiences in keeping his unconscious anger in check intensifies to such a degree that his frustration threatens to undo the diminishing constancy of the ideal.

> All this time I was pressed down to earth, on the one hand, by a sense of the absence of divine comfort, and on the other, by a sense of my inward sins and temptations of every kind. I could not meditate on God, as in times past. I could not keep my heart fixed in

> prayer. I could not love God. I could not love my neighbor. I had lost every good temper. I felt peevishness and discontent. I wished I never had been born or, that my soul and body might die together. I was weary of life, and would have starved myself to death; only for offending God. For the thought of this I could less bear than any other. I had rather have suffered all things, even to eternity, than to commit sin, or omit any the least outward duty (p. 54).

During this time, when Moss tried to pray, his anger intervened and manifested as a sense of demonic presence.

> It seemed as though the enemy were just by me, ready to swallow me up. Sometimes I imagined he leaped upon my shoulders, till my flesh crept upon my bones. Sometimes when I was in bed he seemed to be upon me, with a vast weight (p. 54).

When measured by Wesley's criteria, Moss's heaviness increasingly gave way to darkness, even though he does not backslide into sin at any point. Although his faith is feeble in comparison to his state of mind at the outset of the depression, he manages to preserve some semblance of assurance. For example, excruciating ruminations on eternity and the problem of God's existence eventually drove him to prayer, where he received consolations: "and therein it pleased the Lord generally to relieve me for the present" (p. 54). Moss's phrasing implies that he experienced at least one period of relief. He states that he "continued with no *settled* comfort and peace" (emphasis added; p. 54). His depression finally dissipates while listening to Wesley preach at West-Street. "In the middle of the sermon," he writes, "I felt my soul united to the Lord." Here, the witness of pardon grows steadfast.

> I had closer communion with him than ever. I found his Spirit witnessing with my spirit, not only that I was a child of God, but that he would depart from me no more, that he would abide with me for ever. All sorrow and doubt and fear fled away. I was filled with light and peace. I had such a solid, settled joy in the Holy Ghost, as I was a stranger to, till that hour. I felt a fuller and stronger love to God than ever, as well as to all mankind. And from that time I never lost for a moment the Light of God's countenance (p. 54).

In the previous chapter, my analysis of these extracts emphasized how a sequence of ecstatic episodes allowed for the successive emergence and final consolidation of a unitive ideal. I wish again to stress how the ecstasies convey a series of abstractions that are increasingly generalized or broadened in the scope of their inclusiveness. In the first instance, Moss's idealization of Wesley transforms into a love for God, the preachers and the entire congregation. During the third ecstasy, the abstraction is maximally extended: "I felt a fuller and stronger love to God than ever, as well as to all mankind." This universalizing marks both the termination of the depression and the beginning of a permanent witness. Although Moss depicts his sufferings as extreme, he exercises his admittedly weakened faith so that, with the help of his resolve and the occasional divine consolation, he retains his outward power over sin and endures the vagaries of temptation—grief, doubt, perplexity and even demonic anxiety. If we take him at his word and assume that from this point forward he "never lost the light of God's countenance," we see that the persecutory nature of his aggression, epitomized by the horrifying presence of the "enemy," was significantly modified. Because Moss demonstrates to himself that his love overcomes his hostility, he divests his hostility of its fearsome qualities.

Returning to Jacobson's notion of superego autonomy, we see that the limited margin of emotional vacillations and the stabilization of a basic mood are also associated with an *abstraction*, a uniform articulation of inner standards. Recall that for Moss, the ongoing incubation of an ideal, one that culminates in an equally generalized moral standard—a love for mankind—appears in the beginning as an idealization of a single individual. Kernberg (1966; 1976), whose formulations build on Jacobson's, holds that in normal development the depersonification and abstraction of superego components compliment the increasing synthesis of self and object images. At first, these images are concrete and polarized in terms of good and bad. As this process unfolds, libidinal and aggressive drive-affect components come closer together. *Their raw intensity is attenuated into more stable affective schemas and emotional turbulence decreases.* Moss's faith enables him to tolerate an otherwise intolerable onslaught of psychic pain. His patience is rewarded as the frighteningly archaic quality of the bad object gradually diminishes. The depersonification and integration of these concrete and polarized objects—the idealized Wesley versus the horrifying demon—culminates in an abstracted superego value.

VICISSITUDES OF INFLATION AND DEPRESSION

Methodist autobiographies amply attest to Wesley's post-conversion sequence of inflation and depression. The narratives also show variations attributable to differences in personality. To begin, we observe that the time that intervenes between justification and the second depression can be either brief or considerably long. For example, after his justification, Thomas Hanson "could not hold [his] tongue from speaking of the things of God" (*Arminian Magazine*, 1780, p. 481). His jubilation, however, lasted only briefly.

A few days after my happy conversion, I felt anger at one who persecuted us. Soon after my peace left me. Then the tempter said "He that is born of God sinneth not. But thou hast sinned: therefore thou art not born of God. Thou hast deceived thyself." I was then a great measure ignorant of his devices: so gave up my shield: and was in the depth of distress, ready to chuse strangling for near two hours (p. 481).

Catherine Corbett describes an entirely different scenario. She writes, "For two years after [justification], I felt nothing but love; no trial, no temptation, did the adorable Jesus suffer to disturb me, but all were made easy" (*Arminian Magazine*, 1781, p. 538). Finally, when she realized she lacked "full Sanctification," Corbett reverted to ritual mourning: "And I fought it with all my might, crying day and night, that God would sanctify me wholly" (p. 538).

Various writers explain the factors that triggered the anticipated second depression, as predicted by Wesley's model. There are references to fellow Methodists' progress and remarks made by others who assiduously monitored one's own spiritual progress. The several factors may be expected to have functioned as triggers. We see this process of mutual identification in Thomas Mitchell's narrative. Following his conversion, Wesley placed Mitchell and several others into a class. All of Mitchell's companions eventually "fell back" (*Arminian Magazine*, 1780, p. 315). "Before this," he writes, "I thought my hill was so strong, that I could never be moved" (p. 315).

> But seeing so many fall into sin, I began to see danger in my way. I began to feel an evil heart of unbelief, and was fully convinced, that there must be a farther change in my heart, before I could be established in grace. Afterward I removed to *Kighley*, and had many opportunities of hearing, and profiting by Mr. *Grimshaw*. But feeling my corruptions, with strong temptations, I fell into great doubtings. I was almost in despair, full of unbelief. I could scarce pray at all. I was in this state near half a year, finding no comfort in anything (pp. 315-316).

We also see suggestion and identification in John Atlay's narrative. For three weeks after his justification, Atlay was "unspeakably happy in God, and thoroughly devoted to him" (*Arminian Magazine*, 1778, p. 579). When Atlay's sister informed him of a "much esteemed" (p. 579) friend who had recently lost his joy, Atlay draws an analogy between inflation and Christ's temptation on the Mount, an event that followed his baptism in the spirit. "Ah, poor Johnny!," writes Atlay, "the devil has deceived, as he has many. He has taken him up to the Mount; but he will throw him down, and not leave a whole bone in him" (p. 579). Atlay plainly identifies with his friend's misfortune.

> Immediately I was struck with Horror: I thought, "He is a better judge than me: certainly I am deceived." I was stripped of all. My Love and Joy were gone, and for some weeks I was in the Blackness of despair; and, for fear of being a stumbling block to others, I should have put an end to my wretched Life (p. 579).

We have just seen that Thomas Hanson lost his peace when he grew aware of his anger. This kind of trigger is typical. John Unser provides a vivid example of the eruption of hostility. In a letter to Wesley, Unser reveals that, for two months after he received justification, he was "full of love to God and Man" (quoted in Rack, 1989, p. 426). Soon after, he felt oppressed by feelings of "hatred."

> The scene is quite altered and things has now another face; now all things are past away, behold all things are now become old. But not indeed properly, for I never before felt such a Hell as I now feel. I now am as very a devil as ever was or will be confined in the Everlasting chains of darkness. I now hate God, hate my brother, hate my children, hate all that is good, and what adds much to my sorrow in it, I know God and the Father and our Lord Jesus Christ love me...I am as proud as Lucifer, as covetous as mammon, as hateful as Beelzebub and as lustful. As for my wife, I take no more notice of her
> > Than I do of the spider's web
> > Swept from the wall by the giddy Maid...
> Dr. Sir, what shall I do in this condition? I am just upon the point of breaking off from God, of declaring for the Devil (p. 426).

Unitive ecstasies are so acutely gratifying that they temporarily obscure the distinction between the potential and actual state of the self. The misconception that one is already fully sanctified leads to a decline in "watchfulness," the introspection of impulses and intentions. This lapse allows "sinful" inclinations to pass unchecked into preconscious awareness. They may then find expression unintentionally in certain actions or omissions of duty. Over time, cumulative failures of responsibility cause a diminution or a total disappearance of faith. Richard Rodda describes this process in the following extract.

> Many times that text ran in my mind, I shall never be moved; the Lord of his goodness hath made my hill so strong. I thought my

enemies were all dead, and that my warfare was accomplished. How little did I know at that time of the Christian-Conflict? or the deep import of these words, "unto you is given, in the behalf of Christ, not only to believe in him, but to suffer for his sake."

Through unwatchfulness I fell into levity (a befitting evil) and Satan strove to tear away my shield; but though God suffered him not to do it, yet my joy was greatly damped. My unwatchfulness cost me many an aching heart; and I found I had most need to watch when in company with Professors; where, not suspecting harm, I was often overtaken before I was aware (*Arminian Magazine*, 1784, p. 353).

John Haime expresses himself similarly.

I was truly free; and had I had any to guide me, I need never more have come into bondage. But I was so ignorant, I thought I should know war no more. I began to be at ease in *Sion,* and forgot to watch and pray, 'till God laid his hand upon me again'. I then again went mourning all the day long (*Arminian Magazine*, 1780, p. 212).

The narrative of J. B. of St. Hellier's exemplifies Wesley's understanding of the "middle way." Her faith enables her to remain aware of her anxiety without succumbing to either a depression or the urge to seek premature relief through profane distractions.

Tuesday, 16. I was strongly assaulted by the enemy of the soul: but my faith, instead of being weakened was much confirmed by the conflict. Thursday 18. He endeavored to make me doubt. I retired to my closet, and prayed with uncommon ardor: I did not ask to be delivered from the conflict, but that I might not be overcome by it. While I prayed, I found great power to resist the enemy; and when the Lord gave the victory, the joy was inexpressible (*Arminian Magazine*, 1788, p. 295).

SUMMARY

Methodist justification ecstasies are rooted in previously inaccessible, positive representations of parental images. These images sublimate and manifest as abstract ideals. The virtues that were originally found in the parents are now treated as virtues in their own right. The exhilaration of re-establishing a rapport with these deeply moving qualities, and the enormous relief of temporarily mastering both the persecutory and depressive anxieties of the desolation phase, led the newly converted to overestimate their spiritual status. The intoxicating power of religious ideals creates the illusion that the self has been permanently altered and that no discrepancy remains between the ego and the ego-ideal. Wesley understood this inflation as a confusion, on the one side, between justification and the new birth and, on the other, entire sanctification. The transient disappearance of temptation fostered the illusion. Methodist autobiographies show that the inflation frequently included "manic" trends: loss of sleep and appetite, the urgent need to convert others, and the overestimation of the willingness of others to be persuaded.

The characteristics of inflation, which I view as "unitive distortions," point to a defense against depression or deflation. During repentance, techniques of ritual mourning raised unconscious conflicts into conscious awareness. The positive pole of the split imago became the raw material for the formulation of ideals, while the negative pole of representations, those fraught with the painful legacy of parental authoritarianism, bereavement and judgment fear, were temporarily split off from awareness. In most instances, it was only a matter of time before rage returned in the form of a renewed depression. Wesley, however, understood that this depression allowed believers to exercise their faith and furnished yet another opportunity for spiritual growth.

Some aspects of faith remained dimly accessible throughout the period of heaviness, enabling believers to develop ego-strength in devotion to their ego-ideals. In maintaining what Wesley deemed "the middle way"—a state of equanimity poised between emotional denial and depressive breakdown—and in refusing to mollify the depression by resorting to profane distractions, believers acquired new abilities in the area of impulse control. An internal dialectic came into play. The creation of ego structures that coincided with the imperatives of the ego-ideal garnered a constant sense of superego approval. Wesley called this process "the work of faith." He understood that this "work" led gradually to the permanence of the witness of assurance. As the ego responds to the allure of the ideal, thereby proving its allegiance and devotion, the functions of the positive superego grow correspondingly more reliable and steadfast. In addition to the permanency of the witness, the trial of heaviness also strengthened the fruits of the spirit. These gains further mitigated the split imago and decreased ambivalence, doubt, frustration, and anger.

Seven

The Practice of the Presence

In 1913, Poincaré outlined four stages of the creative process that he named investigation, impasse, illumination, and verification (Fauteux, 1994, p. 230). Incorporating a dialectic between conscious and unconscious forms of mental activity, this sequence became a paradigm for depth psychological approaches to the problem of inspiration. A decade later, Wallas (1926), who introduced what is perhaps the best known stage model of creativity, identified four specific phases similar that of his predecessor: preparation, incubation, illumination and verification. During preparation, one identifies a problem and consciously garners as much material as possible to find a solution. When a satisfactory answer fails to materialize, one pushes current hypotheses to a limit until their possibilities are exhausted. Then one puts the problem aside temporarily. Meanwhile, ideas incubate outside of awareness, and a novel solution develops and spontaneously reveals itself to consciousness in a moment of illumination. An enthusiastic feeling of certainty accompanies the idea. In the final phase of verification, consciousness resumes an active role. "The sense of certainty yields to critical analysis and the inspirations are re-examined, tested, and revised, crafted, or otherwise employed in conscious reasoning and behavior" (Merkur, 2001b, pp. 147-148).

Wallas's model pertained to intellectual problems. Influenced in part by James's work on the relation between religious illuminations and subconscious activity, Batson and Ventis (1982) argue that Wallas's stages apply equally to the resolution of personal and existential problems. Focusing on the rearrangement of cognitive representations of reality, Batson and Ventis transformed Wallas's categories into the following: existential crisis, self-surrender, new vision, and new life. Batson and Ventis's commentary on the new life is particularly interesting. They write, "Analogous to Wallas's verification stage, a dramatic shift in reality should work to produce a dramatic shift in behavior as well. In theological terms, *revelation should lead to sanctification*" (emphasis added; p. 85).

The stages in Wesley's model may readily be aligned with those identified by Batson and Ventis. The desolation phase subsumes both categories of "existential crisis" and "self-surrender." The passive emergence of unitive ideals during justification coincides with the creative solution or "new vision," while the practice of the presence, in combination with another type of meditation—introspective self-examination, or "watching"—is a verification procedure appropriate to the "new life."

Like Batson and Ventis, Fauteux (1994) adapts the model of incubated creativity to his study of unitive states. His work relies heavily on Ernst

Kris's (1952) notion of "regression in the service of the ego," which was itself indebted to Wallas's model. Kris claimed that in healthy creativity, the ego voluntarily regresses so that secondary process thinking may be imaginatively reconfigured by the non-rational play of the primary process. Kris distinguished two stages of creativity: inspiration and elaboration. With respect to elaboration, Fauteux (1994) writes,

> The inspiration stage of creativity is prevented from disintegrating into childish fixation or fear through the artist's expression of that which was inspirational. Kris called this the "elaboration" stage of creativity...Through expressing or elaborating what inspired her, the artist lifts what she experienced out of the precarious unconscious and away from the fixation or psychosis. She expresses her experience in a particular medium, and in the process gives shape to or "grabs hold of"—rather than feeling overwhelmed by—the possibly disturbing or uncontrollable unconscious processes (pp. 89-90).

Echoing Batson and Ventis's discussion of the new life, Fauteux (1994) underscores the idea that ecstatic illuminations and unions that result from contemplative practices constitute inspirations that must be actively engaged and systematically elaborated upon in order to be reparative (pp. 158-191). The raw materials of the illuminations must be recruited by the reality orientation of the secondary process before their meanings can be clarified rationally, differentiated, and applied to worldly practice.

These variations of Poincaré's categories delineate a fundamental principle. *The revelatory character of conversion ecstasies is not transformative in and of itself* (compare: Deikman, 1967). Although conversion ecstasies may provide periods of temporary integration or pseudo-integration, depending upon the degree of distortion, further work is essential if long-term psychic change is to occur. At the turn of the century, Starbuck (1911) had already stated as much. He portrays conversion as "the opening up of an *ideal* that has to be actualised—a vivid foretaste of a life that may become one's own" (emphasis added; p. 354). "Conversion is most frequently an awakening to some truth; but it is a truth which is yet only perceived *and has not yet been worked over into conduct*" (emphasis added; pp. 363-364). For Starbuck, the intervening translation or "elaboration" of truth into conduct is essential to sanctification.

Both Maslow and Merkur insist that peak experiences and self-actualization are independent variables differentiated on the basis of Freud's distinction between "insight" and "working through." For Freud, these terms refer to repressed instinctual derivatives stemming from the id. Because superego materials may also be resisted, Merkur (1996a) argues that the manifestation of ego-ideals during conversion is separate from their prospective integration "within the sense of self" (p. 2) in the ego.

Maslow portrays these distinctions phenomenologically. Peak experiences are "poignant emotional discharges" analogous to "sexual orgasm" (as quoted in Krippner, 1972, p. 113). Characterized by an "autonomic burst," they are transient (p. 113) and linked to dramatic emotional shifts. "The ascending to a great height sort of implies the descending into a valley" (p. 114). In contrast, the "plateau experience" is a "precipitation" of the former. "This type of consciousness has certain elements in common with peak experience—awe, mystery, surprise, and esthetic shock. These elements...are constant rather than climactic" (p. 113). The plateau experience involves a simultaneous recognition of the miraculous and the ordinary. The commonplace acquires "mythic, poetic and symbolic" connotations (p. 113). In contrast to the spontaneous fervor of peak experiences, plateau experiences are inherently serene and voluntarily induced.

> Another aspect I have noticed is that it's possible to sit and look at something miraculous for an hour and enjoy every second of it. On the other hand, you can't have an hour long orgasm. In this sense, the plateau type of experience is better. It has a great advantage, so to speak, over the climactic, the orgasm, the peak (p. 114).

> It is far more voluntary than peak experience are. One can learn to see in this Unitive way almost at will. It then becomes a witnessing, an appreciating, what one might call a serene cognitive blissfulness (Maslow, 1970, p. xiv).

Pahnke suggests that the plateau experience is an outcome of personal growth, while peak experiences serve as "openers" (as quoted in Krippner, 1972, p. 118). Maslow (1970) shares this view. To "take up residence on the high plateau of unitive consciousness," the "transient glimpses" of peak experiences must be subject to "time, work, discipline, study, commitment" (p. xvi). The plateau experience represents "the way the world looks if the mystic experience really takes" (as quoted in Krippner, 1972, p. 115). All of the features that Maslow places at the forefront—sustained effort, personal growth, volition, calm, the simultaneous perception of the sacred and the ordinary (compare Cleary & Shapiro, 1995)—indicate that ecstatic insights have become incorporated into the ego. They are harmonized in terms of perception, reality testing, and will. Maslow states,

> If your mystical experience changes your life, you go about your business as the great mystics did. For example, the great saints could have mystical revelations, but also could run a monastery.

> You can run a grocery store and pay the bills, but still carry on this sense of witnessing the world in the way you did in the great moments of mystic perception (as quoted in Krippner, 1972, pp. 115-116).

The ability to "carry on this sense of witnessing" while participating in worldly endeavors, is integral to "the practice of the presence" of God, a discursive form of meditation that fosters an experiential sense of God's immediate proximity in all things. When practicing the presence, one's everyday activities do not "dissipate" (1984-87, III: pp. 117-125) the illumination. They instead become an inherent part of its expression. Wesley regarded the perfection of the practice of the presence as the crux of sanctification. It was key to the final phase of spiritual development. *The practice of the presence corresponds to the elaboration, or working through stage of creativity.*

In the Wesleyan tradition, sanctification entails the elimination or the working through of "sinful" desires fueled by aggression and narcissistic pride. They are replaced by altruism, which, when actively pursued in daily practice, instills a deep feeling of satisfaction. The ego's actual conformity to a set of moral standards produces more pleasure and satisfaction than the repetitive frustrations and painful self-recriminations that issue from a conflicted attachment to punitive objects. These psychic benefits arise through the systematic use of the practice of the presence and introspection. Together with an all-inclusive style of personal conduct, the two meditative techniques facilitate the final coming to grips with childhood traumas.

How is this procedure accomplished? We are already familiar with the axiomatic notion that the peak experiences of conversion catalyze further spiritual growth. Wesley writes, "It is plain, all these fruits of love are means of increasing the love from which they spring" (1984-87, III: p. 190). Maddox's (1994) study of Wesleyan theology similarly emphasizes the co-operant nature of grace, the dialectic between the passive reception of the spirit and active responsibility of believers.

> [For Wesley] holiness must become a "habitual disposition of the heart" if it is to be manifest in our lives. Such language warrants the recent claim of several Wesley scholars that his model of Christian life is best portrayed in terms of a "character ethic" or "virtue ethic," where meaningful moral actions are grounded in nurtured inclinations (character dispositions). *The crucial implication of this claim is that Wesley's "holy tempers" would not simply be infused by God's sanctifying grace in instantaneous completeness; they would be developing realities, strengthened and shaped by our responsible participation in the empowering grace of God. The di-*

mension of a gradual "growth in grace" would be integral to sanctification (emphasis added; p. 179).

In terms of unitive thinking, so central to the experience of grace, we find that Fauteux's understanding of the transformative potential of mystical states and the way individuals use them to overcome "developmental failures" applies rather well to the Methodist material. Although Fauteux continues to adhere to an outmoded theory of mysticism as a regression to an early period of symbiotic unity between infant and mother, his explanation of the therapeutic dimension of unitive experience remains insightful. He views ecstatic unity in a blend of ego psychological and Winnicottian terms as a "holding environment" (Winnicott, 1971, p. 238) that restores basic trust. Union with God, whose beneficence is felt to be abiding and reliable, "makes the person feel, as in the holding environment of infancy, that when frustrations and unanticipated problems arise, he can express the anxiety and previously forbidden feelings, and God will not vanish" (Fauteux, 1994, p. 144). As a safe maternal space, symbiosis serves as a vehicle through which repression is diminished and "pernicious impulses" are explored. Like Rammage (1967, p. 234) on Methodist conversion, Fauteux (1994) makes use of a clinical analogy. He argues that a symbiotic "self-object" relationship with the therapist produces sufficient courage to confront and resolve "repressed conflicts and hidden needs" (p. 147). This relationship is buttressed by the assurance that the therapist "will not judge, condemn, and especially not abandon [the patient] for expressing the secret feelings...he previously resisted." Similarly, the individual's psychic representation of God (Rizzuto, 1979, pp. 87-173), a transferential object (Merkur, 1995-96), helps "rid the ego of its defensive resistance to unconscious processes" (Fauteux, 1994, p. 147). Freud recognized a connection between mystical practices and psychoanalytic technique.

> Certain practices of the mystics may succeed in unsettling the normal relations between the different regions of the mind, so that, for example, the perceptual system becomes able to grasp the relations in the deeper layer of the ego and in the id which would otherwise be inaccessible to it...we must admit that the therapeutic efforts of psychoanalyses have chosen much the same method of approach (as quoted in Fauteux, pp. 147-148).

Fauteux's argument dovetails with Wesley's portrayal of the final stage of spiritual maturation. For Wesley, the permanence of the witness serves as the very condition through which believers are enabled to engage in an exercise that, as Freud puts it, grasps "the relations in the deeper layer of the unconscious." The durability of pardon, the individual's conviction that God will not condemn and abandon, promotes the discovery of inaccessible thoughts and feelings. Wesley states that the "continual witness" of pardon convinces believers that "they are the children of God" (Wesley & Wesley, 1981, p. 313).

> Then they are indeed *meek* and gentle and teachable, even as a little child. And now first do they see the ground of their heart, which God before would not disclose unto them, lest the soul should fail before him, and the spirit which he had made. Now they see all the hidden abominations there, the depths of pride, self-will, and hell; yet having the witness in themselves: thou art an heir of God, a joint-heir with Christ; even in the midst of this fiery trial, which continually heightens both the strong sense they then have of their inability to help themselves and the inexpressible *hunger* they feel after a full renewal in his image, in *righteousness and true holiness* (p. 313).

For all its merits, Fauteux's study lacks any *specific* data on how the technique of uncovering is accomplished. The omission raises a crucial question because, unlike the analyst in the clinical situation, the religious object of the transference is an object imago that resides in the believer's psyche. Wesley's treatment of the practice of the presence allows us to understand the procedure.

THE PRACTICE OF THE PRESENCE

The practice of the presence is a meditation technique in which one imaginatively summons a continual sense of God's being in and through all things. Writers typically portray the practice as a form of "recollection," a "resituating of the self *toward God*" (Maas, 1990, p. 259). During the meditation, one views the disparate strands of events and circumstances as opportunities for a meaningful and providential dialogue with the divine. The best known treatment of the technique, one which Wesley himself studied and included in his voluminous Christian Library, is entitled *The Practice of the Presence of God* (1977). The volume contains a fragmentary compilation of letters and other writings by Brother Lawrence of the Resurrection, a seventeenth century French Carmelite monk. In it, he portrays the meditation as a "constant conversation" with God (Delaney, 1977, p. 28). The exercise "permeates" every moment of the day so that "all we do becomes prayer" (Nouwen, 1977, p. 12). Inherently object related, the practice promotes an intense attachment to an imaginative and invisible presence.

> [Brother Lawrence explained] that we needed only to know God intimately present in us, to address ourselves to Him at every mo-

ment, to ask His Aid, to discern His will in doubtful things, and to do well those things we see clearly He is demanding of us, offering them to Him before doing them and giving Him thanks for having done them for Him after we have done them...[Brother Lawrence] found the best way of reaching God was by doing ordinary tasks, which he was obliged to perform under obedience, entirely for the love of God (Lawrence of the Resurrection, 1977, pp. 48-49).

Currently, no studies detail the historical transmission of the practice in major Western traditions. Although the Carmelites viewed it as an extension of St. Paul's injunction to "pray without ceasing" (I Thess. 5: 17; Maas, 1990, p. 259), no solid evidence demonstrates that St. Paul referred to the same practice that the Quietist writers, St. Ignatius of Loyola, Brother Lawrence, Jeremy Taylor and others describe. In lieu of a formal genealogy, I have collated materials from a series of Christian texts in order to identify the main features of the practice, and to pinpoint notable variations in technique.

The Quietists coupled the practice of the presence with "stillness," a trance-based cessation of activity (see: Molinos, 1883, pp. 43, 106). However, most other writers incorporate the exercise into their ordinary daily activities. Brother Lawrence (1977) writes:

I adored Him as often as I could, keeping my mind in His holy presence and recalling it as often as it wandered...I did this during the day as often as I did it during the formal time specifically set aside for prayer; for at all times, at every hour, at every moment, even in the busiest times of my work, I banished and put away from my mind everything capable of diverting me from the thought of God (p. 87).

Because the meditation promotes a mild alternate state resembling Maslow's plateau experience, a state that is sustained as one goes about one's life, the practice of the presence may be classed as a form of reverie. The continued activation of what Shor refers to as the "basic reality orientation" (1972a; 1972b), the various core ego functions that are subject to repression in states of hypnotic trance, has crucial implications for Wesley's use of the practice. Reverie maintains an object related stance towards the external world, *and* the ego remains free to engage in lucid introspection, an essential procedure to Wesley's working through process.

In virtually all of the treatments I have surveyed, the authors refer to the gradual refinement or, to use Hartmann's (1939) term, "automatization" of the properly recollected state of mind. For beginners, the concentrated effort to sustain the sense of presence easily gives way to distraction and lapses in mental attention. One must repeatedly draw one's focus back to the exercise.

Over time, persistence cultivates an uninterrupted sense of the presence. For Lorenzo Scupoli, a sixteenth century Italian priest:

> There is yet another form of prayer, which is called standing in the presence of God, when the man who prays is wholly concentrated in his heart and inwardly contemplates God as being present to him and within him...Such a state comes when a man becomes deeply immersed in prayer by word, mind and heart. *If a man prays in the right way and for a long time, these states come to him more and more often, and finally this state can become permanent; then it is called walking before God and is constant prayer* (emphasis added; quoted in Cohen and Phipps, 1992, p. 10).

The following series of characteristics demonstrate what all authors regard as the spiritually beneficial effects of the practice. Note that these categories describe functions of the positive superego: self-soothing, self-observation, the capacity to sustain loss and solitude, and the ability to feel gratitude, as well as concern for others. Lee and Martin (1991), writing from a self-psychological perspective, state that the practice can provide a wholesome self-object experience that facilitates the growth of self-regulating structures: "the subjective experience of having a nourishing, sustaining presence 'inside' seems to have brought great comfort and been of immeasurable help to countless human beings throughout history" (p. 244). "Such a phrase as 'the presence of God'....seems to have been a religious way of expressing the valuable experience of structuralization" (pp. 244-245).

The exercise calms the mind and centers one's attention. Jeremy Taylor (1857), the seventeenth century Anglican divine, states that "it helps to recollection of mind, and refrains the scatterings and looseness of wandering thoughts" (p. 39). Recollection increases when the practice is automatized. According to Lorenzo Scupoli,

> Frequent repetition, becoming established, *collects the mind into one*, standing in the presence of the Lord. Establishing this order within is accompanied by warmth of heart and *by repelling other thoughts*, even simple and not only passionate ones (emphasis added; 1963, p. 159).

When one invokes the sense of presence, one simultaneously invokes the experience of God's scrutiny. St. Ignatius (1992), who calls the practice the "contemplation to attain love," provides the following instruction: "Here it is to see myself as standing before God our Lord, and also before the angels and saints, who are interceeding for me" (p. 94). Taylor (1857) writes:

> In these and all other actions of our lives we always stand before God, acting, and speaking, and thinking in his presence, and that it matters not that our conscience is sealed with secrecy, since it lies open to God, it will concern us to behave ourselves carefully, as in the presence of our Judge (pp. 3-4).

Taylor's extract shows that the fantasy of God's scrutiny bolsters self-observation and the critical awareness of one's actions. Commenting on Brother Lawrence, Maas (1990) explains that not only is the "soul's gaze humbly and trustfully fixed on God," one also places oneself before the "supremely patient and loving" gaze of the almighty (p. 261). Maas writes:

> In the case of recollection, it is particularly easy to see how the practice of this prayer...over a period of time would begin to have ethical consequences...Are there things you would do alone that you would definitely not do in the presence of others? What would it mean, practically speaking, to live as if you were *perpetually* companioned by infinite Love? Doesn't it seem reasonable to expect that the more recollected we are, the more likely the quality of our actions will be affected? (p. 263).

Divine presence promotes a clearer sensitivity to providence. Feeling at all times enveloped by God's beneficent embrace, believers acquire a heightened sense of comfort, trust, and protection. Brother Lawrence (1977) shows how the practice of the presence brought confidence and a sense of competence in performing difficult tasks.

> [He explained that] he had recently been sent to Burgundy to buy wine, that this was difficult for him since he had no head for business matters, was lame in one leg and could not get about on the boat except by hobbling from one cask to another but that he had let none of this bother him...That he said to God that it was His business he was on, and that afterwards he found out everything went smoothly and he had done well. That the previous year he was sent to Auvergne for the same purpose; that he did not know how the business was accomplished, but accomplished it was and very well indeed (p. 41).

For Francis Fenelon (1822), a French Quietist of the seventeenth century, the practice expels obsessional preoccupation with temptations and restores mental composure.

> The second rule is, when tempted, always to turn to God, and not disquiet ourselves by considering whether we have not already in part consented, so as to interrupt the immediate tendency of heart to

God. By examining too closely whether we have not been guilty of some infidelity, we run the risk of being again involved in the temptation...*The practice of the presence of God, is of all others the most sovereign remedy, it comforts, supports and calms us* (emphasis added; pp. 162-163).

As Taylor (1857) shows, one relies on the sense of presence as a means of enduring all manner of hardships.

[The practice of the presence] produces a confidence in God, and fearlessness of our enemies, patience in trouble, and hope of remedy, since God is so nigh in all our sad accidents, he is a disposer of the hearts of men and the events of things, he proportions our trials, and supplies us with remedy, and where his rod strikes us, his staff supports us. To which we may add this, that God, who is always with us, is especially by promise with us in tribulation, to turn the misery into a mercy, and that our greatest trouble may become our advantage by entitling us to a new manner of the Divine presence...he is with us in our natural actions to preserve us, in our recreations to restrain us, in our public actions to applaud or reprove us, in our private to observe us, in our sleeps to watch by us (pp. 35-36).

In the foregoing passage, the notion that God "proportions our trials" shows how the sense of presence provides a self-object function that helps individuals to tolerate the stress of a variety of difficulties and misfortunes. Because the presence represents an idealizing transference, it allows one to contain and process disorganizing emotions, to feel that they are "proportional" to one's own psychic capacities (compare: Kohut, 1977). Brother Lawrence (1977) describes the same principle.

No matter what troubles and ills come our way, they are to be willingly and indeed joyously endured since they come from God, and God knows what he is doing...God never tests us beyond our ability to endure and, as a matter of fact, bestows upon us graces that will enable us to endure as we show our acceptance of whatever He sends our way (p. 28).

Here we see how the exercise promotes a "synchronistic" state of mind by transposing the significance of events into personally meaningful instances of providence (Merkur, 1999, p. 150). Events are viewed as expressions of divine intentionality, a dialogical address or invitation to fulfill the will of God. Faber (1996) traces the subjective perception of meaningful coincidences back to early infancy: "The first and most significant *synchronicity* that we experience as humans is rooted in the caretaker's ability to be there (in time), as the infant expresses his discomfort. When the caretaker meets the infant's needs, answers the infant's frustration, affective attunement results" (p. 106). An experience of divine-human attunement ensues when one views "troubles and ills" as "synchronistic" opportunities granted by God. This modifies frustration and anxiety. When one extrapolates the sense of presence to all persons and things, one situates difficulties within a larger self-object milieu, thereby creating the "graces that will enable us to endure."

The practice of the presence also enables one to deal with grief over loss. In one of his letters, Brother Lawrence (1977) writes:

> If Mr. de N- can take advantage of the loss he has suffered and put his trust completely in God, He will soon give him another friend more powerful and more favorably inclined...think often of God, by day, by night, in all your pursuits and duties; even during your recreations (p. 82).

By emphasizing the theme of ceaseless companionship, Maas (1990) argues that the exercise serves as a means to overcome loneliness and fears of abandonment. All of one's experiences are lovingly mirrored by a divine other whom one experiences as an "endless source of delight and wonder" (pp. 263-64). This idea is significant given the prevalence of separation and bereavement issues among the Methodist population. Bowlby (1980, pp. 161, 166-167) claims that in some cases of unresolved mourning, individuals experience the lost object in the form of a palpably felt presence. Methodists attest to ecstasies involving intellectual visions of presence that occur spontaneously during periods of loss or separation (*Arminian Magazine*, 1795, p. 266; Carvosso, 1835, pp. 57, 103-106). The practice of the presence may have been particularly amenable to individuals whose capacity to be alone was compromised by undue separation anxiety.

Finally, the exercise fosters an altruistic regard for others. In his *Spiritual Exercises*, St. Ignatius describes a prayer that he titled "Contemplation to Attain Love." Commonly deemed "the practice of the presence" by Jesuits, this discursive meditation requires one to remain sensorially aware of the environment. St. Ignatius (1992) accentuates the cultivation of gratitude.

> Love consists in a mutual communication between the two persons. That is, the one who loves gives and communicates to the beloved what he or she has...and the beloved in return does the same to the lover...Each shares with the other...I will call back into my memory the gifts I have received—my creation, redemption, and other gifts particular to myself. I will ponder with deep affection how much God our Lord has done for me, and how much he has given me of

what he possesses...I will consider how God labors and works for me in all the creatures on the face of the earth...I will consider how all good things and gifts descend from above (pp. 94-95).

Scupoli (1963) makes the same point. He writes:

And the place to receive and store [God's] blessings in you is a grateful heart...Giving heed to my words, you will ask: 'How can I set the feeling of gratitude alight in myself and always keep it?" Examine all God's favors to mankind—to our race—and to you yourself, and go over them frequently in your thought, rehearsing them in your memory (p. 181).

As mentioned, Maas (1990) contends that dwelling in the continual presence of another has ethical consequences.

The changes that occur are much more likely to be small and subtle ones: fewer outbursts of temper, more frequent impulses to offer help to someone in need, a willingness to show warmth when you would prefer to give the cold shoulder. The resources for giving more love don't come from within us; they come as a consequence of our dwelling in the presence of Love, and the more we dwell in this presence, the freer we are from our own emotional responses (p. 263).

Because divine presence represens a self-object transference, a partially projected or *externalized* superego, the practice also promotes a certain degree of regressive dependency that centers on the necessity of surrendering to God. The development of trust proceeds from an all-embracing reliance upon God and the disavowal of autonomy. The extent of the regression, however, differs according to the emphases of particular writers, not to mention the personalities of the practitioners themselves. Furthermore, we must differentiate between *actual* loss of autonomy and a subjective shift in one's identity and self-perception. Individuals may objectively retain their autonomy but view their actions in dependent terms, as predicated upon the strength given by the Spirit. In both James's (1985, pp. 53-77) and Merkur's (1999, pp. 95-102) phenomenological surveys of the sense of presence, we see no overt indication of this kind of regression. We may conclude that regression is an independent variable not *intrinsic* to the sense of presence.

The compromise of autonomy is especially apparent in Brother Lawrence's treatment of the practice:

[According to Brother Lawrence, one must] abandon oneself completely to God. Over and over in his letters and conversations he stresses the importance of complete trust and confidence in God's goodness and mercy. "We must trust God once and for all and abandon ourselves to him alone," "It is necessary to put our complete trust in God," "we should surrender ourselves in things temporal and in things spiritual, entirely and with complete abandonment to God," "we have a God of infinite goodness who knows what we need" are just a sampling of the exhortations running throughout the entire work (Delaney, 1977, p. 28).

> [Brother Lawrence's] instructions to "act very simply with God, and speak to him frankly, while asking His help in things as they occur," are a blow to our sense of maturity, independence, and self-esteem. It is as if the call to recollection were a call to a naive and unsophisticated "littleness" (Maas, 1990, p. 264).

The regressive dimension relates to the dynamics of unitive distortions (Haartman, 2001). For Brother Lawrence (1977), dependence is tied to innate sinfulness. Although he places special emphasis on God's infinite mercy and willingness to forgive, his experience of the presence presupposes a guilt that seriously compromises his self-regard.

> My soul has been with God for more than thirty years...*yet I think it is proper that I indicate to you how I consider myself to be before God who I consider as my King*. I regard myself as the most wretched of all men, stinking and covered with sores, and as one who has committed all sorts of crimes against his King (p. 69).

In this instance, guilt produces an abject form of dependence, an affective addiction to God's sustaining presence. "While I am thus with him I fear nothing; but the least turning away from him is hell for me" (pp. 61-62).

In terms of variations in technique, the majority of writers view the practice of the presence as a discursive exercise that requires an imaginative elaboration of thoughts and inspirations concerning the ever present being of God. For the most part, one's consciousness remains alert and diligently engaged with external reality. The meditation fosters a transitional blend of internal and external worlds. By recourse to their own internal representations of deity, practitioners reflect on all aspects of reality as manifestations of the divine. For example, St. Ignatius (1992) writes:

> I will consider how God dwells in creatures; in the elements, giving them existence; in the plants, giving them life; in the animals, giving them sensation; in human beings, giving them intelligence; and finally, how in this way he dwells also in myself, giving me existence, life, sensation, and intelligence; and even further, making me

his temple, since I am created as likeness and image of Divine Majesty...I will consider how God labors and works for me in all the creatures on the face of the earth; that is, he acts in the manner of one who is laboring. For example, he is working in the heavens, elements, plants, fruits, cattle and all the rest—giving them their existence, conserving them, concurring with their vegetative and sensitive activities, and so forth (p. 95)

Taylor (1857) instructs his readers in the same way.

Let *every thing you see* represent to your spirit the presence, the excellency and the power of God, and let your conversation with the creatures lead you unto the Creator; for so shall your actions be done more frequently with an actual eye to God's presence, by your often seeing him in the glass of the Creation. In the face of the sun you may see God's beauty; in the fire you may feel his heart warming; in the water his gentleness to refresh you; he it is that comforts your spirit when you have taken Cordials: it is the dew of Heaven that makes your field give you bread; and the breasts of God are the bottles that minister drink to your necessities (pp.34-35).

The Quietest writers, on the other hand, eschewed the discursive technique. They sought to eliminate the will in order to achieve a passive indifference to salvation. They viewed representational thought as counterproductive because of the immediate link between the senses and bodily desire. According to the French seventeenth century Quietist, Miguel Molinos (1883), the "most secure" kind of prayer is "abstracted from the operations of the imagination" (p. 42). These operations are "always exposed to the tricks of the devil, and the extravagances of melancholy and ratiocination, wherein the soul is easily distracted." The Quietist appropriation of the practice of the presence introduced a dissociative and world renouncing component: "Our indifference to the affairs of this world must give them a dream like quality" (Scupoli, 1978, p. 23). The Quietists used a non-discursive prayer that induced a state of hypnotic trance and led to the cessation of both thought and bodily-motor activity. Consider the following two extracts taken from Molinos's *Spiritual Guide* (1883):

How well is time employed when the soul is dead, dumb, and resigned, in the presence of God, there without any clatter or distraction to receive the Divine influences (p. 43).

The bottom of your souls, you will know, is the place of our happiness. There the Lord shows us wonders. There we engulf and lose ourselves in the immense ocean of His infinite goodness, *in which we are kept fixed and immovable* (emphasis added; p. 106).

Apart from these variations, Wesley's depiction of the practice includes all of the characteristics listed above. He too portrayed the exercise as a discursive technique applied to all facets of daily activity. He regarded the meditations as an acquired skill that enhanced self-observation and with frequent repetition, eventually became automatized or "ceaseless." Moreover, Wesley held that the practice nurtured the self-regulatory dispositions or traits associated with the fruits of the spirit: basic trust, mental calm, confidence and competency, the ability to tolerate loss, altruism and gratitude. In the following chapter, I will examine these, as well as other essential features of Wesley's meditative scheme, and show how they facilitated the long-term personality changes associated with sanctification.

Eight

Watching and Praying
The Paired Meditations of Sanctification

John Wesley's commitment to prayer and meditation owes largely to the influence of his mother (Heitzenrater, 1989, p. 90). As a result of her Puritan background, Susanna Wesley placed great value in "meditation, prayer, self-examination and Holy Communion." "In the Puritan circles in which Susanna was reared, meditation was a hallmark of all serious piety" (Monk, 1966, p. 139). Her father, Dr. Annesley, who insisted on the necessity of daily meditation, refers to the practice of the presence in his devotional writings. He states, "Did you but once a day...solemnly place your selves in God's presence; beg of him the fixing and flowing of your thoughts, that your thoughts might be graciously fix'd, yet as graciously enlarged" (quoted in Monk, 1966, p. 140). Susanna's letters to her children show that she too was familiar with the practice. In a letter to John's elder brother Samuel, she writes,

> Endeavor to get as deep an impression on your mind as is possible of the awful, constant presence of the Great and Holy God. Consider frequently that wherever you are, or whatever you are about, he always adverts to your thoughts and actions, in order to a future retribution. He is about our bed, and about our paths, and spies all our ways. And whenever you are tempted to the commission of any sin, or the omission of any duty, make a pause, and say to yourself, what am I about to do? God sees me (*Arminian Magazine*, 1788, pp. 36-37).

Susanna highlights a certain dread of God's "awful" judgment gaze. However, she portrays a different aspect of the presence in another letter to John—one that imparts a more joyous tone.

> [God] is so infinitely blessed, that every perception of His blissful presence imparts a vital gladness to the heart. Every degree of approach toward Him, is in the same proportion a degree of happiness. And I often think that were he always present to our minds, as we are present to Him, there could be no pain or sense of misery (*Arminian Magazine*, 1778, pp. 84-85).

Both Susanna and her father stressed daily self-introspection, the examination of one's conduct and conscience. Like his forebears, John Wesley combined the practice of the presence with introspection. However, in his mature work, written after 1738, he urged that the combination of these techniques be avoided until after one was justified.

Beginning in the mid-1720s, the Oxford holy club, founded by John Wesley and his brother Charles, used various meditation practices to foster piety and virtue. The exercises they employed were mainly introspective, and "inextricably tied to the whole process of self-examination" (Heitzenrater, 1989, p. 100). Through a set of standardized questions aimed at monitoring one's manners, actions and intentions, the Oxford Methodists carefully measured their "holiness" according to exemplary standards conveyed in such texts as Jeremy Taylor's *Holy Living* and Thomas à Kempis's *The Imitation of Christ* (p.101). Had they been angry? Had they remained simple and recollected? Had they remembered to pray? (p. 90). In addition to the fixed round of daily questions, Wesley employed another scheme similar to that found in St. Ignatius' *Spiritual Exercises* (p. 91). Wesley assigned special virtues for every day of the week; for example, love of God, love of man, humility, and thankfulness. Each virtue was equipped with a further class of corresponding questions. As Heitzenrater (1989) states, "The questions were designed to use the examination of one's performance as a measure of the development of virtue, and thus to gauge the inclination of one's heart and affections, an unfailingly inward focus" (p. 91).

Already in 1729, Wesley and his group engaged in something that approximated the practice of the presence. Wesley writes, "At all times and places one should make fervent returns to the mind of God" (quoted in Tuttle, 1989, p. 75). However, as his printed sermons indicate, it was not until the start of the first Methodist revival proper (that is, 1738 and beyond), that the practice of the presence, as portrayed, for example, by Brother Lawrence, became a *prominent* feature of Wesley's spiritual vision. This prominence may, in part, be due to the fact that during the height of the first revival, he published edited versions of Christian mystical texts (Whaling, 1981, p. 10), many of which endorsed the practice as way of achieving unbroken communion with God (Rack, 1989, pp. 102-103, 401; Tuttle, 1989, pp. 42, 149-150).

Tuttle (1989) argues that it was no earlier than 1764 when Wesley began to emphasize "prayer more and more in [the] mystical sense as a continuous state of mind...as an uninterrupted communion—the practical result of praying without ceasing" (p. 157). This view requires qualification. *The Great Privilege of those that are Born of God*, a sermon that Wesley penned in 1748, examines how one retains God's pardoning presence once it is acquired. Though "the practice of the presence" does not appear as a specific locution, Wesley points to the necessity of the technique as the most reliable way of preserving faith. For example, after describing how the soul becomes sensible of God's omnipresence, or the "invisible world," he goes on to say that this awareness is "continually" perpetuated "by love, by prayer, and praise, and thanksgiving" (1984-87, I: p. 434). In the conclusion of the work, Wesley states:

> [The life of God in the soul] necessarily implies the continual inspiration of God's Holy Spirit: God's breathing into the soul, and the soul's breathing back what it first receives from God; a continual action of God upon the soul, the re-action of the soul upon God; *an unceasing presence of God*, the loving pardoning God, manifested to the heart, and perceived by faith; and an unceasing return of love, praise and prayer (emphasis added; I: p. 442).

Here the basic fundamentals of the practice as a dialogue with the "unceasing presence of God" are inscribed through a metaphor of mutual respiration between the believer's soul and God's Holy Spirit. Tuttle's claim gives the mistaken impression that the practice of the presence was not central in Wesley's earlier writings. I argue that the discrepancy is terminological. If we define the practice from a phenomenological stance, we see plainly that Wesley endorsed it prior to 1764. We must keep in mind that he distinguished among various kinds of prayer: private, public, ejaculatory, petition, intercession, thanksgiving and contemplation (Heitzenrater, 1989, p. 98; Trickett, 1989, p. 364). Given his rejection of Quietistic contemplation, he at first refrained from dubbing the practice as a "continual prayer," for fear that it would condone, by association, the passivist and other-worldly nature of Quietist ideology.

The practice of the presence lay at the heart of Wesleyan spirituality. As Whaling (1981) states, Wesley's "main concern was for spirituality itself, for knowing God in the heart by faith, for practicing the presence of God, for seeking after perfect love" (p. 8). The exercise was a means through which the mindset of the conversion ecstasies were *voluntarily* revived, prolonged, and engaged in living practice. The unitive values of Christian conscience, which originally emerged as emotionally laden abstractions, were "tested" and "verified" through disciplined application. Gradual sanctification consisted in the ongoing consolidation of these values, the attempt to achieve a congruence of intention and deed. The meditative procedures of the practice of the presence—"praying"—and introspection—"watching"—facilitated psychic integration, what Wesley deemed "growth in grace."

> Are you already happy in him? Then see that you 'hold fast' 'whereunto you have attained'! 'Watch and pray, that you may never be 'moved from your steadfastness'. 'Look unto yourselves, that ye lose not what you have gained, but that ye receive a full reward'. In so doing, expect a continual growth in grace, in the lov-

able knowledge of our Lord Jesus Christ (Wesley, 1984-87, III: p. 102).

Wesley intended the practice to help advance the spiritual insights and temperamental shifts of the new birth, to "hold fast" to the fruits of the spirit. Conversion ecstasies provided an experiential glimpse of God's omnipresence, and therefore generated a working model, a cognitive-affective schema for the imaginative elaboration of divine immanence. Wesley stipulated that individuals should begin the practice after they had been justified. In his sermon *On Dissipation*, he challenges William Law, who recommended the practice as a method of conversion (III: p. 123, see footnote 39). Wesley maintains that "the exercise of the presence of God" is unsuitable for those who are as yet "unawakened" and "unconvinced of sin" (III: p. 123).

> This certainly should not be first, but rather one of the last things. They should begin with repentance, the knowledge of themselves, of their sinfulness, guilt and helplessness. They should be instructed next to seek peace with God, through our Lord Jesus Christ. *Then let them be taught to retain what they have received*, to 'walk in the light of his countenance': yea, to 'walk in the light, as he is in the light', without any darkness at all, till 'the blood of Jesus Christ cleanseth' them 'from all sin' (emphasis added; III: pp. 123-124).

Retaining what one has received referred directly to the recollection of mind, to the focusing of one's thoughts upon God, and this required that all one's actions be holistically drawn into the prayer.

> In order to preserve this humble, gentle love, it is needful to do all things with *recollection* of spirit, *watching* against all *hurry* or dissipation of thought, as well as against pride, wrath, or surliness. But this can be no otherwise preserved than by 'continuing instant in prayer', both before and after he comes into the field, and during the whole action; and by doing all in the *spirit of sacrifice*, offering all to God, through the Son of his Love (II: p. 317).

Wesley held that recollection, or being "simple" in all one says and does, corresponds to "what those pious men who are usually styled mystics" meant by the term "introversion" (III: pp. 125).

> Now, the attending to the voice of Christ within you is what they term 'introversion'. The turning of the eye of the mind from him to outward things they call 'extroversion'. By this your thoughts wander from God, and you are properly dissipated; whereas by in-

troversion you may be always sensible of his loving presence (III: pp. 124-125).

The introverted recollection of thoughts spans all forms of action, including transactions with other people. Believers who "begin with a single eye" continue "'looking at Jesus, and talking with him all the time they are with their neighbor" (I: p. 342). Eventually, deliberate recollection becomes automatized, so that prayer is unceasing. "But above all, when once you have learned the use of prayer, you will find that...through every space of life it [will] be interfused with all your employments, and wherever you are, whatever you do, [it will] embrace you on every side" (III: p. 274).

Recollection creates a shift in temporal awareness. The meditation redirects one's attention to the particularities of present circumstances. The Quietists had already recommended this principle. Fenelon (1822) states, "It is one of the greatest rules in the spiritual life to confine our attention to the present moment, without looking any farther" (p. 134). Similarly, in a letter of spiritual counsel written to Philothea Briggs, Wesley states, "It is not always a defect to mind one thing at a time. And an aptness to do so, to employ the whole vigor of the mind on the one thing in hand, may answer excellent purposes" (Wesley & Wesley, 1981, p. 163). Wesley's theological stance reinforced the practice of restricting one's attention to the present moment. In *The Repentance of Believers*, he argues that while faith grants power to refrain from committing sin, sin still "remains in our hearts" and "cleaves to our words and actions" (1984-87, I: p. 341). In line with the reformed tradition, he emphasizes the "utter helplessness" (I: p. 345) of believers, even after they have been born anew.

> They are no more able now *of themselves* to think one good word, or do one good work, than before they were justified; that they have still no kind or degree of strength *of their own*, no power either to do good or resist evil; no ability to conquer or even withstand the world, the devil, or their own evil nature. They 'can', it is certain, 'do all these things'; but it is not by *their own strength*. They have no power to overcome all these enemies; 'for sin hath no dominion over' them. But it is not from nature, either in whole or in part; 'it is the *mere* gift of God'. Nor is it given all at once, as if they had a stock laid up for many years, but from moment to moment (I: p. 345).

Due to the persistence of sinfulness, an inalienable condition of the flesh, Wesley regarded righteousness as a grace in which one participated, as opposed to an *innate* trait that one possessed and identified as one's own. God bestowed his grace through faith. Believers renewed their faith "from moment to moment" (I: p. 349) by contemplation.

> By the same faith we feel the power of Christ every moment resting upon us...whereby we are enabled to continue in spiritual life, and without which, notwithstanding our present holiness, we should be devils the next moment (I: p. 349).

The moment-to-moment recollection of thought fostered a state of "introversion," a mild form of reverie with observable and conspicuous effects. In *A Short Account of the Life and Death of the Reverend John Fletcher*, Wesley states the following:

> It was [John Fletcher's] constant endeavor to maintain an uninterrupted sense of the presence of God. In order to this, he was slow of speech, and had the greatest government of his words. Indeed he both acted, and spoke, and thought, as under the eye of God. And thus setting God always before him, he remained unmoved in all occurrences; at all times and on every occasion possessing inward recollection. Nor did I see him diverted therefrom on any occasion whatever, either going out or coming in, whether by ourselves or in company. Sometimes he took his journeys alone; but above a thousand miles I have traveled with him; during which neither change of company, place, nor the variety of circumstances which naturally occur in traveling ever seemed to make the least difference in his firm attention to the presence of God. *To preserve this uniform habit of soul, he was so watchful and recollected that, to such that were unexperienced in these things, it might appear like insensibility* (Emphasis added; Wesley & Wesley, 1981, pp. 155-156).

Fletcher's recollection was apparent not only in his slow manner of speaking, but also in a demeanor that seemed detached to those unfamiliar with the practice. Wesley implies that what appears as "insensitivity" is the effect of a contemplative preoccupation with the presence, an alternate state of consciousness whose intensity was not so great as to preclude continued commerce with the world.

The provision of spiritual senses that enabled believers to see the invisible world was initially a passive event. However, Wesley also instructed his followers to exercise these senses, to *actively* contemplate the omnipresence of God.

> We are to see the Creator in the glass of every creature; that we should use and look upon nothing as separate from God, which indeed is a kind of practical atheism; but with a true magnificence of

thought survey heaven and earth all that is therein as contained by God in the hollow of his hand, who by his intimate presence holds them in being, who pervades and actuates the whole created frame, and is in a true sense the soul of the universe (1984-87, I: pp. 516-517).

Contemplation required that all actions be viewed as a devotional dialogue expressive of God's presence. Methodists extended the unitive ideals of conscience to all aspects of life. "For it is a great mistake," Wesley states, "to suppose that an attention to those outward things whereto the providence of God hath called us is any clog to a Christian, or any hindrance at all to his always seeing him that is invisible" (I: p. 544). Believers "do all in the name of the Lord Jesus; having only one eye of the soul which moves around on outward things, and one immovably fixed on God" (I: p. 544). Through ceaseless prayer, Methodists deliberately sacralized worldly endeavors. It was not enough to transact one's business with diligence, justice and mercy. "A Christian is called to go still farther—to add piety to justice, to intermix prayer, especially the prayer of the heart, with all the labor of the hands" (III: p. 269).

If you act in the Spirit of Christ you carry the end you at first proposed through all your work from first to last. You do everything in the spirit of sacrifice, giving up your will to the will of God, and continually aiming, not at ease, pleasure, or riches; not at anything this short enduring world can give; but merely at the glory of God. Now can anyone deny that this is the most excellent way of pursing worldly business? (III: p. 269).

As mentioned, Wesley portrayed the practice of the presence as a mutual respiration between the Holy Spirit and the soul of man. The "unceasing return of love, praise and prayer" maximized one's devotion. The metaphor represents a dynamic cycle of intrapsychic reciprocity between the ego and the superego.

[There is] a continual action of God upon the soul, and the reaction of the soul upon God...we may...infer the absolute necessity of this reaction of the soul...in order to the continuance of the divine life therein. For it plainly appears God does not continue to act upon the soul unless the soul re-acts upon God...But if we do not then love him who first loved us; if we will not harken to his voice; if we turn our eye away from him, and will not attend to the light which he pours upon us: his Spirit will not always strive; he will gradually withdraw...He will not continue to breath into our souls unless our souls breathes towards him again (I: p. 442).

Recollection and the prayerful pursuit of ideal standards meet with the approval of the ego-ideal, whose emotional content heightens the sense of presence. In turn, a good conscience increases gratitude and compels the believer to "rejoice" and to do what is "good and acceptable" in the eyes of God (I: p. 266). The failure to exercise one's love interrupts the relationship continuously maintained by the practice. The superego's disapproval then threatens one's self-regard, and the sense of presence inevitably dissipates.

> For as by works faith is made perfect, so the completing or destroying the work of faith, and enjoying the favor, or suffering the displeasure of God, greatly depends on every single act of obedience or disobedience (Wesley & Wesley, 1981, p. 364).

Richard Rodda provides a straight-forward example of the action-reaction principle. After two years of post-conversion depression, Rodda finally regained "a clear sense of [God's] forgiving love." He writes:

> There was not the least doubt remaining of my acceptance through the Beloved. For many days and weeks, I was enabled to rejoice in God my Savior. Every duty was profitable, as it conveyed to me fresh tokens of the divine favor. My understanding was open to behold the power, wisdom and goodness of God; in creating, upholding and governing the world. I saw the whole world was full of his majesty and glory (*Arminian Magazine*, 1784, p. 302).

We see how the rhythm of reciprocity between ego and superego matches Wesley's notion of combined respiration. The sequence begins with Rodda's recovery of the witness as given by God. In response, he "rejoices," determined to abide by the law. "Fresh tokens of divine favor" reconfirm his self-acceptance. In feeling at peace with himself, Rodda experiences a strong sense of divine immanence. "I saw the whole world was full of his majesty and glory."

An extremely important facet of the action-reaction principal pertains to interpersonal relations. "Good works" ensure the perpetuation of the witness, as embodied in the sense of presence. The whole notion of service to others, regarded as an indispensable part of prayer, is predicated on unitive thinking.

> [A believer] doth good, to the uttermost of his power, even to the bodies of all men. He rejoices to 'deal his bread to the hungry', and to 'cover the naked with a garment'. Is any a stranger? He takes him in and relieves him according to his necessities...*And all this he does, not as unto man, but remembering him that hath said,*

'Inasmuch as ye have done it unto one of the least of these my brethren, ye have done it unto me" (emphasis added; Wesley, 1984-87; I: p. 519).

Because all creatures participate in God, service to others is both service rendered unto God and a continuation of the prayer that sustains the object relationship.

Justification ecstasies are vehicles through which unitive ideals of conscience become apparent to consciousness. Unitive abstractions are sublimations of concrete internal object representations. The sense of divine presence encapsulates these two poles of the developmental spectrum. On the one hand, it is the symbolic embodiment of abstract altruistic values expressed in the omnipresence of an "invisible" God whose love (that is, "the law") pervades the entirety of creation. At the same time, the consolidation of these values occurs within a form of "personal mysticism" that involves a dynamic, dialogical object relation (Merkur, 1993, p. 20). In Buber's terms (1958), one conceives of and addresses the presence as a personal "thou." The practice of the presence represents, in actuality, the practice of conscience, the realization of an inclusive whole object relationship.

All the ego-enhancing benefits that derive from this bond are complimented by the fact that the presence is an *imaginary* other. At least in one important respect, the transference relationship to God offers a relatively unique forum for maturational growth, one that differs from that offered by real attachment figures. Insecure individuals often undermine opportunities for secure relationships by repeating conflicts that elicit impatience, rejection and withdrawal in their partners. Writing from the perspective of attachment theory, Kirkpatrick (1995) suggests that these repetitions may be by-passed by a "perceived relationship with God" (p. 455). Such an imaginary yet compelling relationship "characterized by the desired level of intimacy can be maintained over time without being undermined by either 'partner's behavior'." One may successfully establish a growth enhancing attachment "without inadvertently undermining the process through previously established, counterproductive patterns of behavior." The experience of God as a "haven of safety" can give rise "to the same feelings of comfort and security provided by secure human attachments." This formulation coincides with the self-object function of the presence.

An all-encompassing and ceaseless mode of prayer secures the integration of conscience. Wesley understood, however, that in order for the practice to work most effectively, one had to supplement it with another form of meditation—introspection, or "watching." In fact, the two techniques were synergistically aligned: as both a haven of safety and a symbolic manifestation of ideals, the sense of presence served as an indispensable point of departure for the often frightening prospect of self-examination. In essence, the sense of presence brought solace and courage to those fearful of becoming more fully cognizant of their sin. As a manifestation of conscience, it provided self-evident criteria for a coherent exploration of one's motives, feelings, and desires.

MEDITATIVE INTROSPECTION

In the Christian contemplative tradition, the purgative path was the first of three stages in the practice of mysticism. Wesley relocated but otherwise retained the systematic examination of sin, a traditional aspect of the purgative path. One of the earliest instances of this meditative exercise is documented in *The Praktikos* of Evagrius Ponticus, a fourth century monastic author. Using language reminiscent of Buddhist insight meditation, Ponticus describes a finely-tuned awareness of the ebb and flow of one's thoughts and passions. Those who aspire to know God must acquire mental skills to recognize the mercurial nature of sin—the demonic "impurities" and "blasphemies" that impede holy contemplation.

> If there is any monk who wishes to take the measure of some of the more fierce demons so as to gain experience in his monastic art, let him keep careful watch over his thoughts. Let him observe their intensity, their periods of decline and follow them as they rise and fall. Let him note well the complexity of his thoughts, their periodicity, the demons which cause them, with the order of their succession and the nature of their associations. Then let him ask from Christ the explanations of these data he has observed. For the demons become thoroughly infuriated with those who practice active virtue in a manner that is increasingly contemplative. They are even of a mind to "pierce the upright of heart through, under cover of darkness" [Ps 10:3].
>
> Watch carefully and you will discover the two swiftest demons—they are nearly more swift than the speed of thought. Their names: the demon of impurity and the demon of blasphemy against God. Now this latter's attack has a short life-span, and the former will be unable to stand in the way of our contemplation of God if he is unable to stir up in us thoughts filled with passion (Ponticus, 1981, pp. 29-30).

Ponticus lists a set of mental disciplines that are concerned with eradicating narcissism and cultivating moral virtue. He invites contemplatives to track the emotional intensity, duration and associative nexus of their thoughts, many of which are so fleeting, or "swifter than the speed of thought itself," that they tend to go unnoticed unless brought under disciplined scrutiny.

Scupoli (1963), whom Wesley read, refers to a technique that similarly requires affective equanimity and an impassioned kind of introspection of whatever occurs in consciousness.

> The reason why we have wrong judgment of the things we mentioned earlier is that we do not look deeply into them to see what they are, but conceive a liking for them or a dislike of them from the very first glance, judging by appearances. These likes and dislikes prejudice our mind and darken it; and so it cannot form a right judgment of things as they really are. So, my brother, if you wish to be free of this prelest in your mind, keep strict attention over yourself; and when you see a thing with your eyes, or visualize it in your mind, keep a firm grip on your desires and do not allow yourself at the first glance either to conceive a liking for the thing or a dislike for it, but examine it in a detached way with the mind alone. Unobscured by passion, the mind then remains in a state natural to it, which is free and pure, and has the possibility to know the truth and to penetrate into the depths of a thing, where evil is often concealed under a deceptively attractive exterior and where good is sometimes hidden under a bad appearance (p. 35).

For both Ponticus and Scupoli, practitioners who wish to master their sinful natures must stand outside their instinctual willfulness in order to engage in objective self-observation. In keeping with the early Church Fathers, Thomas à Kempis, Scupoli, the Puritan writers and so forth, Wesley regarded self-examination as necessary for repentance. In Wesley's view, repentance, or the self-observation of sin, was not restricted to the crises of desolation. Although the new birth endowed believers with the power to resist temptation, the being of sin continued to inhere in the flesh. Repentance, as "true self knowledge and authentic contrition" (Outler, 1984a, p. 217) did not subside with the acquisition of the witness. Progress in sanctification required an ever deepening understanding of one's divided nature. "Indeed," writes Outler, "since repentance means self-knowledge, the farther Christians are along their way to sanctification, the more sensitive they are to their shortfalls in faith, hope and love" (p. 217). Wesley states:

> Can we fix any bounds to them? Do they not diffuse themselves through all our thoughts, and mingle with all our tempers? Are they not the leaven which leavens, more or less, the whole mass of our affections? May we not, on close examination of ourselves, perceive these roots of bitterness continually springing up, infecting all our words and tainting our actions? (1984-87, I: p. 665).

In the same vein, while commenting on the necessity of "continual watchfulness" in his treatise on *Christian Perfection* (Wesley & Wesley, 1981, p. 371), Wesley writes:

> As the most dangerous winds may enter at little openings, so the devil never enters more dangerously than by little unobserved incidents which seem to be nothing, yet insensibly open the heart to great temptation (p. 371).

Wesley directed his followers to know themselves as God knows them, to continually pray that God reveal the "depth of inbred sin" (1984-87; I: pp. 245). Watchfulness destroys "the whole body of sin": "Thou shalt be 'cleansed from all filthiness both of flesh and spirit'" (I: p. 246). The relationship between watchfulness and sanctification is straightforward. Refined mental acuity brings directly into awareness the "little openings" and "unobserved incidents" that previously evaded conscious recognition. With the assistance of the sense of presence, one can actively repudiate them in consciousness through the initiative provided by conscience. Wesley understood that the practice of the presence, and the idea that God's gaze remained continually focused on the soul of the believer, augmented self-observation. Simply put, God became a co-observer in the process of introspection. "If after having renounced all, we do not *watch* incessantly, and beseech God to accompany our vigilance with his, we shall be again entangled and overcome" (Wesley & Wesley, 1981, p. 371).

The synergistic tie between introspection and the practice of the presence rested on a sound psychological basis that found its theological rationale in Wesley's understanding of the interdependence of faith and repentance (Lindstrom, 1946, p. 116; Maddox 1994, pp. 165, 174). Wesley made a qualitative distinction between two kinds of repentance. Prior to justification, knowledge of sin was not accompanied by the conviction of God's acceptance. With faith and the witness, one "retains the confidence of one's renewed pardoning relationship with God, even as it acknowledges continuing sin and need" (Maddox, 1994, p. 165). As forgiveness, faith granted self-acceptance and trust, thereby assuaging the guilt-ridden consciousness of God's condemnation and wrath. Believers now uncovered sin with greater calm, persistence and precision. Faith and repentance "answer each other" (Wesley, 1984-87, I: p. 349). Faith empowers and is empowered by repentance. Stated psychoanalytically, the practice of the presence provided a space of psychic safety wherein introspection could proceed unhindered by doubt. Enhanced self-esteem made self-criticism tolerable without the immediate risk of depression. The play between introspection and presence is captured in the notion that self-knowledge increases proportionally to the knowledge of God "and the experience of his love" (II: p. 231). For Wesley, faith allows for a depth psychological recovery of the hidden self. Faith alone expedites the process by removing the resistance of fear.

> Is there no condemnation to them which 'walk after the Spirit' by reason of *inward sin* still remaining, so long as they do not give way thereto; nor by reason of *sin cleaving* to all they do? Then fret not thyself because of ungodliness, though it still remain in thy heart...be not afraid to know all the evil of thy heart, to know thyself as thou art known...Let thy continual prayer be:
> Show me, as my soul can bear,
> The depth of inbred sin
> All the unbelief declare
> The pride that lurks within
> But when he heareth thy prayer, and unveils thy heart, when he shows thee thoroughly what spirit thou art of; then beware that thy faith fail thee not, that thou suffer not thy shield to be torn from thee...But still, 'let not thy heart be troubled, neither let it be afraid'. Still hold fast, 'I' even I, 'have an advocate with the Father, Jesus Christ the righteous'. And 'as the heavens are higher than the earth, so is his love higher than even my sins'...Thou shalt love him that loveth thee, and it sufficeth: more love will bring more strength (I: pp. 245-247).

Another aspect of the play between presence and introspection is the fact that a more intimate acknowledgment of sin strengthens the desire to increase one's faith. Here again, we see how the two meditative techniques mutually reinforce each other:

> They are continually ashamed of their wandering thoughts, or of the deadness and dullness of their affections—yet there is no condemnation to them still, either from God or from their own heart...So far are these from driving them away from him in whom they have believed, that they rather drive them closer to him, whom they feel the want of every moment (I: p. 240).

> It is good to have a piercing sense of [sin], and a vehement desire to be delivered from it. But this should only incite us the more zealously to fly every moment to our strong helper...And when the sense of our sin most abounds, the sense of his love should much more abound (Wesley & Wesley, 1981, p. 336).

The combination of presence and introspection, of faith and repentance, provided a crucial opportunity to bring together in consciousness the severed halves of the split imago, to forge a rapprochement between opposing self and object representations. While introspection unearthed the wicked child/angry parent constellation, with its chaotic web of rage, guilt and helplessness, the practice of the presence roused the vitality of the positive superego in an attempt to "purify" the former. The chronic effects of cumulative traumata were placed in a more tolerable psychic milieu, where they were reevaluated and mastered by a mindset infused with self-acceptance, concern, empathy and uncompromised initiative.

> Thus it is that in the children of God repentance and faith exactly answer each other. By repentance we feel the sin remaining in our hearts, and cleaving to our words and actions. By faith we receive the power of God in Christ, purifying our hearts and cleansing our hands. By repentance we are still sensible that we deserve punishment for all our tempers and words and actions. By faith we are conscious that our advocate with the Father is continually pleading for us, and thereby continually turning aside all condemnation and punishment from us. By repentance we have an abiding conviction that there is no help in us. By faith we receive not only mercy, but 'grace to help in *every* time of need'. Repentance disclaims the very possibility of any other help. Faith accepts all the help we stand in need of from him that hath all power in heaven and earth (Wesley, 1984-87, I: pp. 349-350).

The sense of presence stabilizes the unsettling effects of self-observation. Even so, emotional equanimity may give way to vicissitudes not unlike those that follow the new birth. Believers may err in the direction of "presumption," a form of inflation predicated on denial, or they may lapse into a depressive "despair" of ever attaining sanctification. These are the demonic pitfalls of systematic meditation. In terms of denial, Wesley writes:

> Presumption is one grand snare of the devil, in which many of the children of men are taken. They so presume upon the mercy of God as utterly to forget his justice...they flatter themselves that in the end God will be better than his word. They imagine that they may live and die in their sins, and nevertheless 'escape the damnation of Hell' (III: p. 211).

Presumption is a more subtle form of denial than the inflation that ensues after justification. Here believers do not entertain the assumption that they are already sanctified. They acknowledge sin but disavow its significance. The presumptuous simplify the theological equation. They assume not only that they are forgiven, but that their sinfulness is so inconsequential, they deserve to be acquitted (I: p. 345).

In a sermon entitled *Satan's Devices*, Wesley takes up the problems of despair, one of the ways the devil "endeavors to destroy the work of God in the soul" (II: p. 140). The sermon is both a description of the struggle with the bad object, and an instruction manual on how to overcome the struggle via the practice of the presence.

The first of the two main depressive reactions to self-examination is the dampening of joy. According to Wesley:

> [Satan] endeavors to damp our joy in the Lord by the consideration of our own vileness, sinfulness, unworthiness; added to this, that there *must* be a far greater change than is yet, or we cannot see the Lord...that subtle adversary often damps the joy we should otherwise feel in what we have already attained, by a perverse representation of what we have not attained, and the absolute necessity of attaining it. So we cannot rejoice in what we have, because there is more which we have not...Likewise, the deeper conviction God works in us of our present unholiness, and the more vehement desire we feel in our heart of the entire holiness he hath promised, the more are we tempted to think lightly of the present gifts of God, and to undervalue what we have already received because of what we have not received (II: p. 141).

Here despair sets in as a result of the perceived disparity between the ego and the ego-ideal, between one's "corruption" and "the height of the glory of God" (II: p. 144). In effect, perfection is drawn into the traumatizing lure of evangelical nurture and the optimistic promise of redemption turns into an impossible authoritarian demand. The ego-ideal becomes distorted by the bad-object and made into a "perverse representation" whose effect focusses attention on one's failures, on what one has not attained, and "the absolute necessity of attaining it." This distortion and the futility it invokes spark a devaluation of faith so that one feels deprived of a valuable sense of satisfaction.

The demise of joy predictably accompanies a loss of "peace" and the now familiar revival of doubt concerning justification.

> If [Satan] can prevail thus far, if he can damp our joy, he will soon attack our peace also. He will suggest, 'Are you fit to see God? He is of purer eyes than to behold iniquity...How is it possible that *you*, unclean as you are, should be in a state of acceptance with God?...How can you presume then to think that all your sins are already blotted out? How can this be until you are brought nearer to God, until you bear more resemblance to him?'...[This will] bring you back by insensible degrees to the point from whence you set out first: even to seek for justification by works, or by your own

righteousness; to make something in *you* the ground of your acceptance, or at least necessarily previous to it (II: pp. 141-142).

When the supportive influence of the positive superego fades, the upsurge of anxiety dictates a return of the obsessive defense. "Justification by works, or your own righteousness" describes action that is executed by an urgent need for control. In other words, personal righteousness refers to behavior that is not subjectively aligned with the work of the spirit. Instead, such action is again carried out in the shadow of the disapproving parent. It cannot garner the calming approval of the benevolent ideal.

During a depressive crisis, believers should simply resume practicing the presence in order to soothe themselves. The observation of sin necessarily invites the censure of the archaic superego. The anxiety of punishment, threats of abandonment and damnation, can become so overwhelming as to disrupt the mental calm necessary to maintain the practice of the presence. Unitive ideals are punitively distorted. By foregoing the compulsion to reason with the devil, or to engage in obsessive actions, individuals resist the gravitational pull of the bad object and replace it with the therapeutic alliance.

> The more you are tempted to give up your shield, to cast away your faith, your confidence in his love, so much the more take heed that you hold fast that whereunto you have attained. So much the more labor to 'stir up the gift of God which is in you.'...Thus, being filled with all peace and joy in believing, press on in the peace and joy of faith to the renewal of thy soul in the image of him that created thee. Meanwhile, cry continually to God that thou mayest see that prize of thy high calling, not as Satan represents it, in a horrid dreadful shape, but in its genuine native beauty, not as something that *must* be, or thou wilt go to hell, but as what *may* be, to lead thee to heaven. Look upon it as the most *desirable* gift which is in all the stores of the rich mercies of God. Beholding it in this true point of light, thou wilt hunger after it more and more: thy whole soul will be athirst for God, and for this glorious conformity to his likeness (II: p. 149).

Once one re-establishes a rapport with the positive superego, the coercive distortion of the ideal subsides. Sanctification is no longer represented in a "horrid dreadful shape." It ceases to be experienced as an intimidating command—something that "must be" realized to avoid hellfire. The fantasy of achieving perfection regains its ego-syntonic character, a goal that one genuinely desires and voluntarily choses. It is "the most desirable gift," something that "may" be. The movement from an *authoritarian injunction* to a *promise of success* in the future not only instills feelings of mastery or trust in one's own abilities, it also allows one to reposition the self in relation to time. An impending threat paralyzes the ego and makes it is impossible to entertain an optimistic and hopeful vision of self-development. The converse situation is discussed by Loewald (1962) and Lederer (1964), who maintain that the ideals of the positive superego compel the ego to imaginatively project itself forward in time in anticipation of the gratifying fulfillment of those ideals. By refocusing on the sense of presence, a favorable conception of the self as an evolving entity is restored.

> The more you feel of your own vileness the more you rejoice in the confident hope that all this shall be done away. While you hold fast this hope, every evil temper you feel, though you hate it with a perfect hatred, may be a means, not of lessening your humble joy, but rather of increasing it. 'This and this', may you say, 'shall likewise perish from the presence of the Lord. Like as the wax melteth at the fire, so shall this melt away before his face' (Wesley, 1984-87, II: p. 147).

Again, these passages make clear Wesley's conviction that growth in grace was not advanced by darkness, that is, by the depressive trials which arose whenever the effects of the punitive introject were more dominant than those that flowed from the therapeutic alliance. The mystical notion of the dark night of the soul did not play a role in Wesley's understanding of spiritual transformation since it failed to contribute to the consolidation of Christian values (Tuttle, 1989, pp. 106-111). Wesley believed that rendering heartfelt service to God and all his living manifestations intrinsically delighted the soul of true believers. Nurturing these sensibilities to the point of perfection contrasted emotionally with the recurring phases of self-recrimination and dread. Because Wesley held that forgiveness and self-acceptance offered the only conditions conducive to real characterological change, he exclusively endorsed the work of the witness, the identification with the ideal. He knew that introspection was a hazardous endeavor and afflictions of doubt inevitably occurred. However, he did not valorize these crises, nor did he regard them as God-given. "God afflicts, but he never brings darkness" (quoted in Tuttle, 1989, p. 147). Reversing the mystical position, Wesley claimed that believers themselves held responsibility for any bouts of uncertainty. As Tuttle points out, darkness stemmed from a failure "to return to the source of strength" (p. 147).

In a published extract of Bathsheba Hall's diary that appeared in the *Arminian Magazine* (1781), she writes, "There is a season wherein [Christians] are called to inward crucifixion, a being stripped of all sensible enjoyment." Wesley inserted the following editorial comment:

> I cannot find this in the Bible. I do not believe it. We are called of God, *to rejoice ever more*. I know those that have done so for many years: and the *joy of the Lord was their* strength. Tis true, nervous disorders may strip us of this joy: and then God will bring good out of evil. But otherwise we have no more need to be stripped of joy in the Holy Ghost, than of *peace* or *righteousness*. We ought therefore to be *dejected*, that is, grieved and ashamed before God, when we are stripped of all *sensible enjoyment* of God. It is not his will which is the cause of this, but our own: he would have us *always happy* in him (p. 198).

The synergy of the unitive presence and the ego's self-observation, along with the dual complications of presumption and despair, similarly appear in the meditative practices of Theravadin Buddhism. Some of the correspondences to the psychology of Methodist transformation are rather striking. According to Epstein (1986), the ideal personality in the Theravadin tradition, the "arahat," is one in whom unwholesome mental factors such as greed, hatred, conceit, envy, and doubt do not arise. This transformation represents the "fruition of meditation practice," a practice that alters "those psychic structures that embody the individual's internalization of the ideal" (pp. 144-145).

In analyzing the meditations of the Theravadin school, Epstein refers to the "traditional Buddhist division of meditation techniques into 'concentration' and 'insight' practices" (p. 149). The latter technique involves an "attentional strategy," a "moment to moment awareness" of "thoughts, feelings, images, sensations and even consciousness itself" (p. 149). By contrast, concentration practices involve a "one-pointed attention to a single object" and typically culminate in "absorption or trance states."

The technique of Buddhist insight meditation resembles the process of Methodist "watching." "Bare witnessing," as it is termed in Buddhism, is a refined, non-judgmental awareness of whatever occurs in consciousness (Rubin, 1992, p. 97). We see important differences, however, between the Buddhist and Wesleyan worldviews. Generally speaking, Buddhist insight meditation aims to detach from the contents of consciousness and so acquire a first-hand appreciation of the illusory nature of the self. Comparable Christian meditations pay close attention to the unimpeded stream of consciousness, but they seek to dismantle sin and temptation, rather than the ego's self-representation (compare: Engler, 1984, pp. 46-47).

Buddhists use concentrative meditations to attain unitive experiences. Methodists practiced the presence of God to attain similarly euphoric ecstasies. Although the experiences have comparable functions, they also have important differences. The Buddhist experiences are not necessarily theistic in nature, and they involve hypnotic states rather than reveries. The function of pairing concentration with insight nevertheless compares to the value of combining presence and introspection. Both traditions' unitive ecstasies play

bining presence and introspection. Both traditions' unitive ecstasies play a similar role in providing unitive consolations that mitigate the "terrors" (p. 152) of self-examination. "The Buddhist meditative path," writes Epstein, "demands a delicate interplay of the two techniques and consists of a series of alternating plateaus that reflect the affective concomitants of first one strategy and then the other" (p. 149). In this approach, "the emphasis is continually on balancing the forces of concentration and insight, as if the stabilization and gratification of the former allows one to withstand the destabilization of the latter" (p. 154). Concentrative ecstasies of merger produce feelings of contentment, tranquility, rapture and wholeness. "They promote stability, equanimity and equilibrium and are essentially anxiolytic in that they directly counteract mental states of anxiety...and evoke states of well being" (p. 150).

In both the Theravadin and Methodist traditions, the ideational content of adverse reactions depends on their respective ideologies. The range of affective states is comparable, involving persecutory panic, depression, malaise, and so forth. However, Buddhist practitioners suffer from resistances that arise in realizing the "groundless" and "impermanent" character of self-representations, what Epstein calls the "illusory ontology of the self" (p. 153). Methodist anxiety, on the other hand, centers on issues of divine rejection and damnation. In both of these traditions, however, complications subside through meditative exercises that appeal to unitive fantasies representing the ego-ideal. Epstein (1989) argues that concentrative meditation provides "a means of contacting the ego-ideal for ontological security and holding" (p. 69). "The concentration practices clearly promote unity of ego and ego ideal by encouraging fixity of mind in a single object" (Epstein, 1986, p. 152).

Judged from a mental health perspective, we may credit Wesley for bringing together two distinct forms of meditation so germane to each other. The fusion of techniques, one derived from the introspective exercises of the Oxford Holy Club, and the other, inspired by the Moravian doctrine of the immediate witness, was, in Wesley's age, a decidedly original and valuable innovation. Wesley's originality may be measured by the fact that in Puritan spirituality, a tradition steeped in relentless self-examination, no comparable systematic strategy existed that combatted the infamous, widespread crises of doubt. Most spiritual manuals published during the period of Puritan ascendancy devoted themselves to this very problem (Lovelace, 1989, p. 313; Rubin, 1994, p. 35). The Calvinistic core of Puritan theology demanded that examination of sin be coupled with a search for the "experiential evidence of regeneration" (Lovelace, 1989, p. 313), the signs of election, and the mutually exclusive force of these endeavors—the one undermining the other—dictated the inevitable swings into melancholia. The inculcation of depression was precisely Wesley's dilemma during his Oxford days, when he courted the double bind of acquiring holy sincerity by keeping careful track of his failings.

The acute awareness of his shortcomings drove him into increasingly rigid and virtually hypochondriacal regimes of self-scrutiny that exacerbated his uncertainty and brought little respite (Heitzenrater, 1995, p. 53; Rack, 1989, p. 95; Steele, 1994, p. 108). In later years, Wesley identified this vicious circle of obsessional defenses as the futility of relying upon one's own righteousness.

The psychological genius of his later model lay in his insistence that continual watchfulness commence only when one already has the irrefutable evidence of regeneration. Cohen (1986) states that "nothing in seventeenth-century Puritan theory compares to the precision with which John Wesley and his contemporaries ticked off the exact moment of their conversions" (p. 99). For Methodists, the evangelical emphasis on pin-pointing discrete instances of ecstatic conversion ensured that self-examination was grounded in a convincing and enduring sense of divine assurance. Wesley warned believers against "resting" in incomplete manifestations of the spirit. Only the unequivocal witness of pardon could ward off the "perils" of watchfulness.

> Let none rest in any supposed fruit of the Spirit without the witness. There may be foretastes of joy, of peace, of love—and those not delusive, but really from God—long before we have the witness in ourselves, before the Spirit of God witnesses with our spirits that we have 'redemption in the blood of Jesus, even the forgiveness of sins'. Yea, there may be a degree of long-suffering, of gentleness, of fidelity, meekness, temperance (not a shadow thereof, but a real degree, by the preventing grace of God) before we are 'accepted in the Beloved', and consequently before we have a testimony of our acceptance. But it is by no means advisable to rest here; it is at the peril of our souls if we do. If we are wise we shall be continually crying to God, until his Spirit cry in our heart, 'Abba, Father!'...without this we cannot retain a steady peace, nor avoid perplexing doubts and fears (Wesley, 1984-87, I: p. 298).

The practice of the presence continually accentuated the witness of pardon and granted believers the courage to apprehend their ambivalence with a minimal likelihood of stirring a debilitating depression. Strachey (1934) claims that in the analytic situation, the analyst functions for the patient as an auxiliary superego. The patient identifies with and gradually internalizes the analyst's acceptance of the transference, thereby augmenting the harshness of the patient's superego. The analyst's benevolence and commitment to "objective" self-understanding undermines the archaic superego so that the development of a more lenient conscience gives the patient permission to gain insight. Strachey, of course, located this therapeutic action in the patient's transference on to the analyst. In Wesley's model, an analogous process unfolded in relation to the individual's transference onto God, a transference shaped by the facilitating influence of the positive superego.

The sense of presence bolstered introspection by enhancing the normally self-evident criteria of a "good conscience" (Wesley, 1984-87, I: p. 304), the subjective basis of pardon. The ecstatic manifestation of unitive ideals intensified conscience. The expansion of individuals' moral sensibilities, *so constitutive of the invisible knowledge of God*, allowed for a coherent and goal directed examination. It both magnified and illuminated their vision: "And how much sin, if their conscience is awake, may they find *cleaving to their actions* also?" (I: p. 342).

> The joy of a Christian does not arise from any *blindness of conscience*, from his not being able to discern good from evil. So far from it that he was an utter stranger to this joy till the eyes of his understanding were opened, that he knew it not till he had spiritual senses, fitted to discern good and evil. And now the eye of the soul waxeth not dim. He was never so sharpsighted before. He has so quick a perception of the smallest thing as is quite amazing to the natural man. As a mote is visible in the sunbeam, so to him that is walking in the light, in the beams of the uncreated sun, every mote of sin is visible. Nor does he close the eyes of conscience anymore...His soul is always broad awake: no more slumber or folding of the hands in rest! he is always standing on the tower, and hearkening what his Lord will say concerning him; and always rejoicing in this very thing, in 'seeing him that is invisible' (I: p. 311).
>
> It is by faith that beholding 'the light of...the glory of God in the face of Jesus Christ we perceive, as in a glass, all that is in ourselves, yea the inmost motions of our souls (I: p. 304).

Wesley's writing suggests that the refinement of self-observation, together with the intensification of conscience, not only makes ambivalence more apparent to consciousness, but also reveals the defenses used to suppress it. When the "law unveils sin and brings it into the light of day" (Lindstrom, 1946, p. 77), the ego's rationalizations become apparent. "Being stripped even of the poor plea of ignorance, *it loses its excuse, as well as its disguise*, and becomes far more odious both to God and man" (emphasis added; quoted in Lindstrom, 1946, p. 77). Insights concerning both impulses (that is, sin) and defenses (that is, disguise) coincide thematically with Wesley's use of a spatial metaphor and the notion that hidden depths of desire are successively uncovered and brought into awareness.

PSYCHIC INTEGRATION AND CHARACTEROLOGICAL CHANGE

The sense of presence was instrumental in the dynamic uncovering and clarification of sin. Yet, however crucial, insight alone cannot promote characterological change. How exactly did the practice of the presence contribute to the process of working through? To answer this question we must first consider the idea that faith gave believers the strength to overcome the power of sin. According to Wesley, the meditative perpetuation of faith literally expels the force of temptation.

> But 'whosoever is born of God', while he abideth in faith and love and in the spirit of prayer and thanksgiving, not only 'doth not', but 'cannot' thus 'commit sin'. So long as he thus believeth in God through Christ and loves him, and is pouring out his heart before him, he cannot voluntarily transgress any command of God, either by speaking or acting what he knows God hath forbidden—so long that 'seed' which 'remaineth in him' (that loving, praying, thankful faith) compels him to refrain from whatsoever he knows to be an abomination in the sight of God (1984-87, I: p. 436).

As long as one continued to pray, the motivational impetus of unitive ideals minimized the threat of succumbing to temptation. The enormously satisfying effect of the mild alternate state of presence, and the pleasure derived from self-esteem, outweighed the cruder gratification of narcissistic needs and aggressive impulses. The supports helped to preserve an exclusively observational stance where one withstood the lure of the urges. Conversely, lapses in the practice of the presence ruptured the protective space between bare observation and the pull towards action. When prayer is replaced by the fantasy content of temptation, the rapid spread of desire diminishes faith, eclipses the sense of presence, and leaves the individual vulnerable to backsliding. The following extract portrays the sequence of "dissipation" or the "scattering of one's thoughts":

> You see the unquestionable process from grace to sin. Thus it goes on, from step to step. (1). The divine seed of loving, conquering faith remains in him that is 'born of God'. 'He keepeth himself', by the grace of God, and 'cannot commit' sin; (2). A temptation arises, whether from the world, the flesh, or the devil, it matters not; (3). The spirit of God gives him warning that sin is near, and bids him more abundantly watch unto prayer; (4). He gives way in some degree to the temptation, which now begins to grow pleasing to him; (5). The Holy Spirit is grieved; his faith is weakened, and his love of God grows cold; (6). The Spirit reproves him more sharply, and saith, 'This is the way; walk thou in it'. (7). He turns

away from the painful voice of God and listens to the pleasing voice of the tempter; (8). Evil desire begins and spreads in the soul, till faith and love vanish away; (9). He is then capable of committing outward sin, the power of the Lord being departed from him (Wesley, 1984-87, I: p. 440).

When dissipation does not devolve directly into sin, believers tend to resort to an obsessive defense, an embattled dialogue between the ego and the punitive introject. As mentioned, this strategy of self-reliance is commonly referred to as "reasoning." It offers no relief since any attempt to overcome guilt in the absence of the witness produces a cycle of futile appeals and doubt. If one reasons instead of focusing attention on God's presence, the indisputable testimony of a good conscience cannot intervene to allay the anxiety. Robert Roe writes, "When I reason, I have no power, when I [exercise the] the faith I have; and when temptations are offered; immediately faith repels them...If I were to reason for a moment I should be miserable" (*Arminian Magazine*, 1784, pp. 247-248).

Wesley conceded that the effort to resist temptation involved a degree of displeasure, even when practitioners successfully attended to God's presence. To forego the natural inclinations of the will was inherently frustrating, despite the consolations of faith. Wesley regarded instinctual renunciation as a subjection, or "crucifixion" of the flesh (Wesley, 1984-87, I: p. 329). "A cross is anything contrary to our will" (II: p. 243). We recall that during the post-justification period of depression, a tolerable dose of frustration actually makes the ego stronger and more resilient. The same principle of spiritual growth applies to the idea of crucifixion.

> The Lord then sits upon the soul 'as a refiner's fire', to burn up all the dross thereof. And this is a cross indeed; it is essentially painful; it must be so in the very nature of the thing. The soul cannot be thus torn asunder, it cannot pass through the fire, without pain (II: p. 244).

Bathsheba Hall, for example, states that she "still frequently felt anger" and wished "to feel [her] enemies until they were destroyed" (*Arminian Magazine*, 1781, p. 37). Here again, the ability to experience frustration lucidly, without falling into either extreme of presumption or despair, garnered the approval of the positive superego and promoted a more forgiving attitude towards ambivalence, as well as feelings of mastery and self-control. Wesley regarded the sufferings of temptation as "an occasion of thanksgiving" because "the consolations of the Holy One so increase as to overbalance them all" (Wesley, 1984-87, III: pp. 165-166).

> Although they feel the root of bitterness in themselves, yet are they endued with power from on high to trample it continually under foot, so that it cannot 'spring up to trouble them': insomuch that every fresh assault which they undergo only gives them fresh occasion for praise, of crying out, 'Thanks be unto God, who giveth the victory, through Jesus Christ our Lord' (I: p. 236).

Because Methodists viewed temptations as spiritually productive, the evidence suggests that the strengthening of the ego—the development of holiness—was measured in terms of the transformation of impulses. Lee (1936) remarks that "Wesley anticipates modern psychology in his recognition that instinctive attitudes may be sublimated" (p. 195). In *A Plain Account of Christian Perfection*, Wesley explains how appeals to Christ during moments of temptation alter the impulse by *inverting* its meaning and emotional content. Pride turns into humility, anger into love, impatience into patience, and so forth. How can we account for these "sublimations"? Wesley writes the following:

> The bearing men, and suffering evils in *meekness* and silence, is the sum of a Christian life.
>
> God is the first object of our love; its next office is to bear the defects of others. And we should begin the practice of this amid our own household.
>
> We should chiefly exercise our love toward them who most shock, either our way of thinking, or our temper, or our knowledge, or the desire we have that others should be as virtuous as we wish to be ourselves (Wesley & Wesley, 1981, p. 369).

In this passage, Wesley explains how the temptation of intolerance is used as a means to acquire kindness and patience. The realization of such sentiments requires an adjustment of perspective. Wesley describes an implicit sequence of mental events. A charitable disposition towards others arises only after a contemplation of the source of love. "God is the first object of our love; its next office is to bear the defects of others." When the sense of presence remains foremost in one's mind, the array of positive emotions associated with divine acceptance extend magnanimously to others. There is a subtle yet crucial shift in self-observation, one that stems from the super-ego, that is, from the self-observation function carried out by conscience (Freud, 1933, pp. 59-60, 66). By prayerfully invoking God's presence, feelings of intolerance are re-evaluated in fantasy from the perspective of the ideal other. The experiential witness of pardon allows for an imaginative appreciation of God's acceptance of the self, even in light of one's shortcomings. The identification with God's "objective" stance, a view that transcends the ego's usual perspective, encourages one to experience others in an equally empathic and forgiving manner.

The so-called sublimation that reverses impulses can be understood as the result of a shift in self-observation that presupposes a turn to the positive superego. Temptation is welcomed as an opportunity for change, an occasion to understand, manage and finally dispose of troublesome inclinations by aligning oneself with the motivating force of conscience and by adopting the personified perspective of loved and admired ideals. At first, the procedure is entirely voluntary—a conscious and deliberate act of will. Consider, for example, the following extract from the journal of John Nelson (1842):

> I then began to tell [Mr. Ingham] what I had seen at London under Mr. Wesley's preaching. He said, He pitied poor Mr. Wesley, for he was ignorant of his own state; and he spoke as if he believed Mr. Wesley to be an unconverted man; at which words my corrupt nature began to stir. But it came to my mind, "The wrath of man worketh not the righteousness of God;" and I lifted up my heart to the Lord, and my mind was calmed in a moment (p. 50).

In stating his "corrupt nature began to stir," Nelson shows he is quite aware of his indignance towards Ingham. Nelson then recalls an appropriate verse of scripture and lifts up his heart to the Lord. His decision to repudiate his anger by turning to God restores his composure. "I was calmed in a moment."

When the practice of the presence becomes automatized or "ceaseless," the shift in self-observational perspective also occurs automatically, independent of conscious deliberation. *Long-term characterological change, or Sanctification, is achieved when the dictates of conscience are stably incorporated into the ego as preconscious schemas. Ideally, these schemas are durable and comprehensive. They are applied globally.*

> One commends me. Here is a temptation to pride. But instantly my soul is humbled before God. And I feel no pride, of which I am as sure as that pride is not humility.
>
> A man strikes me. Here is a temptation to anger. But my heart overflows with love. And I feel no anger at all, of which I can be as sure as that love and anger are not the same.
>
> A woman solicits me. Here is temptation to lust. But in the instant I shrink back. And I feel no desire or lust at all, of which I am as sure as that my hand is hot or cold...In the instant the soul repels the temptation, and remains filled with pure love. *And the difference is still plainer when I compare my present state with my past, wherein I felt temptation and corruption too* (emphasis added; Wesley & Wesley, 1981, p. 352).

We find an example of an automatized turn to the superego in Richard Moss's autobiographical narrative. Moss's spiritual development exemplifies Wesley's sequence of stages. Early in the narrative, Moss repeatedly tries to restrain his carnal desires: drinking, gambling, falling into "ill company" and associating with "loose women" (*Arminian Magazine*, 1798, p. 48). However, his inability to remain "resolute" drives him into despair. After acquainting himself with the Methodists and listening to Wesley preach, he experiences desolation and ritually mourns his way towards an ecstatic conversion. Justification is followed by an inflation that gives way to a depressive crisis of doubt. Finally, another unitive ecstasy persuades him not only of his forgiveness, but that God's pardon is abiding. At this juncture, Moss begins practicing the presence of God. "I did all my business without distraction. Nothing interrupted or hindered my intercourse with God" (p. 55). In time, he receives a vision of the trinity that signifies his sanctification (p. 56). The narrative comes to close with the story of how he overcomes his reluctance to preach.

> I walked over one day with Mr. Downes, to Burnup-field. I began to speak with him; but he said, "Pray, do not speak, for I want to meditate by myself." Soon after that scripture was strongly fixt upon my mind, wherein Mary is said, to have washed Christ's feet with her tears, and wiped them with the hairs of her head. And presently I was pressed in spirit, to preach on those words. I was surprised, having never had such a thought in my life. I strove to put it out of my mind, but could not: It followed me all the way; and I saw the meaning of the words, and of the whole passage, as I have never done before (pp. 56-57).

When they arrived at Burnup-field, Downes "preached as usual" (p. 57) but took ill the next day. Downes convinces Moss to preach in his stead. With great trepidation, Moss presented his discourse on the meaning of Mary's ministrations. To his surprise, he "found much of the Love of God in speaking, and no want either of matter or words" (p. 57). In light of Moss's imminent turn to preaching, we may assume that he identified with Downes and valued his companionship. Moss's attempt to start a conversation is abruptly refused by the preacher, who prefers to meditate in silence. Moss does not mention any feelings of hurt, disappointment, or anger in being rebuffed. He appears not to have been consciously "tempted." On the other hand, the content of scripture which was immediately "strongly fixed upon his mind" is illuminating. Moss reacts to Downes's rebuff by recalling Mary as she washes the feet of Christ and wipes them with her hair. The image of Mary's humble obedience allows us to infer the missing gap in Moss's response. Keep in mind that for Wesley, when temptations assail those who are only partially perfected, they must willfully resume the practice of the presence so that temptation will give way to holy sentiments. According to the logic of increasing grace, that is, the movement from imperfect to perfect or automatized prayer, if Moss had found himself in a similar situation earlier in his development, his wounded narcissism would have intervened directly and forced him to intensify his prayer. In the present instance, however, feelings of indignation and hurt are by-passed. The shift in observational perspective occurs instantaneously, triggered reflexively in the preconscious. What is more, not only does the image of Mary's submissiveness represent a corrective to Moss's initial impulse, it also preserves Moss's positive identification with Downes, the preacher, and accomplishes an important work of sublimation. As the two men continue walking to the field, Moss silently elaborates upon the content of the inspiration, feeling strangely compelled "to preach on those words." Guilt and resentment do not compromise his push towards autonomy. The following day, Moss delivers his sermon publicly. This event marks the beginning of his career as a circuit preacher.

AUTOBIOGRAPHICAL ACCOUNTS OF WATCHING AND PRAYING

Most references to the practice of the presence and introspection in Methodist autobiographies do not provide a great deal of information. Typically brief and encapsulated, the brevity owes to the fact that the richest sources of personal data are the relatively condensed life histories that appeared in *The Arminian Magazine*. Although more elaborate daily entries taken from diaries were occasionally published, the narrative length of the standard format precluded lengthy accounts of the relation between meditation and spiritual growth. As a result, extensively detailed depictions of meditation are more or less exceptional. Abbreviated descriptions, however, commonly appear in the literature. Albin (1985) found that 33.2% of Methodist sanctification ecstasies occurred in the context of "various types of prayer" (p. 278). We may conclude that a substantial number of Methodists took "watching and praying" seriously.

After a crisis of doubt following his justification, Thomas Hanby's "former peace, love and joy" returned in a moment (*Arminian Magazine*, 1780, p. 481). The distress of losing the witness made him appreciate the necessity of holding fast to his faith.

> My sore trial taught me more watchfulness. After this I walked in great love, and peace, for near two years, buying up every opportunity for prayer, hearing and reading...Oh! what a struggle had I between my unfitness and my love for God (pp. 481-482).

This extract offers a typical example of the generic and unelaborated style of description. Hanby's trial encouraged him to be more watchful and contemplative. In doing so, he comprehends the duality of his love and his "unfitness," or sinfulness. We see a similar pattern in John Mason's narrative, only in this case, he lingered in a post-conversion "darkness" for five years before recovering the "peace and love of God" (*Arminian Magazine*, 1780, p. 653). He writes:

> I was *watchful*, and spent much time in prayer: the word of God was my daily companion, and it was spirit and life to my soul. My faith was now strengthened: my love to God and man increased abundantly. The Lord held me by my hand, and fed me with the bread of life. He gave me to drink of the water of the river of life, and I was happy all the day long. Such was the blessing I continually enjoyed, *I lived near God, keeping Jesus in my view, as my life, my pattern, and my all* (emphasis added, p. 653).

In a post-script to his autobiographical narrative, William Hunter gives a short summary of the events that preceded his sanctification. Here again, references to watchfulness and prayer are presented without intimate descriptions of the experiences he had before he was perfected. "It would be tedious to relate the various exercises I went through for several years" (*Arminian Magazine*, 1779, p. 596). Nevertheless, he states:

> [After being justified] it pleased Infinite Wisdom to open a new scene to me: I began to be exercised with many uncommon temptations, and felt my own heart ready to comply with the same...I began to call in question the work of grace in my soul. O, the pain and anguish I felt for weeks together! Yet all this while I was very earnest with the Lord, my soul clave to him and I often said, *Though he Slay me, yet will I trust in him*. Under this exercise I learned several things: As first, that my nature was not so much changed as I thought: I found many things in me which opposed the grace of God; so that without continual watching and prayer, I was capable of committing the very same sins which I had been guilty of before. 2. I began to be more acquainted with Satan's devices, and found power from God to resist them. 3. I had very affecting views of Christ, as my great high-priest who was touched with a feeling of all my infirmities. 4. The scriptures were precious to me, and I found great comfort in reading them. And lastly, I was conscious of a need of a far greater change in my nature than I had yet experienced...yet I found my mind at times deeply engaged in prayer to be saved from all sin (pp. 594-595).

Note that Hunter "had very affecting views of Christ," who was "touched with a feeling of all [his] infirmities." His sense of presence is personified and experienced as an empathic self-object who is both moved by and appreciatively supportive of Hunter's efforts to subdue his corruptions. For Charles Perronet, the practice of the presence also takes the form of a highly personalized object relationship.

> I talked with him; he seemed to look upon me with precious smiles; became my delightful abode; gave me promises, and made all my existence glory in himself, fixing all my desires upon his Love, and the glorious display of his own person. I could relish only Jesus: to have been a moment with him, I would have given up all besides. I was so engaged with Christ, that the thought he had been despised on earth, drowned my eyes in tears: and the thought that he now possessed all fullness, so satisfied my largest desires that I had no choice whether to exist or not: whatever was myself was no more. It seemed to make no part of my happiness. All centered in Jesus and him alone (*Arminian Magazine*, 1779, p. 202).

Here the personification of presence is imaginatively rooted in the humanity of Christ. Perronet speaks to Jesus, who, in return, grants him "precious smiles" and "promises." Through the play of mutuality, which fosters trust, self-regard and gratitude, Perronet experiences a profoundly empathic tie to Jesus, whose sufferings move Perronet to tears. The intense involvement with the presence of Christ occurs in tandem with the crucial shift in self-observation, a movement from the perspective of the self to that of the ideal other. Because Perronet's narcissistic needs for mirroring and support are taken care of, no anxious or morbid self-involvement intervenes, only an eager devotion to Jesus. "All centered in Jesus and him alone." Indeed, Perronet's relationship to Christ is so all-encompassing that the practice of the presence extends into his dream life as well.

> I seemed in my sleep to be often with Christ. I carried him as an infant in my arms. I heard him speak. I walked with him, and saw him work miracles. I helped to support him in his agony: saw him crucified and was crucified with him. I saw the approaches of the last day, and the trumpet's found. Another time we all stood before Jesus. I cried in an agony to be made fit. I was made so and rejoiced (p. 211).

William Carvosso's (1835) memoir contains several references to watching and praying. In presenting the "remarks" of a certain "Mr. Bramwell," we see how Carvosso aspired "to be taken into God" (p. 122), a condition that he understood as a state of ceaseless prayer.

The following remarks of Mr. Bramwell are striking, and deserve particular notice:—"Justification is great; to be cleansed is greater; but what is justification, or being cleansed, compared with being taken into God? The world, the noise of self,—all is gone; and the mind bears the full stamp of God's image. Here, we talk and walk, and live; doing all in Him and to Him;—continual prayer, and turning all into Christ, in every house, in every company; all things by him, from Him, and to Him" (pp. 122-123).

Carvosso continues with his own commentary:

O! I long to be more filled with God. Lord, stir me up to be more in earnest! I want to be more like Jesus. My soul thirsteth for Thee, O God. I see nothing will do but being continually filled with Thy presence and glory. I know all that Thou hast is mine, but I want to feel a closer union. Lord, increase my faith! (p. 123).

Carvosso's description of faith clearly presupposes the practice of the presence and the use of spiritual senses:

I see if I would get good every where, it must be by striving to keep my outward senses under subjection to those which grace has opened in the soul. By faith I realize the presence of my great Prophet; my ear attends to that still small voice which is not heard in the hurry and tumult of our nature; my eyes gaze on the Divine perfections displayed in the whole economy of nature and grace; and hereby I begin a life that never ends, and obtain enjoyments which shall increase to all eternity. Faith does not merely wait for Divine influence, but actually lays hold of it, as well as on every other purchased and promised blessing; yea, by simple faith, promises and promiser are made all our own…I am desirous of learning his way more perfectly, that I may daily make sensible objects subservient to the realities which faith reveals (pp. 141).

By "striving to keep his outward senses under subjection to those which grace has opened in the soul," Carvosso applies or assimilates the unitive abstraction of presence to the particularities of his sense perception. He makes "sensible objects subservient to the realities which faith reveals." He places emphasis on the voluntary aspect of the exercise. "Divine influence," which includes inspirations of conscience—the "still small voice" of the "great prophet"—is deliberately invoked through meditation. In line with the idea of co-operative grace, Carvosso states that he does not "merely wait for Divine influence," but willingly summons the sense of presence by "actually laying hold of it."

Carvosso's experience of the presence is also personified. A good conscience, expressed as an "approving smile," produces trust, vitality, and confidence.

> He doth now reward my poor services with, His approving smile and continual presence; teaching me in ignorance, strengthening me in weakness, supporting me in trials, blessing my feeble endeavors and labors, fighting for me against every enemy, and making all things work together for my good. O my soul, what mercies! what boundless love! (p. 159).

Carvosso couples the practice of the presence with introspection. "Some days before this, my faith was severely tried; and not without a cause. O what a necessity there is for more self-denial! Lord, keep me ever watching!" (p. 134). In this way, Carvosso participates in the "mystery of faith" that comprehends sin in the light of God's pardon.

> But this is the mystery of faith, that while I have on one hand a painful consciousness of my deserts as a sinner, I have on the other, at the same moment, "boldness to enter into the holiest by the blood of Jesus." "Blessed is the man to whom the Lord imputeth not sin." I thank God through Jesus Christ. He is "the way, the truth, and the life:" we must ever bear in mind, that we can only be saved unto the uttermost while we "come unto God by Him." (p. 266).

Robert Roe's autobiographical narrative includes dated insertions from a personal journal that provide a more detailed account of the difficulties and successes of his meditative experiences. The following extract indicates that he used the practice of the presence, the moment-to-moment renewal of faith, in tandem with self-examination:

> I see plainly we are to come to God by simple faith, and expect grace when we want it, and use it when we have it, day by day, hour by hour, minute by minute...I feel this day the clear witness of God's Spirit, that I am his, and at the same time I have a sense of inbred sin (*Arminian Magazine*, 1784, pp. 360-361).

Roe's introspection frequently gets the better of him, and "trials" and "temptations" disrupt his emotional calm.

> Of late I have been tossed to and fro. Sometimes I have been happy; at other times, almost in despair. Trials from the world;

> temptations from the enemy; and above all, the evils of my own heart, wearied out my spirits: add to this, the weak state of my nerves, which often render me incapable of recollection, so that I cannot persue my business, or properly judge of the state of my soul. Satan always takes advantage of these seasons, and when I lay hold on the promises, he tells me, they are not for thee. Thou art fallen from grace, thou hast sinned away the day of grace, and wilt be damned. I have sunk into despair. Sometimes I would fast, and use all kinds of mortification, to keep under my corruption; but when I found them rise again with equal strength, I was ready to give up all (p. 81).

In permitting himself to feel and explore his ambivalence, Roe undergoes a rapid oscillation of mood states. Strong resistances that manifest as self-accusations and doubt create sufficient anxiety to sabotage his contemplation and leave him "incapable of recollection." Hoping to rekindle the sense of presence, Roe falls back on the standard procedures of ritual mourning. When these prove to be equally ineffective, he sinks into despair. On other occasions, however, he successfully quells his ruminations.

> I was very comfortable, till in placing my books I began to think they were bound too elegantly for a Christian, and fell into reasoning. I had no sooner given way to this, than Satan came in as a flood, and I was almost distracted. The 29th. I was a little comforted; but beginning to reason about speaking, I was soon miserable. I then resolved to cry unto God, and take no thought about speaking. My temptations and misery were gone in a moment, and I had sweet peace and love...April 19th. Since I wrote last, my experience and trials have been various. But this I ever find, when I yield to reasoning and unbelief, the enemy gets the advantage; but if I look to Jesus by faith, it brings present power, peace and love (p. 417).

Distracted by the worldly elegance of his books, and the prospect of preaching, Roe is drawn into an obsessive debate with his tormented conscience. He feels compelled to reason with the devil. But in this instance, instead of ruminating fruitlessly, Roe follows Wesley's instructions. "I then resolved to cry unto God." By reinstating the sense of presence through prayer, which he euphemistically describes as "look[ing] to Jesus by faith," he recovers his equilibrium.

POST-CONVERSION USES OF THE SENSE OF PRESENCE

Although Methodist autobiographers provided only brief references to watching and praying, descriptions of the particular uses of the sense of presence provide a more informative source of data. All occurred after conversion, and some are based on spontaneously occurring ecstasies. I have included this material in the present section because it readily demonstrates how the intellectual vision of presence facilitated the work of the positive superego, helping believers to endure sickness and loss, to overcome the anxieties of preaching, and to engage in moral problem solving.

In much the same way that the sense of presence diminished the physical and mental sufferings of the dying, when Methodists took ill, feelings of divine communion frequently brought them comfort. Carvosso (1835) writes:

> I have been confined to bed four days by an inflammation in my leg. But though the Lord has afflicted my body, my mind has been in perfect peace. My soul has mounted on the wings of contemplation, and I have enjoyed sweet communion with God. His presence makes my paradise (p. 124).

In a rare variation of divine presence, Robert Roe describes a unitive encounter with a "guardian angel," the spirit of a friend.

> The following night I was very ill; but suddenly felt a kindred spirit, with dear ——. The love of God, as soon as I thought of her, warmed my heart, and healed my sorrow. I thought it was impossible to feel such union with any who are in the body. I therefore concluded she was dead; and that her spirit acted as a guardian angel upon mine. I rejoiced at the indisposition of my body, and the expectation of soon following her. The next morning I was tempted to reason; but in the afternoon I found a praying spirit for my dear friends; and the more I prayed, and exercised faith on Jesus, the more I felt heaven opened in my heart (*Arminian Magazine*, 1784, p. 307).

Just prior to his falling ill, Roe grew unhappily estranged from his father who condemned his son's involvement with the Methodists (p. 305-306). Also, on the night before his illness, Roe ministered to a "sick woman," and the encounter left a serious impression upon him. "This was a great cross to me" (p. 307). Although no direct evidence suggests that Roe's sickness was hysterical in nature, we may infer that the stresses of recent events added to his state of mind while he lay convalescing. He suffered due to the guilt over his father's disappointment and the unsettling reminder of human frailty. Roe assumes that he himself is not far from dying. Roe's ecstasy compensates for the "sorrow" or depression associated with the illness. The unexpected intensity of the sense of presence convinces him that his friend must have been deceased, for it seemed "impossible to feel such union with any who are in the body." Because his illness inspires a fear of death, the comforting sense of union with a "kindred spirit," one who has already passed on, augments Roe's separation anxiety. "I rejoiced at the indisposition of my body, and the expectation of soon following her."

Benjamin Rhodes describes a presence ecstasy that occurred while he was still a youth.

> At about twelve years of age, I took a walk one evening into a large, thick wood not far from town. I left the path, and wandered in the thickest part of it, till I was entirely lost. Night began to close in upon me, and I did not know which way to turn my face towards home. It soon became quite dark: I then gave over rambling, and intended to have remained there till the morning, when I hoped to find my way out. In this situation I found my former impressions begin to return with much sweetness. My soul was put in prayer; I was deeply sensible of the presence of God; my heart overflowed with penitential tenderness; and, under a deep sense of my own unworthiness, and of his goodness, mercy, and love, I sung and prayed with much fervor: yea, I was so thankful that the Lord had found me, while lost in a wood, that I would not for all the world have missed such an opportunity (*Arminian Magazine*, 1779, pp. 358-359).

The ecstasy, evoked through prayer, eases Rhodes's fear and loneliness, giving him the patience to wait until his father eventually retrieved him. The experiences documented by Roe and Rhodes illustrate how the sense of presence mitigated separation anxiety. This phenomenon dovetails with the fact that such ecstasies often occured during periods of loss or separation from family and friends. For example, when Zechariah Yewdall first became an itinerant preacher in South Wales, the Lord "condescended to visit [him] in the most gracious manner" (*Arminian Magazine*, 1795, p. 266). The visitation filled his heart "with an abundance of peace and joy in believing." Yewdall explains that the ecstasy was well timed. His departure into the field had "overwhelmed [him] with sorrow" since he was now without the "counsel and support" of his friends. Yewdall experienced his longing as a demonic temptation. "The enemy made cruel and painful suggestions." Even so, the Lord "relieved" him in his time of distress.

After losing his wife, William Carvosso (1835) lived with his son Benjamin, who remained unmarried (p. 57). Benjamin was eventually appointed to a preaching circuit, and forced to leave his father behind. In a letter written one day after his son left, Carvosso states that he prayed to God to assist him in his grief. "[God] so filled my soul with his love, that I have been happy ever since. I am resigned to God's will" (p. 57). Carvosso later received notice that Benjamin was requested to undertake a foreign mission, one that would take him even farther away (p. 103-105). The news left Carvosso stricken with an "indescribable burden," a conflict between his love for his son and his belief that Benjamin had been truly "called of God."

> But on one occasion soon after, while I was in secret pondering over the painful subject, thinking of the separation, and of the various privations and dangers attending such a work, just at the moment when nature shrunk back, and I felt as if I could not consent to make the sacrifice, I seemed suddenly surrounded by Divine presence, and a voice said to me, "I gave my son to die for thee; and canst thou not give thy son to go an errand for me? I will bring him to thee again." I cried out, "Take him, Lord, take him!" The Lord conquered me by his undying love, and never did I offer any thing to God more willingly. Indeed it appeared to me at that time, that, if I had a thousand sons, I would cheerfully have given them all up to God for such a work. Nor have I since changed my views, or had one uneasy thought about him. At the time when I felt the wonderful deliverance, and the Father of mercies Himself condescended to reason with me, it seemed for the moment, I could not tell if I was in the body or out of the body. Time appeared only a moment, compared with that eternity which was opened to my mind; and it was in the full assurance of faith I offered him up, believing that, if I should see him no more in time, we should quickly meet in heaven; seeing the Lord told me He would bring him to me again...When the time came for his departure...and [I] took my final leave of him, I was so supported above myself, that I was perfectly calm and recollected...God has united us; in Him we subsist as one soul, and no "power can make us twain" (pp. 104-106).

The sense of presence functions as an ecstatic manifestation of conscience, assisting Carvosso to resolve a highly charged emotional conflict. The fact that he pondered the "painful subject" while he was in "secret" indicates that Carvosso ritually mourned in order to receive divine guidance. The onset of the sense of presence accompanies an interior dialogue in which the voice of God articulates a moral analogy that clinches Carvosso's decision to surrender his son. "I gave my son to die for thee; and canst thou not give thy son to go an errand for me? I will bring him to thee again." Again we observe the imaginative shift in self-observation from the perspective of the ego to that of the ideal other. Carvosso considers God's sacrificial relationship to his own son, and willingly concedes. In earnestly consenting to his ideal, Carvosso's joy creates a greater sense of trust, and he is enabled to entertain the prospect of reunion, either in this life, or in the next. The satisfaction he experiences in abiding by his conscience heightens his euphoria and gratitude. "The Lord conquered me by his undying love, and never did I offer anything to God more willingly." Interestingly, the ecstasy appears to climax with a brief interlude of trance. For a moment, Carvosso was not certain whether he was still in his body. Perhaps some measure of sorrow felt to be inconsistent with the dominant emotional meaning of the experience led to a momentary, defensive lapse in sense perception. In the end, the gratification of his convictions and the consolations of unitive thinking dissolve his grief. "God has united us; in him we subsist as one soul, and 'no power can make us twain'."

As a source of inner sustainment, courage, conviction, and creative inspiration, the sense of presence gave ample support to Wesley's traveling preachers. Like so many other fledgling preachers, Zechariah Yewdall had difficulty finding the courage to speak in public. He writes, "The first pulpit I went into was at Pudrey Chapel; the Lord was pleased to favor me with such a sense of his presence, as dispelled my fears, and gave me liberty in speaking to people" (*Arminian Magazine*, 1795, p. 218). When confronted by an "unruly" mob that tried to obstruct his passage into a chapel in Monmoth, Yewdall relied on the practice of the presence to subdue his fear. His description underscores how the empathic shift in self-observation helped to preserve his composure.

> When I went first into the pulpit, my mind was much exercised; but in a little time I found serene calm in the midst of the tumult, and a firm reliance upon the protection of the Almighty, especially while I was beseeching him to forgive and have mercy upon those thoughtless men, who knew not what they were doing. A friend conducted me home safely, and I was unfeignedly thankful that the Lord had given me a heart to pity and pray for my enemies...I found how much better it was to be persecuted for righteousness sake, than to follow a lawless multitude to do evil" (p. 268).

In addition to taking on the perspective of the other, Yewdall's bravery, his willingness to risk attack and suffer ridicule, was reinforced by the self-esteem derived from living up to his ideals in the midst of danger.

Because verbal and intellectual inspirations of conscience are an integral part of the alternate state of presence, Methodist preachers like Thomas Olivers sometimes felt themselves prompted to speak on themes and ideas that they believed were passively and spontaneously mediated by the spirit. On one occasion, while traveling as a circuit preacher in Scotland, Olivers awoke in the early hours of the morning and began to "call upon God." "In an instant," he writes, "I was filled with such sweetness as I had not tasted for a long time" (*Arminian Magazine*, 1779, p. 142). Olivers writes that the positive effect of this "visitation" endured and was tied to an equally remarkable infusion of grace given to him while he addressed his congregation.

> The effect of this visitation lasted a considerable time, and was of greater use to me, both in preaching and living. Some time after, I was preaching on the barren fig tree, a few words proceeded from me in such a manner, as I can scarce describe. The congregation seemed as if they had been electrified. One who had long been bowed down, cried out amain; and said afterwards, that under those words, she felt as if she was dropping into hell. I have since thought that if the word was always attended with such power, very few would stand before it (p. 142).

We find a particularly fascinating example of the courage individuals derived from the sense of presence in John Haime's narrative. In this case, the blissfulness of divine presence reinforces an *adaptive* denial of extreme anxiety. Convinced of his invulnerability, Haime is literally swept up in manic exaltation during a brutal military encounter with the French army.

> For my part, I stood the hottest fire of the enemy, for above seven hours. But I told my comrades, "The French have no ball made, that will kill me this day." After about seven hours, a cannon ball killed my horse under me. An officer cried aloud, "Haime where is your God now?" I answered, "Sir, he is here with me; and he will bring me out of this battle." Presently a cannon ball took off his head. My horses fell upon me, and some cried out, "Haime is gone!" But I replied, "He is not gone yet." I soon disengaged myself and walked on praising God. I was exposed both to the enemy and to our own horse; but that did not discourage me at all: for I knew I had the God of Jacob with me. I had a long way to go through all our horse, the balls flying on every side. And all the way, multitudes lay bleeding, groaning, dying, or just dead. Surely I was in the fiery furnace; but it did not singe a hair of my head. The hotter the battle grew, the more strength was given me. I was as full of joy as I could contain (*Arminian Magazine*, 1780, p. 262).

> My heart was filled with love, peace and joy, more than tongue can express. I was in a new world! I could truly say, "Unto you that believe he is present." I stood the fire of the enemy seven hours (p. 217).

We have previously seen how William Carvosso used the sense of presence to assuage the sadness of being separated from his son. The ecstasy also served, however, as a vehicle or manifestation of conscience. The emotional power of the ideal strengthened Carvosso's will and brought closure to a painful moral dilemma. John Cennick provides another example of the relation between ecstatic presence and moral problem solving. Although Cennick was an early follower of Methodism, his Calvinist leanings kept him from fully embracing several of Wesley's core theological tenets, including the doctrine of Christian perfection, and Wesley's insistence that conversion did not guarantee "final perseverance," or the impossibility of backsliding (Towsland, 1957, 106-107). Cennick also disapproved of the eccentricity of "scenes," the panic attacks, convulsive seizures and paralyses that Wesley, during his ministry at Fetter Lane, regarded as the "work of God" (p. 106). Torn between his allegiance to Wesley, and his own personal convictions, Cennick resolved the conflict in the following way:

> One day I walked by myself into the wood, and wept before the Savior, and got again a sensible feeling of His presence and determined thenceforward to preach nothing but Him and his righteousness. And so all fits and crying out ceased wherever I came, and a blessing attended my labors. Only this opened a way for Mr. Wesley and me to jar and dispute often, because, firstly, I could not believe or preach Perfection, and, secondly, I resolved to mention only the righteousness of Christ and the final perseverance of souls truly converted (quoted in Towsland, 1957, p. 107).

Like Carvosso, Cennick deliberately induced the ecstasy through ritual mourning. He found a secluded spot in the woods and exacerbated his distress by weeping and appealing to Christ. Upon acquiring a "sensible feeling" of the savior's presence, Cennick overcame his resistance to taking a moral stance that genuinely reflected his own convictions. In deciding to follow his conscience, Cennick's self-esteem and sense of integrity allowed him to tolerate his guilt. In short, he was enabled to assert his autonomy. The experience left him confident enough to "jar and dispute" with Wesley, to reassert a previously inhibited set of religious values, and to preach the gospel in accordance with his beliefs.

SUMMARY

Anticipating the current consensus of writers in the psychology of religion, Wesley understood that the revelatory character of conversion ecstasies were not wholly transformative in and of themselves. For long-term characterological change to occur, ecstatic insights needed to be systematically engaged, elaborated, and carried forward in worldly practice. For this reason, he recommended the simultaneous use of two meditative exercises, the practice of the presence and introspection. The combination of these techniques coincided theologically with the interdependence of faith and repentance, both of which were the necessary prerequisites of gradual sanctification.

The practice of the presence, a discursive exercise involving the imaginative contemplation of God's immanence, was predicated on the memory of the original conversion ecstasies. The technique preserved and prolonged the state of mind associated with the new birth. Because Methodists regarded all forms of action as expressions of prayer, they applied the emotional and cognitive content of unitive ideals, the foundation of Christian conscience, to their daily affairs, where, ideally, the ideals eventually stabilized as permanent dispositions.

The practice of the presence induced a mild alternate state of consciousness that compares with what Maslow calls the plateau experience. Two aspects of this state are crucial for understanding how the practice could bring about the personality changes associated with sanctification. First, the unitive dimension of the sense of presence, as both a form of personal communion and an abstraction that organized one's perception of the cosmos, provided a holding environment, a space of psychic safety where self-examination proceeded with a minimal likelihood of incurring a depression. Secondly, the alternate state was based on reverie, so that core ego functions remained intact. Consequently, individuals could maintain the mental flexibility necessary to balance the continual "day dream" of divine immanence with lucid introspection.

In essence, we may say that the practice of the presence represented an intensification of conscience. This simple formulation illuminates what I refer to as the synergistic tie between watching and praying. Inasmuch as the practice of the presence perpetuated the witness of pardon, believers in possession of a good conscience found themselves far more able to withstand the anxieties and depressive reactions that typically accompanied the apprehension of sin. The "shield" of faith permitted an intensive moment-to-moment examination of impulses resistant to a fuller realization of altruistic values. Also, inasmuch as the alternate state was a symbolic, that is, personified embodiment of conscience, it provided self-evident criteria for introspection. Wesley held that an awakened conscience not only brought one's sins into the light of day, it also revealed their "disguises," or the rationalizations used to deny hypocrisy. Wesley delineated an insight model of spiritual development, one that presupposed a depth psychological metaphor, a penetration into the "depth" and "ground" of one's heart.

Even though the practice of the presence minimized the psychological threats of introspection, resistances occurred all the same. Wesley identified two common reactions or "unitive distortions": presumption and despair. In the former case, practitioners experienced a subtle form of inflation that involved a denial of the significance of sin. Despair, on the other hand, was characterized by an exaggerated preoccupation with the seemingly unbridgeable gap between one's own corruptions and the "height and glory of God." Here the psychic residue of evangelical nurture distorted the hope of acquiring holiness. With the return of the bad object, the promise of perfection—the confident hopefulness rooted in an unconflicted ideal—devolved into an impossible authoritarian demand. Wesley's advice to those who found themselves stymied by doubt was straightforward. Instead of "reasoning with the devil," a phrase that signified an obsessive and ultimately futile debate between the ego and the punishing superego, believers should resume the practice of the presence in order to revive the witness of pardon.

Because the practice of the presence maintained the ego's rapport with the loved and admired ideals of conscience, the motivating impetus of the ideals gave "power" to overcome the temptations of sin. The important gratifications that accompanied the alternate state of presence, not the least of which was the ego's sense of satisfaction in living up to its ideals, were more compelling than those derived from the guilt ridden impulses of sin, such as worldly pride, indiscriminate sexual longings, anger, and intolerance. Methodists endured the frustrations of instinctual renunciation, but the frustrations were attenuated by the pleasure of self-esteem. As structures of impulse control continued to form in the ego, individuals became more and more able to tolerate and contain psychic pain and tension. This process was due, in large measure, to the self-regulatory functions of the positive superego. As I have shown, the sense of presence helped Methodists to endure the ravages of sickness, the grief of loss, the anxieties of preaching, and the conflicts of moral problem solving. Methodists regarded temptations as welcomed opportunities for spiritual growth. The insight obtained in observing rather than acting on one's impulses promoted characterological change in tandem with the imaginative dimension of the practice of the presence. In other words, the meaning and consequences of undesirable impulses were re-evaluated, in fantasy, from the perspective of the ideal other, from the superego's point of view. Long-term characterological transformation, or sanctification, corresponded to the automatization of this shift in self-observation. Wesley characterized sanctification as the perfection of contemplation, a state of ceaseless, uninterrupted prayer.

Nine

Concluding Reflections

Freud brought psychoanalytic anthropology into existence with the publication of *Totem and Taboo* (1913). By employing essentially the same deductive method found in his individual case histories, Freud reconstructed the origins of human social structure and cultural life, that is, organized communal existence, the incest taboo, and the beginnings of religion. By designating the Oedipus complex as the impetus for the creation of cultural forms, and by charting an evolution of religious ideas that reflected the need to manage the universal problems of oedipal rebellion and guilt, Freud established a "defense" conception of culture that became axiomatic in later streams of psychoanalytic anthropology. For writers such as Roheim (1971), Kardiner (1946), Whiting (1961) and Spiro (1965), collective symbolism reproduces and reinforces optimal compromise formations between the ego and the unconscious. Whereas the actual clinical practice of psychoanalysis aims, ideally, at the resolution of neurotic conflict, prevailing psychoanalytic theories of cultural symbolism tend to highlight themes of conflict management.

Although useful as a methodological tool, the defense conception poses theoretic limitations if we view it as the primary metaphor for a working definition of culture. For example, while conceding that symbol systems may function as defenses, Obeyesekere (1990, p. 19) holds that the foregoing writers, in emphasizing regressive themes, implicitly assume an isomorphism between cultural symbols and symptoms. From his field work in Sri Lanka, Obeyesekere describes the experiences of an ecstatic priestess who, through an emotional identification with, and the ritual manipulation of cultural symbolism, transformed and transcended the "archaic terrors of childhood" in a manner comparable to the "working through" of unconscious fixations in clinical psychoanalysis (pp. 11-12). If cultural symbolism can effect such resolutions, we need to augment the defense conception and devise a more inclusive theory. In other words, if cultural symbolism is, in itself, primarily symptomatic, how can it possibly contribute to the genuine resolution of symptoms?

The restriction of our understanding of cultural symbols to the defense metaphor invokes a subtle ethnocentric and rationalistic bias. Obeyesekere challenges Devereux's contention that ethnic symbolism may promote social "adjustment," but not "introspective awareness" or "curative insight" (p. 21). Devereux (1980, pp. 17-18) argues that a shaman provides a mode of treatment which, at most, "leads to a repatterning of defenses," "a changeover from idiosyncratic conflicts and defenses to culturally conventional conflicts and ritualized symptoms." Insights that constitute a "psychiatric cure" reside exclusively in the analytic session. Obeyesekere (1990, p. 21) argues that this position raises an "embarrassing" implication: "one has to assume that prior to the invention of psychoanalysis, all of us went our ways in the abysmal dark of ignorance." Clinical psychoanalysis, a product of a modern and demystified worldview, promotes a specific kind of reflexivity in the form of rational self-reflection. Cultural and religious symbols also permit curative reflexivity, but in a different *idiom*.

Obeyesekere's discussion of symptoms versus personal symbols offers a decisive methodological distinction that supplements the defense conception. Individual symptoms possess "little range of variation or capacity for continual displacements, or substitutive flexibility" and therefore tend to "exhibit near identity cross-culturally" (p. 14). Personal symbols, on the other hand, are the product of culturally transformed symptoms. Predicated on a publicly recognized symbol system made available by the cultural sphere, personal symbols create a space for active self-reflection. They replace the compulsive rigidity of symptoms whose limited meanings are by definition inaccessible to consciousness. Obeyesekere explains that although both of these terms presuppose motive and meaning, symptoms are dominated by motive rather than meaning. Their regressive character engenders very little reflexivity in that reflections habitually "hover" around infantile motivations (p. 12). Personal symbols, on the other hand, channel fixated motivations into a galaxy of cultural signifiers whose cognitive richness and intersubjective character afford a range of psychologically adaptive options not available to the private neuroses. Personal symbols provide greater degrees of remove from the archaic motivations of childhood. Unlike idiosyncratic symptoms, personal symbols require public consensus. Shared intentionality fosters meaningful communication with others and enhances self-reflection. The "mindlessness" of the limited and private repertoire of symptom-symbolism is replaced by the "mindful" play of polyvalent symbols whose existential meanings encourage therapeutic insight. Obeyesekere holds that the process of symbolic remove, the work of culture, is inherently tied to ideals and their potential for sublimation. Within these "higher levels of symbolization," "the Freudian notion of idealization and sublimation prevails; it is here that symbols prospectively and progressively move away from the sources of motivation to the realm of the sacred and the numinous" (p. 68).

Pfister's (1932) analysis of shamanic healing in a Navaho context demonstrates how ritual uses of religious symbolism resolve neurotic conflict and promote conscious insight in symbolic form. Certain kinds of religious healing constitute an "instinctive psychoanalysis" by an unwitting "[penetration] to the unconscious motivation of the psycho-neurotic disturbance" (p. 250). In stipulating that the unconscious "reacts more quickly to the language of symbols than the propositions of reason" (p. 251), Pfister brings instances of successful religious healing into line with play therapy where insight and the recession of symptoms relies on the use of figurative language.

Obeyesekere's and Pfister's views coincide with the way that Wesleyan spirituality systematically utilized religious symbolism in tandem with both alternate states of consciousness and meditative techniques. Methodists regarded the pursuit of holiness as a renewal of the whole person. Holiness presupposed significant personality transformation based on the long-term integration of religious and altruistic values. In keeping with scripture, Wesley regarded sin as a disease entity. He understood sanctification as a process of personal healing. Prior to conversion, the soul's alienation from God was not only a moral dilemma. It was also the root of strife, the source of discontent and suffering. Wesley knew well that many of his followers wrestled with despair. His rendering of the Gospel message spoke directly to this ailment. Methodists continually invoked God's benevolence and grace to overcome an array of symptomatic states that were all organized by a core depression and a sense of futility.

In Wesleyan spirituality, religious symbolism produced insights capable of healing psychic conflict and depression. Wesley's portrayal of a merciful God, along with his attempt to induce an immediate, perceptual sense of God's forgiving presence, generated a potentially "curative" insight: "I am worthy of love." This kind of insight differs from that initially intended by Freud, who emphasized the conscious acknowledgment of repressed instinctual strivings. To be sure, the realization that one is worthy of love departs from the traditional mode of psychoanalytic insights epitomizing the passions of infantile sexuality and the Oedipus complex. If anything, the former is an expression of self-esteem, which, in terms of Freud's structural model, relates to the superego. However, since ego psychologists stipulate that superego as well as id materials are subject to repression (Rangell, 1974), we may view the recovery of ideas pertaining to self-worth as a legitimate class of insight.

The three traumas of eighteenth century British childrearing—evangelical nurture, bereavement, and the early pre-occupation with death and damnation—led to disruptions and complications in emotional development. The splitting of self and object representations interfered with the consolidation of the positive superego such that the development of reliable values, non-conflicted ego-motivation and autonomy, self-esteem, regulation of drive and affect, intimacy and interpersonal relatedness were significantly compromised by aggression. Wesley's method of spiritual development and the techniques used to achieve sanctification led gradually to a reconciliation of psychic splits. The pursuit of sanctification required individuals to bring together separated currents of love and hostility in direct apprehension of the presence of God. The method mitigated conflict by strengthening the ego's ability to maintain an alliance with the positive superego and the ideals of conscience.

The process of Wesleyan sanctification parallels contemporary claims made by humanistic and transpersonal psychologists, who see a link between peak experiences and the transformation of values and personality structure. In the Methodist context, conversion, or "justification" is a unitive ecstasy characterized by the immediate sense of God's loving presence. Methodists used two meditation techniques side by side: the discursive "practice of the presence"; and "watching," a variety of introspective mindfulness. The paired meditations consolidate, as long-term structures, the moral insights of the conversion ecstasy. These techniques foster a potentially significant resolution of psychic conflict and promote long-term gains in both content and accessibility of the positive superego. For Wesley, God's love and mercy represent the most fundamental features of his moral attributes (Maddox, 1994, p. 53). Watching and praying promote a perceptible—that is, a cognitive and affective—apprehension of divine grace that gradually modifies previously depressing views of God as distant, critical and unforgiving. Wesley's definition of religion symbolically describes the ego's permanent acceptance by the ego-ideal.

> The knowledge of God in Christ Jesus; 'the life that is hid with Christ in God'; the being joined unto the Lord in one Spirit'; the having 'fellowship with the Father and the Son'; the 'walking in the light as God is in the light'; the being 'purified even as he is pure'—this the religion, the righteousness he thirsts after. Nor can he rest till he thus rests in God (Wesley, 1984-87, I: pp. 497).

We can compare the integrative potential of Methodist spirituality to Klein's notion of the depressive position (see: Hinshelwood, 1991, pp. 138-155). The genius of Wesley's technique lies in the *concurrent* acknowledgment and assimilation of one's aggression or "enmity" in the light of God's abiding forgiveness. Ideally, the simultaneous knowledge of hate and love, of sin and absolution, gradually decreases the fluctuating cycles of depression and elation. The sense of God's presence dramatically manifested in conversion, and later sustained by meditative practice, reduces the anxiety connected to aggression and allows for the systematic introspection of sin without the crippling fear of God's wrath (Lindstrom, 1946, p. 116).

Unitive ecstasies are key in this process. They afford new opportunities for constructive identifications with an idealized imago (Haartman, 1998b, pp. 216-219). While the ego maintains an identificatory alliance with the latter, action is no longer dominated by unconscious rage stirred by the demands of a negative superego. A new locus of psychological motivation forms. A dramatic boost in self-esteem accompanies one's conformity to recovered ideals. God's Pardon provides the courage to examine compulsive sinning, motivated in part by the need to act out or "rebel" against the internal bad object. These behaviors are gradually relinquished out of love. With the upsurge in self-esteem, they are replaced by aspirations reflecting the new value system. In Wesley's terms, this corresponds to receiving power from God to resist sin.

The practice of the presence and watchfulness reinforce two processes that lead to the durable integration of the initial peak experience. Recurring identification with God's presence consolidates unitive values, while introspection strengthens the awareness that sin no longer brings gratification or compels action. Wesley's method created the opportunity for achieving greater integration between the ego and the positive superego, due to the ego-syntonic nature of religious ideals. Through the ecstatic invocation of love, rage separates from these ideals, allowing the ego gradually to adopt them. Psychological integration, the amelioration of the split imago, is concurrent with the intensification of empathy, and the transformation of moral sensibility.

As a developmental ideal, sanctification corresponds to what Brierley (1947) terms the "integration of sanctity," a "total surrender of ego-direction to super-ego control" (p. 47). In a very significant sense, Maslow's notion of self-actualization illuminates Methodist sanctification. Both presuppose a more or less permanent alignment of the ego and the ego-ideal. On the other hand, the integration of sanctity does not envisage a "democratic harmonization of id, ego and super-ego systems" (p. 47). Although abstract, these formulations raise an important question as to the integrative limitations of Wesleyan spirituality. Similarly, Obeyesekere (1990, p. 62) in his discussion of the work of culture and the process of symbolic remove, hints at the problem of symbolic constraints, or the extent to which cultural, and, more particularly, religious discourses are able to promote the working through of archaic motivations.

A truly thorough analysis of the limitations of early Methodism, as measured from the perspective of psychic integration, would require another study. Yet we may usefully conclude with a brief delineation of the problem as it bears on avenues of future research. As I see it, the integrative constraints of Wesleyan holiness were rooted in a historical paradox: the attempt to overcome the scars of evangelical nurture continued to bear the unmistakable signature of the very regime that inflicted these wounds. Because Wesley and his followers could not erase their own psychic histories, it is too easy to analyze Methodist spirituality in terms of repetitions and compromise formations, an approach that obscures new developmental achievements, as well as the resolution of conflict. On the other hand, no form of cultural practice, be it spiritual healing or clinical psychoanalysis, effects a wholesale rupture from the past. A clean slate is both impossible and meaningless. The formative events of early life are indelibly laid down in the unconscious, shaping our identity, character, and core beliefs. However, in tandem with new experiences, formative events provide the raw materials for psychic change and growth. Integration involves a more inclusive reconfiguration of past experiences, a transformation of internal representations and their emotional meanings, leading to a richer subjectivity and the undoing of rigid defenses.

In one sense, the whole notion of sanctification as the *perfection* of holiness continued to perpetuate the ethos of authoritarian childrearing. It is true that Wesley advocated a qualified definition of perfection, one that mercifully tolerated the "defects inseparable from life on earth," that is, the imperfections of knowledge and the shortcomings of bodily infirmities (Lindstrom, 1946, p. 145). Even so, the doctrine preserved the essential traces of infancy by enshrining a set of moral standards both exacting and difficult to achieve. In this sense, the lofty ideals internalized in the context of evangelical nurture remained essentially the same. The crucial difference is that Wesley resuscitated a primal love for the good parent, one that had been previously compromised by disappointment, rage and trauma. The symbolic re-emergence of this attachment, now manifesting as a good conscience, meant that one could eagerly and voluntarily embrace one's ideals with a minimum of conflict. However, because the trace of the bad parent remained inscribed within the moral objectives of sanctification, anger and depression punctuated every step of the process. Moreover, the majority of published narratives and extracts that entered into the public domain attested to the benefits and successes of Methodist holiness. Like any other organization geared towards consolidating power and attracting greater membership, Methodism was not particularly interested in disseminating the accounts of those who, despite their efforts, continually failed to thrive and remained unenriched by grace. For this reason, we cannot adequately assess the number of individuals who failed to surmount their depression, who remained untouched and unredeemed by the spirit, or those who, after tasting the fruits of conversion, backslid permanently.

If we conceptualize early Methodist spirituality as a metaphoric system that facilitated insight in symbolic form, we may say that the persistence of the bad object limited its therapeutic potential. Without question, Wesley's theology did much to soothe terrifying depictions of God the father. He adamantly opposed the Calvinist doctrine of predestination, replacing the inscrutable arbitrariness of divine judgment with images of God's unconditional mercy and his willingness to save all who chose to accept Christ. The rejuvenating power of the witness radically diminished the paralyzing effects of a troubled conscience. In the end, however, the fear of God was never wholly exorcised. The unconditionality of his grace was guaranteed only as long as one continued to abide by his word. Methodists understood that a significant decline in personal holiness would drive them back into the realm of the angry

God where they would once again grapple with the his ominous vengeance. Wesleyan spirituality went a long way in healing the split imago, but the split never *fully* disappeared. Although Wesley eventually modified the tactics of his early sermons in which he graphically portrayed the sufferings of the damned, his later works attest to the fact that he did not completely abandon this approach (see: 1984-1987, III: pp. 31-44). What is more, some of Wesley's circuit preachers clearly garnered reputations as hell fire preachers (*Arminian Magazine*, 1780, pp. 98, 309, 479). Not surprisingly, the periods of darkness and heaviness so frequently described in the autobiographical narratives revolved around the problem of doubt and the stubborn dread of damnation.

Besides fear, we also see evidence of identification with the aggressor, a defense that contradicts the otherwise dominant sensibilities of Christian Holiness. For example, Rack (1980) points out that "all Methodists...believed in 'particular providences'—the manifestation of the direct action of God through events" that, among other things, "wrought judgments on evil doers and scoffers" (p. 432). The sadism in these celebrated instances of providence is undisguised.

> As a warning to drunkards, for example, the *Magazine* recorded how a man was drunk on the Sabbath as usual and died in his sleep. A blasphemous gardener dreamt that he met two devils and beat one of them. On waking he joined his drinking companions and later went to his hot-house. Here he was found to be on fire with his nose burnt off, his lips preserved but his blasphemous tongue burnt out of his mouth (p. 432).

Wesley himself imagined that divine intervention ruthlessly disposed of several of his detractors.

> During the course of Wesley's fifty-one years as a traveling evangelist, some of his local opposers were removed out of his way, as he thought, providentially. One "dropped down and spoke no more"; another hanged himself in "his own necessary house"; two in the same parish were "snatched away by a fever" (Abelove, 1990, p. 11).

Finally, we see the persistence of the bad object and splitting in the fact that Methodists, according to Rack (1989), "inhabited a world which had strong elements of dualism" (p. 434).

> The devil and his demons afflicted them during their conversion struggles, and their visions and visitations seemed vividly to symbolize the struggle for the soul between good and evil powers. And

indeed Wesley himself believed in good and evil angels as agents of God and the devil (p. 434).

Abelove (1990) argues that in spite of its evangelical concerns, Methodists' relationship with non-Methodists remained dualistic. A pronounced ingroup-outgroup mentality held sway. Wesley's followers had no difficulty in observing his rule "that they love each other and help each other in business" (p. 108). As Wesley traveled throughout the British countryside, he consistently noted the ties of affection that so tenaciously bound his followers to each other. He described them as having "one heart and one mind." They were "lovingly and closely knit together," "united" like a "family of love" (quoted in Abelove, 1990, p. 45). But they did not so easily extend the ethic of mutual reciprocity to outsiders. Abelove claims that Methodists' "generosity seldom resulted in anything more than money or spiritual advice." "So strong was their sense of union with one another that no outsiders were really tolerable to them, unless of course the outsiders wanted to join" (p. 108). The following account of a Sheffield man is, according to Abelove, a "typical" representation "of how the reaction to an outsider would go" (p. 108).

> He says that once when "a strange family" had moved into the neighborhood, he went to call on them. He told them, "after some introductory remarks," that he was a Methodist, that he "feared God," and "had lately begun to inquire the way to heaven." He added that he and his family wished them well and would be glad to do them any feasible "office of kindness," but on one condition only: that they turned out to be "like-minded with reference to the salvation of their souls." If they were not, then, he could have no "familiarity or acquaintance with them," because "the friendship of the world was enmity against God" (pp. 108-109).

Whether or not this example truly characterized the attitude of most Methodists, it certainly illustrates the realistic imperfections of empathy as compared to the scriptural ideal of universal love. In the end, Wesley and his flock were all too human. The legacy of the past continued to inhere in the present. Yet, whatever theoretic criteria we use to characterize psychic integration—the achievement of self-awareness and insight, the resolution of conflict, the movement into the depressive position, and the strengthening of the ego—we must remember that these indices are never absolute. They exist on a spectrum and can only be measured by degrees. Moreover, we may reasonably suggest that Wesley's technique of watching and praying might foster an even greater degree of integration in the context of a more liberal, modern theology—one less encumbered by unresolved splitting. Be that as it may, if Wesley's "method" promoted what Brierley calls the "integration of sanctity," the therapeutic gains derived from the relationship between the ego and the positive superego represented a significant developmental achievement, one that, despite its limitations, attests to the crucial role of ideals and conscience in mental life.

Bibliography

Abelove, Henry. (1990). *The Evangelist of Desire: John Wesley and the Methodists*. Stanford: Stanford University Press.

Aberbach, David. (1987). Grief and mysticism. *International Review of Psychoanalysis*, 14, 509-526.

Albin, Thomas R. (1985). An empirical study of early Methodist spirituality. In *Wesleyan Theology Today: A Bicentennial Theological Consultation*, Theodore Runyan (Ed.). Nashville: Kingswood Books.

Alexander, Donald L. (Ed.). (1989). *Christian Spirituality: Five Views of Sanctification*. Downers Grove: Intervarsity Press.

Arbman, Ernst. (1963-1968). *Ecstasy or Religious Trance: In the Experience of the Ecstatics and from the Scientific Point of View*, vols. 1 & 2. Stockholm: Svenska Bokforlaget.

Arminian Magazine. (1778 ff.). John Wesley (Ed.). London: J. Fry and Co.

Assagioli, Roberto. (1990). *Psychosynthesis: A Manual of Principals and Techniques*. Mandala: London.

Ayling, Stanley. (1980). *John Wesley*. Nashville: Abingdon Press.

Bacal, Howard A. & Newman, Kenneth, M. (1990). *Theories of Object Relations: Bridges to Self Psychology*. New York: Columbia University Press.

Batson, C. Daniel & Ventis, W. Larry. (1982). *The Religious Experience: A Social-Psychological Perspective*. New York & Oxford: Oxford University Press.

Bayne-Powell, Rosamond. (1939). *The English Child in the Eighteenth Century*. London: John Murray.

Benson, Peter L. & Spilka, Bernard, P. (1977). God image as a function of self-esteem and locus of control. In *Current Perspectives in the Psychology of Religion*, H. Newton Malony (Ed.). Grand Rapids: William B. Eerdmans Publishing Company.

Bergmann Martin S. (1971). Psychoanalytic observations on the capacity to love. In *Separation-Individuation: Essays in Honor of Margaret S. Mahler*, John B. McDevitt & Calvin F. Settlage (Eds.). New York: International Universities Press.

Bexton, W. H., Heron, W., & Scott, T. H. (1954). Effects of decreased variation in the sensory environment. *Canadian Journal of Psychology*. 8, 70-76.

Blanck, Gertrude & Blanck, Rubin. (1979). *Ego Psychology II: Psychoanalytic Developmental Psychology*. New York: Columbia University Press.

Blatt, Sidney J., Auerbach, John S., & Levy, Kenneth, N. (1997). Mental representations in personality development, psychopathology, and the therapeutic process. *Review of General Psychology*, 1, 351-374.

Bowlby, John. (1960). Grief and mourning in infancy and early childhood. *Psychoanalytic Study of the Child*, 15, 3-39.

_____. (1980). *Attachment and Loss, Vol. 3: Loss, Sadness and Depression*. London: Hogarth Press.

_____. (1988). *A Secure Base: Parent-Child Attachment and Healthy Human Development*. New York: Basic Books.

Bowmer, John C. (1951). *The Sacrament of the Lord's Supper in Early Methodism*. London: Dacre Press.

Breen, Hal J. (1986). A Psychoanalytic approach to ethics. *Journal of the American Academy of Psychoanalysis,* 14, 255-275.
Brenner, Charles. (1982). *The Mind in Conflict.* Madison: International Universities Press.
Brierley, Marjorie. (1951). *Trends in Psycho-Analysis.* London: Hogarth Press.
Buber, Martin. (1958). *I and Thou.* New York: Charles Scribner's Sons.
_____. (1985). *Ecstatic Confessions.* Trans. Esther Cameron. San Francisco: Harper & Row.
Byman, Seymour. (1978). Child raising and melancholia in Tudor England. *Journal of Psychohistory,* 6, 67-92.
Carter, John D. (1981). Personality and Christian maturity: A process congruity model. In *Psychology and Christianity: Integrative Readings,* J. Roland Fleck & John C. Carter (Eds.). Nashville: Abingdon Press.
Carvosso, William. (1835). *The Efficacy of Faith in the Atonement of Christ: Exemplified in a Memoir of Mr. William Carvosso.* London: Wesleyan-Methodist Book-Room.
Cell, George C. (1935). *The Rediscovery of John Wesley.* New York: Holt Rinehart.
Chadwick, Owen. (1975). Indifference and morality. In *Christian Spirituality: Essays in Honor of Gordon Rupp,* Peter Brooks (Ed.). London: SCM Press Ltd.
Chasseguet-Smirgel, Janine. (1985). *The Ego Ideal: A Psychoanalytic Essay on the Malady of the Ideal.* New York: W. W. Norton & Company.
Church, Leslie F. (1948). *The Early Methodist People.* London: Epworth University Press.
Clapper, Gregory S. (1989). *John Wesley on Religious Affections: His Views on Experience and Emotion and Their Role in the Christian Life and Theology.* Metuchen: Scarecrow Press.
Cleary, Tom S. & Shapiro, Sam I. (1995). The plateau experience and the post-mortem life. *Journal of Transpersonal Psychology,* 27, 1-21.
Cohen, Charles, L. (1986). *God's Caress: The Psychology of Puritan Religious Experience.* New York: Oxford University Press.
Cohen, Eric (1981). Holiness and health. In *Psychology and Christianity: Integrative Readings,* J. Roland Fleck & John C. Carter (Eds.). Nashville: Abingdon Press.
Cohen, J. M. & Phipps, J.F. (1992). *The Common Experience: Signposts on the Path to Enlightenment.* Wheaton: Quest Books.
Committee on Psychiatry and Religion [Furst, Sidney S., Leavy, Stanley A., Lewis, Richard C., Lubin, Albert J., Ostow, Mortimer & Zales, Michael R.]. (1976). *Mysticism: Spiritual Quest or Psychic Disorder?* Group for the Advancement of Psychiatry, Volume IX, Publication No. 97, November 1976.
Conn, Walter E. (1986). Adult conversions. *Pastoral Psychology,* 34, 225-236.
Corderoy, Edward. (1873). *Father Reeves the Methodist Class Leader: A Brief Account of Mr. William Reeves, Thirty-Four Years a Class Leader in the Wesleyan Methodist Society, Lambeth.* London: Wesleyan Conference Office.

Davidoff, Leonore & Hall, Catherine. (1987). *Family Fortunes: Men and Women of the English Working Class, 1780-1850*. Chicago: University of Chicago Press.

Davies, Rupert E. (1963). *Methodism*. London: Epworth Press.

Deikman, Arthur J. (1967). The overestimation of the mystical experience. In *Do Psychedelics Have Religious Implications?*, D.H. Salman & R. H. Prince (Eds.). Montreal: Bucke Memorial Society.

Delameau, Jean. (1990). *Sin and Fear: Re-Emergence of a Western Guilt Culture 13th-18th Centuries*. New York: St. Martin's Press.

Delaney, John J. (1977). Introduction. In Brother Lawrence of the Resurrection, *The Practice of the Presence of God*, John J. Delaney (Trans.), 13-30. Garden City, NY: Image Books-Doubleday & Company.

Devereux, George. (1980). *Basic Problems of Ethnopsychiatry*. Chicago: University of Chicago Press.

Dieter, Melvin E., Hoekema, Anthony, A., Horton, Stanley M., McQuilkin, J. Robertson, & Walvoord, John F. (1987). *Five Views on Sanctification*. Grand Rapids: Acadamie Books.

Dimond, Sydney G. (1926). *ThePsychology of the Methodist Revival: An Empirical and Descriptive Study*. London: Oxford University Press.

Dryer, Frederick. (1983). Faith and experience in the thought of John Wesley. *American Historical Review*, 88, 12-30.

Dupré, Louis. (1989). Jansenism and Quietism. In *Christian Spirituality: Post-Reformation and Modern*, Louis Dupré & Don E. Saliers (Eds.). London: SCM Press.

Earle, Peter. (1989). *The Making of the English Middle Class: Business, Society and Family Life in London: 1660-1773*. Los Angeles: University of California Press.

Edwards, Tilden. (1995). *Living in the Presence: Spiritual Exercises to Open Our Lives to the Awareness of God*. San Francisco: Harper Collins.

Eigen, Michael. (1993). *The Electrified Tightrope*, Adam Phillips (Ed.). New Jersey: Jason Aronson.

Ellwood, Robert S. (1980). *Mysticism and Religion*. New Jersey: Prentice-Hall.

Engler, Jack. (1984). Therapeutic aims in psychotherapy and meditation: Developmental stages in the representation of self. *Journal of Transpersonal Psychology*, 16, 25-61.

Epstein, Mark. (1986). Meditative transformations of narcissism. *Journal of Transpersonal Psychology*, 18, 143-158.

_____. (1989). Forms of emptiness: Psychodynamic, meditative, and clinical perspectives. *Journal of Transpersonal Psychology*, 21, 61-67.

Faber, Mel D. (1996). *New Age Thinking: A Psychoanalytic Critique*. Ottawa: University of Ottawa Press.

Fauteux, Kevin. (1994). *The Recovery of Self: Regression and Redemption in Religious Experience*. New York: Paulist Press.

Fenelon, Franz. (1822). *Part of the Spiritual Works of the Celebrated Francis Fenelon*, vol. I. Dublin: C. Bentham.

Fraser, Robert M. (1988). *Strains in the Understanding of Christian Perfection in Early British Methodism.* Unpublished doctoral dissertation, Vanderbilt University.
Freeman, Daniel M. A. (1981). Mythological portrayal of developmental processes and major intrapsychic restructuralizations. *Psychoanalytic Study of Society,* 9, 326-340.
Freud, Sigmund. (1953-1974). *Standard Edition of the Complete Psychological Works of Sigmund Freud,* 24 vols, trans. & ed. James Strachey. London: Hogarth & New York: Macmillan.
_____. (1900). The interpretation of dreams. *Standard Edition,* 4-5.
_____. (1913). Totem and taboo. *Standard Edition,* 13.
_____. (1914). On narcissism: An introduction. *Standard Edition,* 14.
_____. (1923). Two encyclopedia articles. *Standard Edition,* 18.
_____. (1933). New introductory lectures on psychoanalysis. *Standard Edition,* 21.
Frick, Willard B. (1983). The symbolic growth experience. *Journal of Humanistic Psychology,* 23, 108-125.
_____. (1987). The symbolic growth experience: Paradigm for a humanistic-existential learning theory. *Journal of Humanistic Psychology,* 27, 406-423.
_____. (1990). The symbolic growth experience: A chronicle of heuristic inquiry and a quest for synthesis. *Journal of Humanistic Psychology,* 30, 64-80.
Furer, Manuel. (1967). Some developmental aspects of the superego. *International Journal of Psychoanalysis,* 48, 277-280.
Giovacchini, Peter, L. (1987). *A Narrative Textbook of Psychoanalysis.* Northvale: Jason Aronson.
Goldsmith, Joel S. (1991). *Practice of the Presence: The Inspirational Guide to Regaining Meaning and a Sense of Purpose in Your Life.* San Francisco: HarperCollins Publishers.
Green, V. H. H. (1961). *The Young Mr. Wesley: A Study of John Wesley and Oxford.* Oxford: London E. Arnold.
Greven, Philip. (1977). *The Protestant Temperament: Patterns of Childrearing, Religious Experience and the Self in Early America.* New York: Alfred A. Knopf.
_____. (1991). *Spare the Child: The Religious Roots of Punishment and the Psychological Impact of Physical Abuse.* New York: Knopf.
Grof, Christina & Grof, Stanislav. (1990). *The Stormy Search for the Self.* Los Angeles: Jeremy Tarcher/Perigee.
Grof, Stanislav. (1976). *Realms of the Human Unconscious: Observations from LSD Research.* New York: E.P. Dutton and Co.
Grossman, Lee. (1993). The significance of religious themes and fantasies during psychoanalysis. *Journal of the American Psychoanalytic Association,* 41, 755-764.
Gunter, W. S. (1989). *The Limits of 'Love Divine'.* Nashville: Kingswood Books.
Haartman, Keith. (1998). On the role of the positive superego in religious uses of alternate states. *International Journal for the Psychology of Religion,* 8, 205-220.

_____. (2001) On unitive distortions: A contribution towards a differential assessment of religious ecstasy. *Psychoanalytic Review*, 88, 811-836.
Harrison, Irving B. (1986). On "merging" and the fantasy of merging. *Psychoanalytic Study of the Child,* 41, 155-170.
Hartmann, Heinz & Loewenstein, Rudolph M. (1962). Notes on the superego. *Psychoanalytic Study of the Child*, 17, 42-81.
Hartocollis, Peter. (1974). Mysticism and violence: The case of Nikos Kazantzakis. *International Journal of Psychoanalysis*, 55, 205-210.
_____. (1976). Aggression and mysticism. *Contemporary Psychoanalysis*, 12, 214-226.
Harvey, E. Ruth. (1975). *Inward Wits: Psychological Theory in the Middle Ages and the Renaissance.* London: Warburg Institute-University of London.
Hauerwas, Stanley. (1985). Characterizing perfection: Second thoughts on character and sanctification. In *Wesleyan Theology Today: A Bicentennial Theological Consultation,* Theodore Runyon (Ed.). Nashville: Kingswood Books.
Heitzenrater, Richard P. (1989). *Mirror and Memory: Reflections on Early Methodism.* Nashville: Kingswood Books/Abingdon Press.
_____. (1995). *Wesley and the People Called Methodists.* Nashville: Abingdon Press.
Hempton, David. (1996). *The Religion of the People: Methodism and Popular Religion 1750-1900.* New York: Routledge.
Heron, Woodburn, Doane, B. D., & Scott, T. H. (1956). Visual disturbances after prolonged perceptual isolation. *Canadian Journal of Psychology*, 10, 13-18.
Hildebrant, Franz. (1951). *From Luther to Wesley.* London: Lutterworth Press.
Hinshelwood, R. D. (1991). *A Dictionary of Kleinian Thought.* London: Free Association Books.
Holland, Bernard. (1973-74). "A species of madness": The effect of John Wesley's early preaching. *Proceedings of the Wesley Historical Society*, 39, 77-85.
Hollenback, Jess Byron. (1996). *Mysticism: Experience, Response and Empowerment.* University Park: The Pennsylvania State University Press.
Hood, Ralph W. (1995). The facilitation of religious experience. In *Handbook of Religious Experience*, Ralph W. Hood (Ed.). Birmingham: Religious Education Press.
Horton, Paul C. (1973). The mystical experience as a suicide preventative. *American Journal of Psychiatry*, 130, 294-296.
_____. (1974). The mystical experience: Substance of an illusion. *Journal of the American Psychoanalytic Association*, 22, 364-380.
Ignatius of Loyola, St. (1992). *The Spiritual Practices of Saint Ignatius.* Chicago: Loyola University Press.
Jacobson, Edith. (1964). *The Self and the Object World.* New York: International Universities Press.
James, William. (1985). *The Varieties of Religious Experience.* Toronto: Penguin Books.
Josephs, L. (1989). Self psychology and the analysis of the superego. *Psychoanalytic Psychology*, 6, 73-86.
Kakar, Sudhir. (1991). *The Analyst and the Mystic: Psychoanalytic Reflections on Religion and Mysticism.* Chicago: University of Chicago Press.

Kernberg, Otto. (1966). Structural derivatives of object relations. *International Journal of Psychoanalysis,* 47, 236-253.
_____. (1976). *Object Relations and Clinical Psychoanalysis.* New York: Jason Aronson.
King, John O. (1983). *The Iron of Melancholy: Structures of Spiritual Conversion in America from the Puritan Conscience to Victorian Neurosis.* Connecticut: Wesleyan University Press.
Kirkpatrick, Lee A. (1995). Attachment theory and religious experience. In *Handbook of Religious Experience,* Ralph W. Hood (Ed.). Birmingham: Religious Education Press.
Klauber, John. (1974). Notes on the psychical roots of religion with particular reference to the development of Western Christianity. *International Journal of Psychoanalysis*, 55, 249-259.
Klein, Melanie. (1988). *Love, Guilt and Reparation.* London: Virago Press.
Kohut, Heinz. (1977). *The Analysis of the Self: A Systematic Approach to the Psychoanalytic Treatment of Narcissistic Personality Disorders.* New York: International Universities Press.
Knox, Ronald A. (1950). *Enthusiasm: A Chapter in the History of Religion.* New York: Oxford University Press.
Kris, Ernst. (1952). *Psychoanalytic Explorations in Art.* New York: International Universities Press.
Krippner, Stanley (1972). On plateau experience. *Journal of Transpersonal Psychology,* 2, 107-120.
Kurland, Albert A., Grof, Stanislav, Pahnke, Walter, N., & Goodman, Louis E. (1973). Psychedelic drug assisted psychotherapy in patients with terminal cancer. In *Psychopharmacologic Agents for the Terminally Ill and Bereaved,* Ivan Goldberg, Sidney Malitz, & Austin Kutscher (Eds.). New York: Columbia University Press.
Lakoff, George & Johnson, Mark. (1980). *Metaphors We Live By.* Chicago: University of Chicago Press.
Laplanche, J. & Pontalis, J. B. (1988). *The Language of Psychoanalysis.* London: Karnac Books.
Laski, Marghanita. (1961). *Ecstasy in Secular and Religious Experience.* Los Angeles: Jeremy P. Tarcher.
Lawrence of the Resurrection, Brother. (1977). *The Practice of the Presence of God.*, John J. Delaney (Trans.). Garden City, NY: Image Books-Doubleday & Company.
Lederer, Wolfgang. (1964). *Dragons, Delinquents, and Destiny: An Essay on Positive Superego Functions.* New York: International Universities Press.
Lee, R. R. & Martin, J. C. (1991). *Psychotherapy After Kohut: A Textbook of Self Psychology.* Hillside: The Analytic Press.
Lee, Umphrey. (1931). *The Historical Backgrounds of Early Methodist Enthusiasm.* New York: Columbia University Press.
_____. (1936). *John Wesley and Modern Religion.* Nashville: Cokesbury Press.
Lewin, Bertram. (1951). *The Psychoanalysis of Elation.* London: The Hogarth Press.

Lichtenberg, Joseph B. (1989). *Psychoanalysis and Motivation.* Hillsdale: Analytic Press.
Lilly, John. (1956). Mental effects of reduction of ordinary levels of physical stimuli on intact, healthy persons. *Psychiatric Research Reports,* 5, 1-9.
Lindstrom, Harald. (1946). *Wesley and Sanctification: A Study in the Doctrine of Salvation.* London: Epworth.
Linn, Louis & Schwartz, Leo. (1958). *Psychiatry and Religious Experience.* New York: Random House.
Locke, John. (1964). *Some Thoughts Concerning Education.* New York: Barron's.
Lorence, Bogna W. (1974). Parents and children in eighteenth-century Europe. *History of Childhood Quarterly: The Journal of Psychohistory,* 2, 12-30.
Lovelace, Richard C. (1989). Puritan spirituality: The search for a rightly reformed church. In *Christian Spirituality: Post-Reformation and Modern,* Louis Dupré & Don E. Saliers (Eds.). New York: SCM Press.
Lovin, Robin W. (1985). The physics of true virtue. In *Wesleyan Theology Today: A Bicentennial Theological Contribution.*, Theodore Runyon (Ed.). Nashville: Kingswood Books.
Maas, Robin. (1990). Practicing the presence of God: Recollection in the Carmelite tradition. In *Spiritual Traditions for the Contemporary Church*, Robin Maas & Gabriel O'Donnell (Eds.). Nashville: Abingdon Press.
_____. (1990). Wesleyan spirituality. In *Spiritual Traditions for the Contemporary Church.*, Robin Maas & Gabriel O'Donnell (Eds.). Nashville: Abingdon Press.
MacNutt, Francis. (1984). *Overcome by the Spirit.* Old Tappan: Chosen Books.
Maddox, Randy L. (1994). *Responsible Grace: John Wesley's Practical Theology.* Nashville: Kingswood Books.
Mahler, Margaret S., Pine, Fred, & Bergman, Anni. (1975). *The Psychological Birth of the Human Infant: Symbiosis and Individuation.* New York: Basic Books.
Maslow, Abraham. (1968). *Toward a Psychology of Being*, Second Ed. Toronto: Van Nostrand Reinhold.
_____. (1970). *Religions, Values and Peak Experiences.* New York: Viking Press.
_____. (1971). *The Farther Reaches of Human Nature.* New York: Viking Press.
Mathews, Rex D. (1985). "With the eyes of faith": Spiritual experience and the knowledge of God in the theology. In *Wesleyan Theology Today: A Bicentennial Theological Consultation,* Theodore Bunyan (Ed.). Nashville: Kingswood Books.
Mavromatis, Andreas. (1987). *Hypnagogia: The Unique State of Consciousness Between Wakefulness and Sleep.* New York: Routledge.
McDevitt, J.B. & Mahler, M. S. (1989). Object constancy, individuality and internalization. In *The Course of Life, Vol. II: Early Childhood,* S. I. Greenspan & G.H. Pollock (Eds.). Madison: International Universities Press.
Meissner, W. W. (1984). *Psychoanalysis and Religious Experience.* New Haven: Yale University Press.
Menninger, Karl. (1938). *Man Against Himself.* New York: Harvest Books.
Merkur, Dan. (1989a). The visionary practices of Jewish apocalyptists. *Psychoanalytic Study of Society,* 14, 119-148.

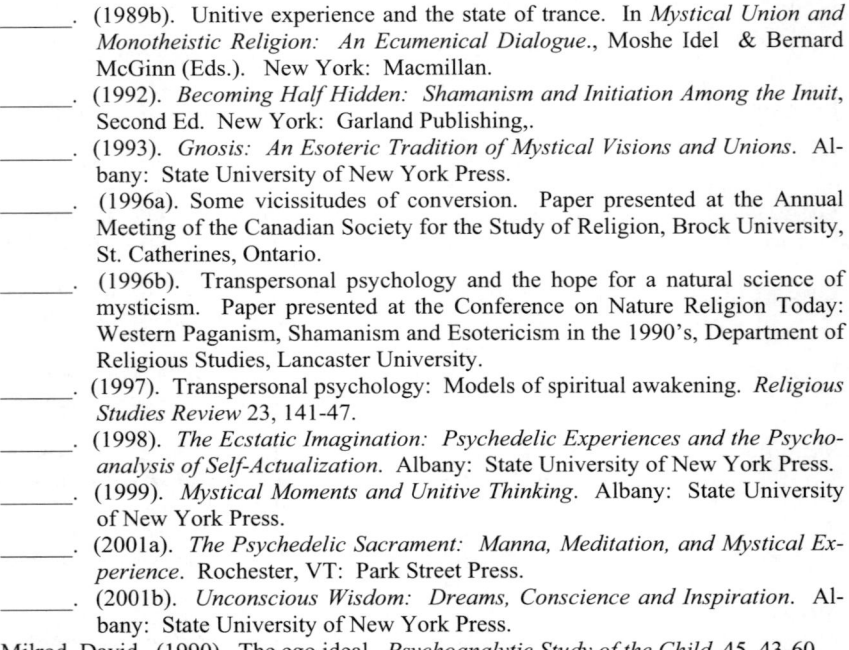

_____. (1989b). Unitive experience and the state of trance. In *Mystical Union and Monotheistic Religion: An Ecumenical Dialogue.*, Moshe Idel & Bernard McGinn (Eds.). New York: Macmillan.
_____. (1992). *Becoming Half Hidden: Shamanism and Initiation Among the Inuit*, Second Ed. New York: Garland Publishing,.
_____. (1993). *Gnosis: An Esoteric Tradition of Mystical Visions and Unions.* Albany: State University of New York Press.
_____. (1996a). Some vicissitudes of conversion. Paper presented at the Annual Meeting of the Canadian Society for the Study of Religion, Brock University, St. Catherines, Ontario.
_____. (1996b). Transpersonal psychology and the hope for a natural science of mysticism. Paper presented at the Conference on Nature Religion Today: Western Paganism, Shamanism and Esotericism in the 1990's, Department of Religious Studies, Lancaster University.
_____. (1997). Transpersonal psychology: Models of spiritual awakening. *Religious Studies Review* 23, 141-47.
_____. (1998). *The Ecstatic Imagination: Psychedelic Experiences and the Psychoanalysis of Self-Actualization.* Albany: State University of New York Press.
_____. (1999). *Mystical Moments and Unitive Thinking.* Albany: State University of New York Press.
_____. (2001a). *The Psychedelic Sacrament: Manna, Meditation, and Mystical Experience.* Rochester, VT: Park Street Press.
_____. (2001b). *Unconscious Wisdom: Dreams, Conscience and Inspiration.* Albany: State University of New York Press.
Milrod, David. (1990). The ego ideal. *Psychoanalytic Study of the Child,* 45, 43-60.
Modell, Arnold H. (1968). *Object Love and Reality: An Introduction to a Psychoanalytic Theory of Object Relations.* New York: International Universities Press.
Molinos, Miguel. (1883). *Golden Thoughts from The Spiritual Guide of Miguel Molinos, the Quietest.* Glasgow: David Bryce and Son.
Moller, Herbert. (1962). Affective mysticism in Western civilization. *Psychoanalytic Review,* 52, 258-274.
Monk, Robert C. (1966). *John Wesley: His Puritan Heritage.* New York: Abingdon Press.
Moore, Robert L. (1974). Justification without joy: Psychohistorical reflections on John Wesley's childhood and conversion. *History of Childhood Quarterly: The Journal of Psychohistory,* 2, 31-52.
Morentz, Paul E. (1987). Conversion: A way of resolving conflict. *Pastoral Psychology,* 35, 254-262.
Mounteer, Carl. (1981). Guilt, martyrdom and monasticism. *Journal of Psychohistory,* 9, 145-171.
Nelson, John. (1842). *The Journal of John Nelson, Preacher of the Gospel.* London: John Mason.
Newton, John A. (1968). *Susanna Wesley and the Puritan Tradition in Methodism.* London: Epworth Press.

Nixon, Laurence. (1995). Personal loss and emotional support in the lives of four Hindu mystics. Paper presented at the Annual Conference of the South Asia Council of the Canadian Asian Studies Association, Montreal, Quebec.

———. (1996a). The mystical quest as a transformed search for a lost caregiver: The case of Paramahansa Yoganda. Paper presented at the American Academy of Religion Upper Midwest Regional Meeting, St. Paul, Minnesota.

———. (1996b). The origins of creativity and mysticism: A comparative study of Charles Darwin and Therese of Lisieux. *Advanced Development*, 7, 81-100.

Nouwen, Henri J. M. (1977) Foreword. In Brother Lawrence of the Resurrection., *The Practice of the Presence of God.*, John J. Delaney (Trans.). Garden City, NY: Image Books-Doubleday & Company.

Oakland, James A. (1981). Self-actualization and sanctification. In *Psychology and Christianity: Integrative Readings*, J. Roland Fleck & John D. Carter (Eds.). Nashville: Abingdon Press.

Obeyesekere, Gananath. (1990). *The Work of Culture: Symbolic Transformation in Psychoanalysis and Anthropology*. Chicago: University of Chicago Press.

Ortony, Andrew. (Ed.). (1993). *Metaphor and Thought*, Second Ed. Cambridge: University Press.

Ostow, Mortimer. (1975). Psychological defense against depression. In *Depression and Human Existence*, E. James Anthony & Therese Benedek (Eds.). Boston: Little, Brown and Company.

Outler, Albert C. (Ed.). (1964). *John Wesley*. New York: Oxford University Press.

———. (1981). Preface. In John and Charles Wesley, *Selected Writings and Hymns*, Frank Whaling (Ed.). Toronto: Paulist Press.

———. (1984a). An introductory comment on "The way to the kingdom." In *Sermons*. Albert Outler (Ed.). Volume 1 of *The Bicentennial Works of John Wesle*, 217. Nashville: Abingdon Press.

———. (1984b). An introductory comment on "The righteousness of faith." In *Sermons*. Albert Outler (Ed.). Volume 1 of *The Bicentennial Works of John Wesley*, 200-202. Nashville: Abingdon Press.

———. (1984c). An introductory comment on "The spirit and bondage of adoption." In *Sermons*. Albert Outler (Ed.). Volume 1 of *The Bicentennial Works of John Wesley*, 248. Nashville: Abingdon Press.

———. (1987). An introductory comment on "On faith." In *Sermons*. Albert Outler (Ed.). Volume 4 of *The Bicentennial Works of John Wesley*, 187-188. Nashville: Abingdon Press.

Pahnke, Walter N. (1969). The psychedelic mystical experience in the human encounter with death. *Harvard Theological Review*. 62, 3-21.

Pahnke, Walter N., Kurland, Albert A., Goodman, Louis E., & Richards, William A. (1969). LSD-assisted psychotherapy with terminal cancer patients. *Current Psychiatric Therapies*, 9, 144-152.

Pfister, Oskar. (1932). Instinctive psychoanalysis among the Navahos. *Journal of Nervous and Mental Diseases*, 76, 234-254.

Pinchbeck, Ivy & Hewitt, Margaret. (1969). *Children in English Society: From Tudor Times to the Eighteenth Century*. Toronto: University of Toronto Press.

———. (1973). *Children in English Society: From the Eighteenth Century to the Children Act 1948*. Toronto: University of Toronto Press.

Pine, Fred. (1990). *Drive, Ego, Object and Self: A Synthesis for Clinical Work.* New York: Basic Books.
Plumb, J. H. (1975). *The First Four Georges.* Toronto: Hamlyn Press.
Pollack, Linda A. (1983). *Forgotten Children: Parent-Child Relations from 1500-1900.* Cambridge: Cambridge University Press.
_____. (1987). *A Lasting Relationship: Parents and Children Over Three Centuries.* London: Fourth Estate.
Ponticus, Evagrius. (1981). *The Praktikos: Chapters on Prayer.* Kalamazoo: Cistercian Publications.
Prince, Morton. (1906). The psychology of sudden religious conversion. *Journal of Abnormal Psychology,* 1, 42-54.
Prince, Raymond & Savage, Charles. (1965). Mystical states and the concept of regression. In Raymond Prince (Ed.). *Personality Change and Religious Experience.* R. M. Bucke Memorial Society for the Study of Religious Experience, Proceedings of the First Annual Conference, January 15-16, 1965. Montreal. Reprinted *Psychedelic Review* 8 (1966), 59-81.
Pruyser, Paul W. (1974). *Between Belief and Unbelief.* New York: Harper and Row.
Rack, Henry D. (1987). Early Methodist visions of the trinity. *Proceedings of the Wesley Historical Society,* 46, 38-44, 57-69.
_____. (1989). *Reasonable Enthusiast: John Wesley and the Rise of Methodism.* London: Epworth Press.
Rahner, Karl. (1979). The doctrine of the "spiritual senses" in the Middle Ages. In *Theological Investigations, Volume XVI: Experience of the Spirit: Source of Theology,* David Morland (Trans.), 104-134. New York: Seabury Press.
Rambo, Lewis R. (1993). *Understanding Religious Conversion.* New Haven: Yale University Press.
Rammage, Ian. (1967). *Battle for the Free Mind.* London: George Allen and Unwin Ltd.
Rangell, Leo. (1974). A psychoanalytic perspective leading currently to the syndrome of the compromise of integrity. *International Journal of Psychoanalysis.* 55, 3-12.
Reich, Annie. (1953). Narcissistic object choice in women. *Journal of the American Psychoanalytic Association,* 1, 22-24.
_____. (1954). Early identifications as archaic elements in the superego. *Journal of the American Psychoanalytic Association,* 2, 218-238.
_____. (1960). Pathologic forms of self esteem regulation. *Psychoanalytic Study of the Child,* 15. New York: International Universities Press.
Rendle-Short, John. (1960). Infant management in the 18th century with special reference to the work of William Cadogan. *Bulletin of the History of Medicine,* 34, 97-122.
Rizzuto, Ana-Maria. (1979). *The Birth of the Living God: A Psychoanalytic Study.* Chicago: University of Chicago Press.
Rogers, Hester Ann. (1832). *An Account of the Experience of Hester Ann Rogers.* New York: Carlton & Lanahan.
Roheim, Geza. (1971). *The Origin and Function of Culture.* New York: Anchor Books.

Ross, Nathaniel. (1968). Beyond the "Future of an illusion." *Journal of Hillside Hospital,* 17, 259-276.
Rubin, Jeffrey. (1992). Psychoanalytic treatment with a Buddhist meditator. In *Object Relations Theory and Religion,* Mark Finn & John Gartner (Eds.). Westport: Praeger.
Rubin, Julius H. (1994). *Religious Melancholy and Protestant Experience in America.* New York: Oxford University Press.
Rycroft, Charles. (1973). *A Critical Dictionary of Psychoanalysis.* Totowa: Littlefields, Adams and Co.
Sagan, Eli. (1988). *Freud, Women and Morality: The Psychology of Good and Evil.* New York: Basic Books.
Sandler, Joseph. (1960). On the concept of the super ego. *Psychoanalytic Study of the Child,* 15, 128-162.
Sargant, William. (1959). *Battle for the Mind: A Physiology of Conversion and Brainwashing.* New York: Perennial Library.
_____. (1976). *The Mind Possessed: From Ecstasy to Exorcism.* London: Pan Books.
Saul, L. J. (1970). Inner sustainment: The concept. *Psychoanalytic Quarterly,* 15, 163-188.
Schafer, Roy. (1960). The loving and beloved superego in Freud's structural theory. *Psychoanalytic Study of the Child* 15, 163-188.
Schecter, David E. (1979). The loving and persecuting superego. *Contemporary Psychoanalysis,* 15, 163-188.
Schilder, Paul & Kauders, Otto. (1956). *The Nature of Hypnosis.* New York: International Universities Press, 1973.
Scupoli, Lorenzo. (1963). *Unseen Warfare.* London: Faber and Faber.
_____. (1978). *The Spiritual Combat and a Treatise on Peace of the Soul.* New York: Paulist Press.
Segal, Hanna. (1974). *Introduction to the Work of Melanie Klein.* New York: Basic Books.
Shadford, George. (1866). The life of George Shadford. In *The Lives of the Early Methodist Preachers,* Thomas Jackson (Ed.)., vol. VI. London: Wesleyan Conference Office.
Shor, Ronald E. (1972a). Hypnosis and the concept of the generalized reality orientation. In *Altered States of Consciousness,* Charles T. Tart (Ed.). Garden City: Anchor Books.
_____. (1972b). Three dimensions of hypnotic depth. In *Altered States of Consciousness,* Charles T. Tart (Ed.). Garden City: Anchor Books.
Siegel, Allen. (1996). *Heinz Kohut and the Psychology of the Self.* New York: Routledge.
Silverman, Lloyd H., Lachmann, Frank M., & Milich, Robert H. (1982). *The Search for Oneness.* New York: International Universities Press.
Sommerville, John C. (1978). English Puritans and children: A social-cultural explanation. *Journal of Psychohistory,* 6 , 113-137.
Southey, Robert. (1820). *The Life of Wesley: and Rise and Progress of Methodism.* New York: W. B. Gilley.

Spiro, Melford, E. (1965). Religious systems as culturally constituted defense mechanisms. In *Context and Meaning in Cultural Anthropology,* Melford E. Spiro (Ed.). New York: Free Press.
Stace, W. T. (1961). *Mysticism and Philosophy.* London: Macmillan and Co. Ltd.
Starbuck, Edwin Diller. (1911). *The Psychology of Religion: An Empirical Study of the Growth of Religious Consciousness.* New York: Walter Scott Publishing Company.
Steele, Richard B. (1994). *"Gracious Affection" and "True Virtue" According to Jonathon Edwards and John Wesley.* Metuchen: Scarecrow Press.
Steiner, John. (1993). *Psychic Retreats: Pathological Organizations in Psychotic, Neurotic, and Borderline Patients.* New York: Routledge.
Stern, Daniel N. (1985). *The Interpersonal World of the Infant: A View from Psychoanalysis and Developmental Psychology.* New York: Basic Books.
Strachey, James. (1934). The nature of the therapeutic action of psychoanalysis. *International Journal of Psychoanalysis,* 15, 127-159.
Taves, Anne. (1993). Knowing through the body: Dissociative religious experience in African and British American Methodist traditions. *Journal of Religion,* 73, 201-221.
Taylor, Jeremy. (1857). *The Rule and Exercises of Holy Living.* London: Bell and Daldy Street.
Thompson, E .P. (1963). *The Making of the English Working Class.* London: Gollancz.
Told, Silas. (1954). *The Life of Silas Told.* London: Epworth Press.
Towlson, Clifford W. (1957). *Moravian and Methodist: Relationships and Influences in the 18th Century.* London: Epworth Press.
Trickett, David. (1989). Spiritual vision and discipline in the early Wesleyan movement. In *Christian Spirituality: Post-Reformation and Modern,* Louise Dupré & Don E. Saliers (Eds.). New York: SCM Press.
Tuttle, Jr., Robert Gregory. (1989). *Mysticism in the Wesleyan Tradition.* Grand Rapids: Zondervan.
Ullman, Chana (1989). *The Transformed Self: The Psychology of Religious Conversion.* New York: Plenum Press.
Waelder, Robert. (1930). The principle of multiple function. In *Psychoanalysis: Observation, Theory, Application,* S. A. Guttman (Ed.). New York: International Universities Press.
Wallas, Joseph. (1926). *The Art of Thought.* New York: Harcourt, Brace.
Werner, Julia S. (1984). *The Primitive Methodist Connexion: Its Background and Early History.* Wisconsin: The University of Wisconsin Press.
Wesley, John (1984-1987). *Sermons.* Albert Outler (Ed.). Volumes 1-4 of *The Bicentennial Edition of the Works of John Wesley.* Nashville: Abingdon Press.
Wesley, John & Wesley, Charles. (1981). *Selected Writings and Hymns.,* Frank Whaling (Ed.). The Classics of Western Spirituality. Toronto: Paulist Press.
Wesley, Susanna. (1997). *The Complete Writings,* Charles Wallas Jr. (Ed.). London: Oxford University Press.

Whaling Frank, (1981). Introduction. In John and Charles Wesley: *Selected Writings and Hymns,* Frank Whaling (Ed.), 1-64. The Classics of Western Spirituality. Toronto: Paulist Press.
White, Charles E. (1986). *The Beauty of Holiness: Phoebe Palmer as Theologian, Revivalist, Feminist, and Humanitarian.* Grand Rapids: Francis Asbury Press.
Whiting, W. H. M. (1961). Socialization process and personality. In *Psychological Anthropology,* Francis L. K. Hsu (Ed.). Homewood: Dorsey Press.
Winnicott, D. W. (1971). *Playing and Reality.* New York: Basic Books.
Zaehner, R. C. (1957). *Mysticism Sacred and Profane.* London: Oxford University Press.
Zales, Michael R. (1978). Mysticism: psychodynamics and relationship to psychopathology. In *Expanding Dimensions of Consciousness,* A. Arthur Sugarman & Ralph E. Tarter (Eds.). New York: Springer.

Index

A. B., Mrs., 75
Abelove, Henry, 218
Aberbach, David, 137-38
Aggression, unconscious, 25, 45-46, 86
Albin, Thomas R., xii, 44, 76, 197
Anglicanism, 1, 2, 18-19, 92
Arlow, Jacob A., ix
Arminian Magazine, xii, 1, 19, 44, 187
Assagioli, Roberto, 133
Atlay, John, 71, 151-52

Bacal, Howard A., x
Batson, C. Daniel, 155
Bernard of Clairvaux, St., 41
Bipolar mechanism, 42-43, 87
Blatt, Sidney, 27
Bonaventure, St., 95
Bowlby, John, 19, 20, 25, 165
Breen, Hal J., 113
Brierley, Marjorie, 9, 218
Briggs, Philothea, 175

Bright, Timothy, 50
Brown, George, 116
Buber, Martin, 179
Buddhist meditation, 188-89
Bunyan, John, 20, 57. 73, 74
Burton, Robert, 50

Calvinism, 3, 57, 208, 216
Carter, John D., 8, 9
Carvosso, William, 75, 82, 84-86, 199-201, 203, 204-6, 208
Cennick, John, 63-64, 65, 208
Chasseguet-Smirgel, Janine, x, 111
Childrearing, eighteenth century, 12-27, 53, 69, 69, 185, 213
Church, Leslie F., 6
Clapper, Gregory S., 5
Cohen, Eric
Cohen, Charles L., 58-59, 190

Cohen, Eric, 9
Colman, Benjamin, 57
Conn, Walter E., 111
Conscience, ix, 3, 4, 11, 12, 20, 22, 23, 24, 43, 44, 50, 52, 53, 56, 108, 109, 111-13, 118, 123, 128, 130, 142, 144, 145, 147, 163, 171, 173, 177, 178, 179, 180, 182, 190, 191, 193, 194, 195, 200, 201, 202, 205, 206, 207, 208, 209, 210, 214, 216, 219
Conversion, 1, 7-9, 20, 21, 22, 29, 36, 43-44, 50, 58, 66, 73, 76, 85-86, 90, 102, 106, 107, 111, 114-16, 119, 120-21, 123, 130, 135, 137, 139, 140, 147, 151, 153, 154, 156-60, 173, 174, 178, 190, 196, 208-9, 214, 216, 217. *See also* Justification
Convulsions, 51, 61, 62, 63, 64, 65, 67, 68, 208
Cooper, Jane, 118-19
Corbett, Catherine, 151
Crosby, Sarah, 28-29, 63, 68-70, 110-11
Cultural symbolism, 211-13, 215, 216

Davidoff, Leonore, 18
Death crisis, 42, 62, 65, 83, 84, 85, 139
Delameau, Jean, 20
Depression, 3, 7, 14 ,20, 22-27, 29, 35, 39-47, 49, 51, 70, 71, 74, 76, 78-79, 81, 86, 87, 89, 95, 109, 116, 120, 128, 133, 134, 136-40, 142-45, 147-151, 153-54, 178, 182, 184-87, 189, 190, 193, 196, 204, 209, 213, 214, 216
and mysticism, 40-43
Desolation, 29, 40, 43, 47, 49, 53, 54, 61, 64, 67-68, 71, 74, 85, 87, 114, 140, 153, 155, 181, 196
Devereux, George, 211

Dimond, Sydney G., 8-9, 61, 65, 102
Dissociation, xi, 51, 64, 65, 124, 139, 168
Dryer, Frederick, 2, 100
Dual consciousness, 76, 78-80

Earle, Peter, 15, 16, 18
Ecstasy, defined, 90
Edwards, Jonathan, 56-57
Ego ideals. *See* Ideals
Eigen, Michael, x, 130-31, 139
Empathy, x, 12, 14, 25, 44, 47, 89, 108, 109, 110, 111, 113, 120, 128, 139, 184, 194, 199, 206, 215, 218
Enthusiasm, 2, 33, 92, 93, 100, 129, 135
Epstein, Mark, 188, 189
Equanimity, 117-19, 128, 154
Evagrius Ponticus, 180-81
Evangelical nurture. *See* Childrearing, eighteenth century

Faber, Mel D., 164-65
Faith, 2, 34-37, 71, 91-92, 94-106, 111-12, 115, 146-47, 154, 182-83, 192, 209
Fasting, 42, 70-73, 76, 81, 120, 148, 202
Fauteux, Kevin, xi, 138, 155-56, 159, 160
Fenelon, Francis, 163-64, 175
Fenichel, Otto, 68
Fletcher, John, 176
Fraser, Robert M., 33
Freeman, Daniel M. A., 25
Freud, Sigmund, 11, 46, 111, 139, 159, 211, 213
Frick, Willard B., 130, 131
Furer, Manuel, 110

Galen, 50
Greven, Philip, 12, 13, 28

Grieving, 70, 76-79, 81, 82, 126-27, 143, 151
Grof, Stanislav, 42, 139
Gunter, W. S., 100

Haime, John, 153, 207
Hall, Bathsheba, 187-88, 193
Hall, Catherine, 18
Hall, Ruth, 60-61, 125
Hanby, John, 75, 76, 197-98
Hanson, Thomas, 84-85, 124-25, 150-51, 152
Hartmann, Heinz, 129, 161
Hartocollis, Peter., 137
Hauerwas, Stanley, 46
Haydon, John, 64
Heitzenrater, Richard P., 172
Hewitt, Margaret, 17
Hippocratic writers, 50
Holland, Bernard, 51, 58-59, 65
Hollenbeck, Jess Byron, 93
Hopper, Charles, 23-24, 121-22
Horton, Paul C., 140
Hunter, William, 29, 198-99
Hypnosis, 64, 65, 91, 124, 161, 168, 188
Hysteria, 51, 59, 61, 63-66, 73, 82, 84, 86, 203

Ideal(s), x, xi, 7, 8, 11, 27, 31, 37, 40, 43, 46, 54, 69, 83, 84, 85, 86, 87, 99, 106, 108, 109, 111, 114, 115, 116, 117, 118, 119, 123, 125, 127, 128, 129, 130, 131, 133, 134, 135, 138, 139, 140, 143, 144, 145, 146, 148, 149, 150, 153, 154, 155, 156, 157, 177, 178, 179, 185, 186, 187, 188, 189, 191, 192, 194, 195, 199, 205, 206, 207, 209, 210, 212, 214, 215, 216, 218, 219

Index

Idealization, x-xi, 3, 27, 28, 30, 44, 126, 127, 129, 136, 137, 138, 149, 150, 164, 212, 214
Imaginal vision, 100, 101, 102, 103
Imago, 4, 27-31, 44, 47, 58, 59, 6-67, 69, 86, 87, 130, 142, 150, 160, 210, 215, 216-17
Incubation, unconscious, 97, 43-44, 78, 150, 155
Inflation, 44, 120, 123, 133, 134-37, 140, 141, 145, 146, 147, 150, 151, 154, 184, 196, 210
Insight (psychoanalytic), x, 3, 8, 47, 87, 125, 128, 156, 157, 190, 191, 192, 209, 210, 211, 212, 213, 216, 218
Inspiration, x, 43, 45, 79, 85, 92, 106, 111, 118, 124, 125, 129, 155, 156, 167, 197, 200, 206
Integration, ego-superego, ix, xi, 8-10, 25, 27, 30, 45, 46, 49, 108, 133, 139, 146, 150, 156, 157, 173, 179, 213, 215, 216, 218
Internal object. *See* Imago
Introject. *See* Imago
Introspection, ix, 3, 30, 35, 45, 118, 136, 143, 145, 152, 155, 158, 161, 171, 172, 173, 179, 180, 181, 182, 183, 184, 187, 189, 191, 197, 201, 209, 214, 215

J. B. of St. Hellier's, 72-73, 103, 125-26, 153
Jacobson, Edith, 114, 144, 150
James, William, 7-8, 40-41, 43, 155, 166
Janeway, James, 21
Jenkins, Marg, 93-94
John of the Cross, St., 41
Jones, Joseph, 59-60
Josephs, L., 11
Joyce, Thomas, 125
Justification, ix, 2, 6, 9, 15, 20, 29, 33, 36-37, 38, 40, 43-47, 49, 53, 68, 71, 76, 78, 79, 85, 87, 89-96, 99, 102, 106-7, 109-11, 115, 116, 118-22, 124-26, 128-29, 134, 135, 137, 138, 142, 144, 147, 148, 150-54, 155, 172, 174-75, 179, 182, 184-86, 193, 196-98, 200, 214

Kakar, Sudhir, x, 41
Kardiner, Abram, 211
Kempis, Thomas à, 34, 172, 181
Kernberg, Otto, 150
King, John O., 73, 79-80
Kirkpatrick, Lee A., 108, 179
Klauber, John, 14
Klein, Melanie, 4, 26, 57, 67, 138, 214
Kohut, Heinz, x
Kris, Ernst, 137, 155-56

Laski, Marghanita, 40, 41
Law, William, 16, 34, 146, 174
Lawrence of the Resurrection, Brother, 160-61, 163, 164, 165, 166-67, 172
Lederer, Wolfgang, 11, 12, 187
Lee, R. R., 162, 194
Lewin, Bretram., 137, 138
Libidinal object constancy, 29, 45, 46, 140, 142, 144-48
Lichtenberg, Joseph B., 25
Lindstrom, Harald, 5, 108
Linn, Louis, 137
Locke, John, 16-17, 93
Lockean empiricism, 34, 99
Loewald, Hans, 12, 187
Loewenstein, Rudolph M., 129
Lorence, Bogna W., 16
Loyola, St. Ignatius, 95, 161, 162, 165-66, 167-68, 172
Luther, Martin, 56

Maas, Robin, 163, 165, 166
Maddox, Randy L., 105, 108, 158-59
Mahler, Margaret S., 138

Mallit, S., 75
Manic defense, x, 44, 45, 120, 121, 135-38, 140, 144, 154, 207
Manic-depression, 41
Martin, J. C., 162
Maslow, Abraham, 8, 9, 90, 106-110, 115, 117, 118, 129, 133-34, 156-57, 161, 209, 215,
Mason, John, 120, 121, 198
Mather, Cotton, 57
Mathers, Alexander, 125
Mathews, Rex D., 95, 100
Meditation, ix, 34, 43, 45, 74, 75, 90, 93, 104, 107, 136, 143, 148, 155, 158, 160-61, 165, 167, 169, 171-73, 175, 179-80, 183-84, 188, 189, 192, 196, 197, 200, 201, 209, 213-14. *See also* Introspection; Watching; Presence, practice of the.
Meditation, concentrative, 188-89
Meditation, Insight, 180, 188, 189. *See* Mindfulness
Melancholy, 23, 40,41, 49-50, 70, 71, 74, 75, 78, 79, 133, 140, 142, 145-46, 148, 190. *See* Depression
Menninger, Karl, 72
Merkur, Dan, xii, 8, 9, 40, 42, 43, 76, 87, 90-91, 93, 109, 111, 113-14, 128, 156, 166
Mindfulness, 214. *See* Meditation, insight
Mitchell, Thomas, 15
Modell, Arnold H., 67, 137
Molinos, Miguel, 168-69
Moore, Robert L., 15
Moravian Brothers, 1, 3, 35-37, 95, 97, 189
Moss, Richard, 19, 22, 71-72, 126-28, 147-50, 196-97
Mounteer, Carl, 72
Mystics, French, 35, 104-6

Mystics, intellectual, 93

Narcissistic defense, 53, 135
Newman, Kenneth M., x
Nelson, John, 19, 71, 122-23, 137, 195
New birth, 15, 55, 59, 51, 53, 62, 89, 92, 96, 102, 119, 121, 122, 125, 126, 128, 134, 141, 154, 174, 181, 184, 209. *See also* Conversion, Justification
Nixon, Laurence, 20

Oakland, James A., 8, 9
Obeyesekere, Gananath, 211-212, 213, 215
Oedipal phase, 144
Oedipal triumph, x
Oedipus complex, 114, 144, 211, 213
Olivers, Thomas, 99, 206-7
Origen, 95
Ostow, Mortimer, 40
Outler, Albert C., 3, 181

Pahnke, Walter N., 129, 157
Panic attacks, 22, 28, 50, 51, 59, 73, 83-84, 86, 189, 208
Paul, St., 8, 91, 146, 161
Pawson, John, 74-75, 76-79
Payne, Thomas, 19
Perfection, xi, 2, 3, 5, 6, 27, 33, 34, 35, 37, 38, 50, 53, 54, 102, 104-5, 112, 122, 133, 137, 143, 144, 146, 173, 178, 185, 186, 187, 196, 197, 198, 200, 203, 205, 208, 210, 216, 218
Perronet, Charles, 102, 199
Pfister, Oskar, 212-13
Pinchbeck, Ivy, 17
Plumb, J. H., 17, 21
Poincaré, Henri, 155
Pollack, Linda A., 15, 18

Post-conversion, 133, 134, 140, 143, 150, 198, 203
Praying, ix-x, 2, 21, 22, 28, 29, 30, 33, 34, 38, 42, 43, 50, 61, 63, 72, 75, 76, 77, 78, 82, 84, 85, 103, 104, 110, 116, 118, 123, 124, 126, 127, 128, 136, 147, 148, 149, 151, 153, 160, 161, 162, 163, 165, 168, 171-75, 177-79, 182-83, 192, 194, 196-200, 202-206, 209-10, 214, 218
Preconversion, 25, 80, 213
Presence of God, intellectual vision of, 89, 93, 97, 98, 99, 100, 103, 104, 105, 106, 129, 165, 168, 172, 174, 176, 177, 188, 200, 203, 213
Presence of God, practice of, ix, 104, 155, 158, 160, 163-65, 167-68, 171-74, 177, 179, 182-86, 188-90, 192-93, 195-97, 199-201, 206, 209, 210, 214-15
Presence of God, sense of, 7, 26, 28, 35, 43, 47, 69, 72, 84, 86, 94, 98-99, 103, 116-18, 122, 124-25, 127, 128, 142, 144, 146-48, 161-67, 171-73, 175-76, 178-80, 182, 184, 187, 191, 192, 194, 199, 201-10, 214
Prince, Morton, 135
Prince, Raymond, 137
Pruyser, Paul W., 114
Psychedelics, 42, 89, 91, 119, 129, 133, 139, 140
Psychic depth, 64
Puritans, 1, 15, 17-18, 20-21, 29, 50, 57, 58, 73, 74, 172, 181, 189, 190

Quietism, 104-6, 161, 163, 168, 173, 175

Rack, Henry D., 6, 7, 15, 16, 51, 57, 101, 102, 217
Rambo, Lewis R., 133
Rammage, Ian, 7, 15, 57, 66-67, 137, 159
Rankin, Thomas, 19, 82-84, 85, 86, 116-17, 136
Reeves, Father, 120, 124
Reich, Annie, x
Repentance, ix, 5, 14, 15, 39-40, 43-45, 49-54, 56-61, 66, 71, 73, 74, 77, 79-82, 84-85, 87, 94, 109, 112, 120, 123, 141, 154, 174, 181, 182-84, 209
Repentance attacks, 61-70
Reverie, 90-91, 93, 102, 105, 124, 129, 161, 176, 188, 209
Rhodes, Benjamin, 135-36, 204
Ritual mourning, 39, 40, 42, 49, 70-71, 76, 79-81, 151, 154, 202, 208. *See also* Fasting, Grieving, Solitude
Rizzuto, Ana-Maria, 130
Rodda, Richard, 152-53, 178
Roe, Robert, 193, 201-2, 203-4
Rogers, Carl, 8
Rogers, Hester Ann, 18-19, 22, 119, 137
Rogers, James, 19, 23, 102, 123-24
Roheim, Geza, 211
Ross, Nathaniel, 110
Rubin, Julius H., 12, 14, 72
Ryan, Sarah, 29-30

Sanctification, ix, xi, 2, 5, 6, 7, 8, 9, 20, 30, 31, 33, 34, 36, 37, 38, 44, 45, 76, 76, 96, 102, 134, 136, 147, 151-59, 169, 171, 173, 181, 182, 184, 186, 195, 196, 197, 198, 209, 210, 214
Sandler, Joseph, 11, 113
Sargant, William, 65
Saul, L. J., 11
Savage, Charles, 137
Schafer, Roy, 11
Schecter, 1979
Schwartz, Leo, 137

Scougal, Henry, 34
Scupoli, Lorenzo, 162, 166, 181
Self-esteem, ix, 11, 29, 68, 87, 108-9, 111, 128, 129, 139, 144, 151, 167, 182, 192, 206, 208, 210, 213, 215
Sensory deprivation, 76, 91
Separation, 18, 19, 20, 26, 27, 41, 52, 53, 66, 69, 81, 83, 85, 86, 165, 204, 205
Shadford, George, 107
Shor, Ronald E., 161
Sleep deprivation, 70, 75, 76, 120
Solitude, 42, 70, 71, 73-76, 79, 81, 104
Sommerville, John C., 17
Southey, Robert, 65
Spiritual development, ix-x, 33, 36, 37, 38-47, 134, 209, 213
Spiritual senses, 89, 93, 95, 96, 97, 100, 112, 122, 172, 200
Spiro, Melford E., 211
Starbuck, Edwin Diller, 7, 43, 107, 156
Steele, Richard B., 5
Steiner, John, 138-39
Stone, Lawrence, 15
Strachey, James, 190
Sublimation, ix, x, 11, 12, 114, 118, 127, 143, 153, 179, 194, 195, 197, 212
Superego, x, xi, xii, 4, 8, 9, 11-12, 14, 25, 27, 39, 43, 44, 45, 76, 84, 87, 108, 109, 111, 115, 119, 128, 129, 137, 140, 142, 143, 144, 150, 154, 156, 162, 166, 177, 178, 184, 186, 187, 190, 191, 193, 195, 196, 210, 211, 213, 214, 215, 219

Taves, Anne, ix
Taylor, Jeremy, 16, 34, 161, 162-63, 164, 168, 172
Taylor, Thomas, 102
Tennant, Thomas, 22-23
Teresa of Avila, St., 41

Therapeutic alliance, ix, 39, 45, 49, 68, 76, 79, 83, 84, 86, 87, 140, 142, 146, 186, 187, 214
Todd, Silas, 74
Trance, 29, 55, 82, 90-91, 105, 125, 129, 161, 168, 188, 206
Transference, ix, x, 46-47, 49, 56, 126, 138, 160, 161, 166, 179, 190, 191
Transference neurosis, ix, 49, 76, 80-81
Tuttle, Jr., Robert Gregory, 172, 173, 187

Ullman, Chana, 114
Unitive distortions, 139-40, 154, 167, 186, 210
Unitive ecstasy, ix=xi, 20, 40, 42-44, 67, 76, 89, 100, 103-6, 109, 111, 117, 125, 137-39, 147, 152, 155, 159, 188, 189, 191, 196, 203, 214
Unitive thinking, 40, 44, 97, 98, 106, 108, 110-114, 122, 124, 125, 127-31, 134, 139, 140, 145, 149, 155, 157, 159, 173, 177, 178, 179, 186, 189, 191, 200, 206, 209, 215
Unser, John, 152

Ventis, W. Larry, 155

Waelder, Robert, x
Wallas, Joseph, 155
Watching, ix-x, 118, 136, 152, 153, 155, 171, 173, 174, 176, 179, 180, 182, 188, 192, 197, 198, 199, 201, 203, 209, 214, 215, 218. *See also* Introspection
Wesley, Charles, 172
Wesley, John, ix, xi-xii, 1-7, 9, 11, 13-15, 21-22, 25, 27, 33-39, 40, 43, 44, 49, 50-66, 68-72, 80, 81, 89, 91-115, 117-119, 126, 127, 128, 134-135, 140-47, 148, 149, 150, 151, 153, 154, 158, 159-60, 161,

169, 172, 173-87, 189-95, 196, 202, 208-9, 210, 214-16, 217-18
and mysticism, 104-106
Wesley, Susanna, 12-13, 15, 25, 171
Wesley's method, ix, xi, 34-35, 218
Whaling, Frank, 104, 173
Whatcoat, Richard, 121
Whiting, W. H. M., 211
Winnicott, D. W., 108, 140, 159
Wright, Duncan, 110

Yewdall, Zechariah, 61, 78, 204, 206

Zaehner, R. C., 41